MORE PRAISE FOR *THE PROFESSOR IS IN*

"**Explains in exquisite detail exactly how to land a tenure track job.** In her genial yet unabashedly thorough book, Kelsky coaches readers through the critical topics they need to know. **I wouldn't want to navigate the inhospitable weirdness of the academic job market without it.**"

—Adam Ruben, author of *Surviving Your Stupid, Stupid Decision to Go to Grad School*

"It's tough out there, but no one understands how academic jobs are landed better than Karen Kelsky. **If you are a graduate student, *The Professor Is In* offers sound, realistic advice, and it may be the most valuable book you ever read if you intend to have an academic career.**"

—William Pannapacker, professor of English at Hope College and columnist, *Chronicle of Higher Education*

"**Karen Kelsky levels the playing field, providing practical insider knowledge to demystify the job market and help you improve the odds.**"

—David M. Perry, columnist, *Chronicle of Higher Education*, and director of Undergraduate Research, Dominican University

"**Getting a job is about more than being smart; read this book if you want to be prepared, professional, and on your game.**"

—Elizabeth Reis, professor and chair, Women's and Gender Studies department, University of Oregon

"A realistic account of what it takes to turn a Ph.D. into a job when all the jobs seem to be disappearing, *The Professor Is In* offers sobering, impeccable advice from one of the most honest voices in higher education today."

—Greg M. Colón Semenza, author, with Garrett Sullivan, of *How to Build a Life in the Humanities: Meditations on the Academic Work-Life Balance*

"**This is the book I wish I had when I was a grad student.** In *The Professor Is In*, Karen Kelsky delivers generous, savvy advice for academic job seekers. Unflinching, supportive, and honest, there is no other book like it. **All Ph.D. students (and their advisors) should have a copy on their shelves.**"

—Carole McGranahan, associate professor of anthropology, University of Colorado

THE
PROFESSOR
IS IN

THE ESSENTIAL GUIDE TO
TURNING YOUR PH.D. INTO A JOB

Karen Kelsky, Ph.D.

THREE RIVERS PRESS

New York

Copyright © 2015 by Karen Kelsky

All rights reserved.
Published in the United States by Three Rivers Press,
an imprint of the Crown Publishing Group, a division of
Penguin Random House LLC, New York.
www.crownpublishing.com

Three Rivers Press and the Tugboat design are registered trademarks
of Penguin Random House LLC.

Some of the material in this work was previously published on the
author's blog "The Professor Is In."

Library of Congress Cataloging-in-Publication data
is available upon request.

ISBN 978-0-553-41942-9
eBook ISBN 978-0-553-41943-6

Printed in the United States of America

Book design by Nicola Ferguson
Cover design by Michael Morris
Cover photograph: (certificate in suitcase) Alexandr Sidorov/Dreamstime.com

10

First Edition

To Kellee, who inspires
To Miyako, who questions
To Seiji, who challenges

CONTENTS

·····················

PART III. THE NUTS AND BOLTS OF
A COMPETITIVE RECORD

PART IV. JOB DOCUMENTS THAT WORK

PART V. TECHNIQUES OF THE ACADEMIC INTERVIEW

PART I

· · · · · · · · · · · · ·

DARK TIMES IN THE ACADEMY

ONE

·······

The End of an Era

It's a balmy fall evening in Eugene, Oregon. The air is soft, the setting sun glows, and the leaves shimmer in shades of red, yellow, and orange. A murmur of voices blends with the clink of glasses as a crowd of professors, staff, and graduate students gathers on the spacious deck of a senior faculty member's elegant house. It is a retirement party. A longtime professor is bidding good-bye after twenty-five years at the University of Oregon. The ceremony unfolds as the professor and his colleagues regale the assembled crowd with stories of the students he taught, the programs he built, the family he raised, and the pleasures of his years of sabbatical travel. One of the resident faculty eccentrics (decked out in mauve velvet beret and dashing smoking jacket) laughingly recalls the professor's fierce affection for white-water rafting, and the many, many faculty meetings missed as a result.

As they talk, I pause to ponder the event through the eyes of the graduate students in the crowd. It looks beautiful and soothing, a vision of a career and a life lived at a peaceful, gracious pace, filled with teaching and leisure, colleagues and family. I wonder if they know that the life being feted here this evening is already a relic of the past. I suspect they do not. I suspect that they come to this party, and others like it, mingle in the lovely faculty home, drink the wine, eat the food, hear the stories, and believe that this, too, will someday be theirs.

Nobody will tell them that they are wrong.

The American academy is in crisis. Decades of shrinking funding and shifting administrative priorities have left public universities strapped for cash and unable to sustain their basic educational mission. As state legislatures have slashed funding to their state university systems, what money remains increasingly goes to pay for bloated administrative ranks, and the expensive dorms and recreational facilities that can be used to attract students and justify skyrocketing tuition dollars. A few facts and figures tell the story.

States spent 28 percent less per student on higher education in 2013 than they did in 2008. Eleven states have cut funding by more than one-third per student, and two states—Arizona and New Hampshire—have cut their higher education spending per student in half. Graph 1, from a 2014 report by the Center on Policy and Budget Priorities, illustrates.[1]

To compensate for declining state funding, public colleges and universities across the country have drastically raised tuition. Tuition growth has outpaced inflation for the past thirty years. Annual inflation-adjusted tuition at four-year public colleges grew by $1,850, or 27 percent, between 2008 and 2014, with states such as Arizona and California increasing tuition at four-year schools more than 70 percent. Graph 2 from the Center on Budget and Policy Priorities demonstrates.

According to the *Wall Street Journal*, in 1975, a University of Minnesota undergraduate could cover tuition by working six hours a week year-round at a minimum-wage job. Today, a student would have to work thirty-two hours a week—close to full-time—to cover the cost.[2]

The result of these hikes to tuition is escalating student debt. The Institute for College Access and Success reported that 71 percent of the class of 2012 had debt at graduation, and the average debt of $29,400 was up 25 percent compared to 2008 figures.[3] Currently student debt in America totals approximately $1 trillion, and default rates on these loans have climbed for six straight years.

Astoundingly, in the midst of this crisis, universities have chosen to vastly increase hires at the highest end of the pay scale—university administrators such as deans, provosts, and the like. According to

Graph 1: State Funding for Higher Education Remains Far Below Pre-Recession Levels in Most States

Percent change in state spending per student, inflation adjusted, FY08–FY14*

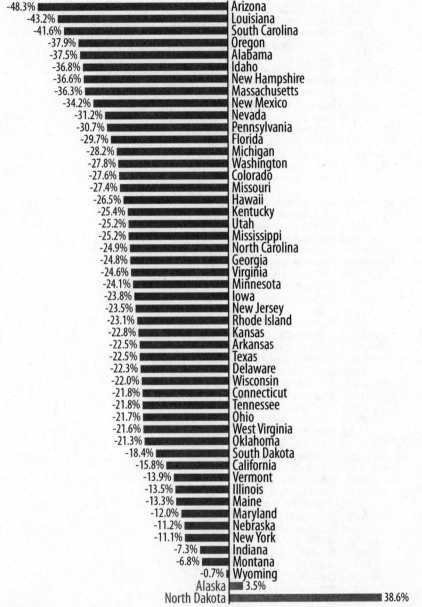

-48.3%	Arizona
-43.2%	Louisiana
-41.6%	South Carolina
-37.9%	Oregon
-37.5%	Alabama
-36.8%	Idaho
-36.6%	New Hampshire
-36.3%	Massachusetts
-34.2%	New Mexico
-31.2%	Nevada
-30.7%	Pennsylvania
-29.7%	Florida
-28.2%	Michigan
-27.8%	Washington
-27.6%	Colorado
-27.4%	Missouri
-26.5%	Hawaii
-25.4%	Kentucky
-25.2%	Utah
-25.2%	Mississippi
-24.9%	North Carolina
-24.8%	Georgia
-24.6%	Virginia
-24.1%	Minnesota
-23.8%	Iowa
-23.5%	New Jersey
-23.1%	Rhode Island
-22.8%	Kansas
-22.5%	Arkansas
-22.5%	Texas
-22.3%	Delaware
-22.0%	Wisconsin
-21.8%	Connecticut
-21.8%	Tennessee
-21.7%	Ohio
-21.6%	West Virginia
-21.3%	Oklahoma
-18.4%	South Dakota
-15.8%	California
-13.9%	Vermont
-13.5%	Illinois
-13.3%	Maine
-12.0%	Maryland
-11.2%	Nebraska
-11.1%	New York
-7.3%	Indiana
-6.8%	Montana
-0.7%	Wyoming
Alaska	3.5%
North Dakota	38.6%

*FY=Fiscal year

Source: CBPP calculations using data from Illinois State University's annual Grapevine Report and the State Higher Education Executive Officers Association. Illinois funding data is provided by the Fiscal Policy Center at Voices for Illinois Children. Because enrollment data is only available through the 2013 school year, enrollment for the 2013–14 school year is estimated using data from past years.

Center on Budget and Policy Priorities | cbpp.org

Graph 2: Tuition Has Increased Sharply at Public Colleges and Universities

Percent change in average tuition at public, four-year colleges, inflation adjusted, FY08–FY14*

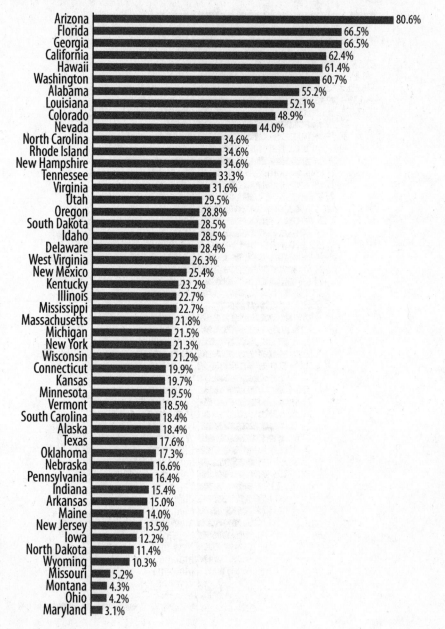

State	Percent change
Arizona	80.6%
Florida	66.5%
Georgia	66.5%
California	62.4%
Hawaii	61.4%
Washington	60.7%
Alabama	55.2%
Louisiana	52.1%
Colorado	48.9%
Nevada	44.0%
North Carolina	34.6%
Rhode Island	34.6%
New Hampshire	34.6%
Tennessee	33.3%
Virginia	31.6%
Utah	29.5%
Oregon	28.8%
South Dakota	28.5%
Idaho	28.5%
Delaware	28.4%
West Virginia	26.3%
New Mexico	25.4%
Kentucky	23.2%
Illinois	22.7%
Mississippi	22.7%
Massachusetts	21.8%
Michigan	21.5%
New York	21.3%
Wisconsin	21.2%
Connecticut	19.9%
Kansas	19.7%
Minnesota	19.5%
Vermont	18.5%
South Carolina	18.4%
Alaska	18.4%
Texas	17.6%
Oklahoma	17.3%
Nebraska	16.6%
Pennsylvania	16.4%
Indiana	15.4%
Arkansas	15.0%
Maine	14.0%
New Jersey	13.5%
Iowa	12.2%
North Dakota	11.4%
Wyoming	10.3%
Missouri	5.2%
Montana	4.3%
Ohio	4.2%
Maryland	3.1%

*FY=Fiscal year

Source: College Board, "Trends in College Pricing," 2013

the U.S. Department of Education, between 2001 and 2011, the number of administrators hired by colleges and universities increased 50 percent faster than the number of instructors. Between 2008 and 2012, university spending on administrator salaries increased 61 percent, while spending on students increased only 39 percent.[4] The University of Minnesota system added more than one thousand administrators between 2001 and 2012, for an increase of 37 percent, two times the growth of both teaching staff and student body.[5]

To balance the loss of funding combined with the added salary burden of new administrative positions, colleges and universities have slashed educational programs, cut faculty positions, eliminated course offerings, closed campuses, shut down computer labs, and reduced library services. Arizona's university system, for example, cut more than 2,100 positions between 2008 and 2013, and merged, consolidated, or eliminated 182 colleges, schools, programs, and departments, while closing eight extension campuses entirely. During the same period the University of California laid off 4,200 staff and eliminated or left unfilled another 9,500 positions; instituted a system-wide furlough program, reducing salaries 4 to 10 percent; consolidated or eliminated more than 180 programs; and cut funding for campus administrative and academic departments by as much as 35 percent.[6]

With fewer faculty and more students, who is teaching the classes? Temporary, contingent faculty known as adjuncts. Adjuncts have replaced traditional tenure track professors as the majority of instructional staff on campuses: in 2013 approximately 75 percent of university faculty were contingent and only 25 percent permanent tenure line. Forty years ago, these proportions were exactly the reverse.[7] Between 1975 and 2011, the number of full-time tenured or tenure track positions increased just 23 percent, to about 310,000, but part-time appointments rose almost 300 percent to 762,000, according to the 2012–13 annual report of the American Association of University Professors.[8] Graph 3 from the AAUP shows the shift.

Adjuncts, who are also sometimes called instructors, lecturers, teaching professors, teaching postdocs, or visiting assistant

Graph 3: Trends in Instructional Staff Employment Status, 1975–2011

All Institutions, National Totals

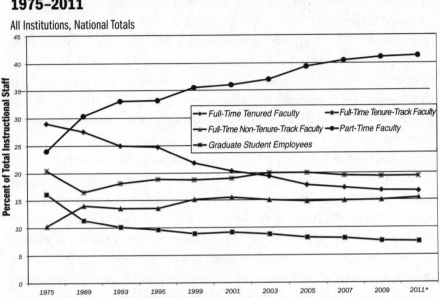

- Full-Time Tenured Faculty
- Full-Time Non-Tenure-Track Faculty
- Graduate Student Employees
- Full-Time Tenure-Track Faculty
- Part-Time Faculty

Notes: Figures for 2011 are estimated. Figures from 2005 have been corrected from those published in 2012. Figures are for degree-granting institutions only, but the precise category of institutions included has changed over time. Graduate student employee figure for 1975 is from 1976. Percentages may not add to 100 due to rounding.

Source: US Department of Education, IPEDS Fall Staff Survey.

professors, often have Ph.D.'s and scholarly records equivalent to those on the tenure track, and teach the same classes. However, they are paid a fraction of the salary. Where a tenure line faculty member in 2014 could expect to earn an average salary (encompassing all ranks) of close to $102,000 at doctoral institutions, and $75,317 at liberal arts colleges, an adjunct was likely to be paid a mere $1,800 to $2,700 per course for a maximum annual salary of around $23,000 per year.[9] When the hours of required work are factored in, adjuncts' hourly take-home pay of about $9 is less than that earned by a typical Walmart worker. Seventy-nine percent of adjuncts do not receive health insurance at work, and 86 percent do not receive retirement benefits.[10] Adjuncts at institutions of every rank often qualify for welfare and food stamps. The number of people with advanced degrees receiving public assistance more than doubled between 2007 and 2010, from 111,458 to 272,684. *Washington Post* writer Coleman McCarthy wrote of the "hordes of adjuncts" who "slog like migrant workers from campus to campus."

"Teaching four fall and four spring courses at $2,700 each," he continued, "generates an annual salary of $21,600, below the national poverty line for a family of four."[11] As the *Los Angeles Times* recently observed, "The lives of many adjunct professors are ones of Dickensian misery."[12]

Added to this financial struggle is the escalating student debt borne by those with advanced degrees. Graduate student debt is the fastest growing type of student debt, and graduate students now owe an average of $57,600. One in four graduate students owes almost $100,000.[13]

Adjuncts also lack access to the basic resources and tools of university teaching, such as an office, a phone line, a library card, or even photocopying privileges. They are typically told of their teaching assignment just days or weeks before the first day of class, and must scramble to prepare. When adjuncts arrive on campus, 94 percent receive no campus or department orientation.[14] Despite their qualifications, skills, and dedication, adjuncts cannot manage, with their impoverished resources and precarious employment status, to provide a quality of student experience equivalent to that provided by professors with job security and full access to university resources.

As tenure track faculty member turned adjunct Alice Umber (a pseudonym) wrote in her *Chronicle of Higher Education* column "I Used to Be a Good Teacher": "I'm not suggesting that adjuncts are poorer teachers than tenure-track professors (except in the fiscal sense), only that the very limited institutional support so many of us receive undermines our teaching; at least it has mine. No matter how dedicated I am to my teaching or how hard I work, I simply can't do for students as an adjunct what I could when I was an integral part of a department and a university."

She elaborated on how adjunct teaching falls short, hampered by isolation and exclusion. While adjunct professors usually bring great passion and dedication to their work, the lack of institutional inclusion means that they have little knowledge of, or impact on, the integrated curriculum that is supposed to govern the content and sequence of courses in a major. "I teach in a vacuum," she explained. "While I'm assigned classes and (sometimes) given course outlines or sample syllabi, after that initial exchange of information, I teach my courses in almost total isolation. In my previous job, one of the first things I learned was how the sequence of required courses in the major fit together to create a foundation, continuity, and a discipline-specific education for our majors. That I ever possessed such knowledge now seems like such a luxury to me."[15]

In order to survive, adjuncts usually must cobble together a set of courses at several different universities, driving frantically across the city or state to assemble a piecemeal income from three or four different campuses. Called "freeway flyers," they have no time or space to conduct the research necessary to keep their courses vibrant and demanding, to meet with students, or to publish the kind of work that is required to get a permanent position and leave behind adjuncting once and for all.

Students (and their tuition-paying parents), of course, have no ability to discern the difference between a tenure line and an adjunct professor. To students and parents, they are both "professors." The adjunctification of the university has flourished as an open secret, hollowing out the university education even as the costs of that education have skyrocketed.

The cost of adjunctification for undergraduate students may be hidden, but the costs for those earning Ph.D.'s are anything but. Adjunctification has openly decimated the career prospects of new Ph.D.'s, particularly in the traditional humanities and social sciences, where nonacademic uses of advanced degrees are still relatively unusual. Thousands of Ph.D.'s emerge onto the tenure track job market each year, expecting to find permanent and secure tenure line work at a university commensurate with their years of advanced training, only to discover that there is almost no such work to be had.

In some corners of a field such as English, a single job opening can draw nine hundred to one thousand applications. In less overcrowded fields, the number may be closer to three hundred to five hundred. In all fields, candidates grow increasingly desperate. They stay on the job market for years, eking out a living by adjuncting. They quickly become enmeshed in a self-destructive adjunct cycle—adjuncting to make ends meet while searching for a tenure track job, but unable to research and publish enough to compete for a tenure track job due to the time demands of adjuncting.

The tenure track job market in recent years has been likened to a lottery system, a Ponzi scheme, the Hunger Games, and a drug gang.[16] In response to this state of affairs, increasing numbers of adjuncts are organizing in advocacy groups such as New Faculty Majority, Adjunct Action, and Coalition of Contingent Academic Labor (COCAL).[17] Because agitation for better working conditions can lead to the immediate dismissal of individual adjuncts, they have also begun to unionize. Adjuncts and other contingent faculty have successfully unionized at American University and Georgetown, among other institutions, and have been incorporated into faculty unions at the University of Oregon and a few other places.[18] Progress, however, has been slow, for reasons I'll discuss in chapter 2.[19] In all cases, the universities have fought these efforts. Northeastern University retained one of the country's most aggressive antiunion law firms to fight adjuncts' unionization efforts there.[20]

Despite these upheavals, most ranking graduate programs still consider any Ph.D. who doesn't land a tenure track job a failure or an aberration. "Doctoral education in the humanities socializes idealistic, naïve, and psychologically vulnerable people into a profession with a very clear set of values," critic and columnist William Pannapacker wrote. "It teaches them that life outside of academe means failure, which explains the large numbers of graduates who labor for decades as adjuncts, just so they can stay on the periphery of academe."[21]

Graduate students absorb this value system and judge themselves harshly. Adjuncts and those who can't find tenure track positions suffer not just from debt and poverty, but debilitating feelings of shame and failure. As Robert Oprisko observed, "A substantial and deeply meaningful of your core identity is tied to your profession [and] losing your position represents the death of your identity, the annihilation of your self. Your identity is contingent not on publishing or getting high marks in teaching. . . . It is contingent on being employed, which is beyond your power to control."[22] Rebecca Schuman calls not getting a tenure track job a "cataclysmic, total failure."[23]

Many tenured faculty advisors in the departments that produce all of these Ph.D.'s maintain a studied silence on the question of, in Oprisko's words, "being employed." Rare is the advisor or department that acknowledges the employment needs of their Ph.D.'s. or provides hands-on training in the tactical professionalization graduate students need to either compete for scarce positions, or retool themselves for nonacademic work.

That is where this book comes in.

The Professor Is In: The Essential Guide to Turning Your Ph.D. into a Job reveals the unspoken norms and expectations of the job market so that graduate students, Ph.D.'s, and adjuncts can grasp exactly what is required in the tenure track job search, and accurately weigh both their chances of success and the risks of continuing to try.

With this book I hope to empower you, whether you're a current or future Ph.D. job seeker, to understand how the job market works, make informed choices about your career, and protect your financial security and mental health.

TWO

·······

Breaking Out of the Ivory Tower

The advice in this book draws from my four years of writing and consulting as "the Professor" at The Professor Is In, a blog and business dedicated to demystifying the tenure track job search in this time of contraction of the academic job market. It also stems from the fifteen years I spent as a tenure track and tenured professor, and the five years I spent as a department head. My primary field is cultural anthropology, with a secondary focus on Japan. After completing my Ph.D. at the University of Hawai'i in 1996, I held joint positions in anthropology and East Asian studies at two R1 research universities, the first that I call West Coast U and the second that I call Midwestern U. I was head of the East Asian Studies Department at Midwestern U. As a humanistically oriented cultural anthropologist and the head of a humanities department, my career from start to finish evenly straddled the social sciences and the humanities.

From my earliest days as an ABD job seeker ("all but dissertation"—the status you are awarded after completing all program requirements and defending your dissertation proposal), I was fascinated by the unspoken cultural norms, biases, and expectations of the tenure track job market, and determined to analyze them. I led my first "job market workshop" for my graduate school friends in 1996, when, still a Ph.D. student myself, I had just received my first tenure track job offer after two years of searching. I continued to lead similar events every year as an assistant professor, and to incorporate professionalization training in every one of the graduate seminars I taught. I served on or chaired more than ten search committees and participated as a faculty voter on many more, and in those capacities observed the painful errors made by candidate after candidate—errors that eventually came to show a consistent and predictable pattern of misapprehension of the actual judgments governing our hiring decisions. It was clear, from these experiences with visiting candidates and with graduate students at my institutions, that the need for Ph.D. career advising was urgent and the supply virtually nonexistent. Indeed, the sum total of job market advice I received as a graduate student was from my department head at our new student orientation in 1990, in which he told us, "You'll never get an academic job, so don't even bother trying." As a tenure track and tenured faculty member I knew that my tenured colleagues rarely spoke of the job market or of the need to train our graduate students to prepare for it. When I did so in a variety of formal and informal ways, my colleagues were generally, at best, bemused. Nobody I encountered in the academy, including my cultural anthropologist colleagues, found the cultural practices of tenure track hiring a compelling or worthy subject of investigation.

I left the academy—and an ostensibly successful career—in 2009. This was a highly unusual move. People rarely leave tenured positions. As the department head of a small humanities department at a major research institution in the Midwest, I made an excellent salary, had funded graduate students, generous summer research funding, and few obligations beyond the ones for which I was paid: holding faculty meetings, balancing the department budget, running searches, meeting staffing needs, handling tenure cases, filing faculty paperwork, and calculating faculty raises, on the occasions there were any. I was busy and stressed, but not nearly as busy and stressed as I had been as a new assistant professor. And I had far more to show for it at the end of the day. Unexpectedly, I enjoyed administration.

In the end I left because of two fundamental problems: 1) I needed to remove my children from a bad custody situation; and

2) my soul was dying at Midwestern U. I described my situation at Midwestern U and my reasons for leaving in detail in a guest blog post called "Death of a Soul on Campus," on Amanda Krause's *Tech in Translation* blog.[1] The outcome of the difficult situation in which I found myself was that my partner and I made a joint decision: If she found a job back in our beloved Pacific Northwest that could support the family, I would leave behind academic work entirely. This was not a completely wrenching decision for me to make. I was ready to leave academia. Faced with the choice between money and status at Midwestern U, and no money and no status back in the Northwest, I chose the latter.

The year that followed my departure from a successful career and identity as an academic was bewildering and painful. I struggled to imagine fulfilling work that would offer something of value to the world. Eventually, I decided to turn my painstakingly gathered fund of knowledge about the job market, and my determination to share it with desperate job seekers, into a blog, and eventually, a business. I began blogging on The Professor Is In five days a week in late 2010, aiming to build an online body of freely available advice for all tenure track job seekers, covering essential information about basic job application documents, the elements of a competitive record, interviewing practices, and search committee attitudes. The response was immediate and gratifying. Tentatively, I hung out my virtual shingle offering job market related assistance in June 2011. Within a week, I had my first client. Soon I had a roster. My instincts were correct: People needed this help, and were not getting it anywhere, certainly not in their departments.

It was when I published a column called "To: Advisors. Re: Your Advisees" in the *Chronicle of Higher Education* in September 2011 that things took off. The essay opens with this: "Dear faculty members: I sell Ph.D. advising services on the open market. And your Ph.D. students are buying. Why? Because you're not doing your job."

The column asks, "Why am I the pinch-hitter for an absentee professoriate?" and points out the thundering absence of anyone willing to teach desperate graduate students career-related skills such as deciphering a job ad, constructing a CV, delivering the elevator speech about the dissertation, planning a publishing trajectory, cultivating well-known reference letter writers, and writing effective job applications. "You are sending your Ph.D. students out onto this job market so unprepared that it would be laughable if the outcome weren't so tragic," I wrote. "Meanwhile, when students ask for help with their job search, too many of you respond with some version of 'not my problem' or the tired incantation: 'The Ph.D. is not professional training.' When one of my clients asked her advisor for career help, he accused her of trying to 'game the system.'" I noted that, ironically, the awful job market has become a rationale for refraining to advise. "'Well, the job market's impossible,' my former colleagues would say, airily, 'of course I always tell them that.'"

More broadly, the column accuses advisors of mystifying the financial foundations of academic work. It critiques advisors' failure to acknowledge graduate students—and themselves—as workers who operate within an existing money economy, and their denial that scholarly accomplishments require a living wage. I wrote:

> To be sure, my clients tell me that advising occurs—endless advising of "the dissertation project." As if that project, and its minutiae of citations and shades of meaning, is the point of graduate school. It is not the point of graduate school. It is simply a document that demonstrates a mastery of a discipline and a topic. The point of graduate school, for the actual graduate students themselves, is preparation for a career. A career like yours, with benefits and a retirement plan, to the extent that still exists.
>
> That kind of career derives far less from a thick wad of dissertation pages than from the quantity of one's publications, the impressiveness of one's grant record, the fame of one's reference writers, and the clarity of one's ambition. I don't find it problematic to say any of that openly. But apparently you do. You reject it as "vulgar" and "careerist"—as if wanting to have health insurance is vulgar and wanting to not go on food stamps is careerist.

I concluded, "Your job is to tell [your graduate students] the truth. . . . And to extend an ethos of care beyond their writing and research to encompass their material existence. Because your students need work, even when it's not the coveted tenure track job. Work is good. You work. So should your Ph.D.'s."

I published this column with great trepidation; I expected to be excoriated. And, to a degree, in the comment thread, I was. But I was also thanked, effusively (by graduate students). The immediate outcome of the column was a deluge of pleas to my fledgling business for help. Emails came by the (literally) thousands, from desperate, panicked Ph.D. candidates and tenure track job seekers. They came from the Ivy Leagues, from the Public Ivies such as Berkeley and Michigan, from second and third tier programs, and from campuses around the world. They came from new ABDs fearing their first foray onto the market, longtime adjuncts who'd been fruitlessly searching for jobs for years, and assistant professors seeking to move out of stressful and unfulfilling positions.

New clients came telling two versions of a single tale. Either version A: "My advisor, X, barely reads my material, barely writes a recommendation letter for me, and has nothing whatsoever to say about the job market." Or version B: "My advisor, X, is really nice, tries to be very supportive, does a great job in terms of my dissertation, and has nothing whatsoever to say about the job market."

When I inquired why the advisors were so unhelpful, my new clients described several scenarios: Some advisors understand their advising responsibilities to end with the writing and defense of the dissertation manuscript. Other advisors who obtained their degrees and jobs in a far different era are devastatingly ignorant of the conditions of the new university hiring economy. And then there is advisor selfishness, laziness, and indifference—factors in many client stories. One tactic some professors employ to silence intensifying graduate student requests for help is exceptionalism based on institutional rank or field. Rhetoric and composition faculty believe their field immune to market forces, while Ivy League advisors typically scoff at the notion—in the face of all evidence—that their Ph.D.'s don't sail effortlessly into top-ranking tenure track positions. "My advisor told me everyone in the program gets good jobs," said one client from Yale, who went on, "but I know the cohorts of the last few years, and only two made it onto the tenure track. He's delusional, living in some outdated fantasy of institutional prestige."

But more than anything, the desperate emails I received then and continue to receive daily reveal the enduring "Work of the Mind" cultural mythology of the academy.[2] This mythology dictates that nobody must ever associate intellectual endeavor with payment. It is unseemly and crass to speak openly of the wages of intellectual work, let alone to teach students the strategies and practices necessary to build a paying career. These efforts are held as contemptible "careerist" betrayals of the pursuit of pure scholarship. As higher education critic David Perry observed in a recent *Chronicle Vitae* post about the resistance of nearly everyone in the academy to unionization: "Many academics, especially those in the tenure track, just resist seeing themselves as laborers." He continued, "Still we persist with the myth that the university is a special space, exempt from the power and pressures of capitalism and the neoliberal worldview."[3]

The academic blogger and commentator Ian Bogost remarked, at the close of a blog post about the tactics of midcareer hiring, "I'm sure I'll receive a host of insults that include the word 'neoliberal' for suggesting we think tactically about the reality of the organizational-political moil of academic job-seeking."[4] He went on, "But there's a flipside to academic freedom. We might cheekily call it 'academic paydom': the need to tend to our own professional situations in a way that allows us to do the rest of our jobs effectively—including the idealistic intellectualism."

The Work of the Mind stance of intellectual purity often casts itself as a noble critique of neoliberal logic, which is a logic of pure monetization, in which intellectual pursuits are useless that do not yield immediate patentability or profit. Neoliberal values have taken over budgetary decisions by both the Left and the Right in modern-day America, and lie behind the wholesale assault on (and determined defunding of) the university as a mostly wasteful and self-indulgent space of "pointless" research. On this side academic critics insist that the purity of intellectual pursuit must be defended against the encroachments of money values. And indeed, those critics look with horror at my business as the complete capitulation to neoliberal logic, in that I urge my clients to commit themselves to an entirely instrumentalizing relationship to scholarly pursuits, packaging everything into quantifiable units of productivity for the purposes of job market competition.

Are they right? Am I reinforcing the same logic that has created the job market crisis?

Yes and no. The Work of the Mind is indeed valuable. But it cannot be pursued without adequate income. Nobody on public assistance, sleeping in a car, or living with two children in their parents' basement has the luxury to do this work. For me, the overriding ethical imperative is not to parrot proper political critique, but to assist desperate people. Ph.D. candidates, like other workers, first and foremost need secure paying work.

All successful tenure line professors draw regular salaries and enjoy health insurance, benefits, and retirement plans. Tenured professors enjoy (for now) a job security unheard of in any other sector of the economy. Professors know perfectly well that their own career progress rests on tangible outcomes in the form of publications, grants, and conference papers, and often pursue these with tactical precision. They also know that they would toss posthaste any application for a tenure track position in their own departments that did not include most or all of these same elements of a competitive professional record. Yet they fail to support—sometimes even actively discourage—their own graduate advisees in the same tactical thinking. As I wrote in my *Chronicle* column, "The irony of faculty 'work' ('I'm working on a project on death and the abject') is its scrupulous denial of any acknowledged kinship to the actual wage-work for which [faculty] do, indeed, draw a salary."

This discourse of intellectual purity meanwhile functions to disguise the truth that the modern university system systematically requires an unending supply of young, vulnerable idealists to work for poverty wages as graduate student teaching assistants (and, of course, adjuncts). The advanced degree these students earn is, as Marc Bousquet has argued, simply a by-product of this systemic exploitation, and not meant to carry value forward as a basis for high-wage employment.[5] Faculty who encourage bright undergraduates to enter Ph.D. programs, and current graduate students to remain in them, are, from this point of view, engaged in a form of unscrupulous "subprime lending" (which I discuss more in chapter 57) meant to funnel resources from this vulnerable population both to wealthy universities and their well-compensated administrators, and to the banks, through the systematic debt that is now a core part of most graduate school education.

Activist and writer Ann Larson tells a story from a 2011 event in her English graduate program, when two illustrious Marxist rhetoric and composition scholars, John Trimbur and John Brereton, came to speak.[6] During the Q and A, one graduate student spoke up: "The job market is terrible right now," she said. "What advice do you have for us? Where can we find hope?" Larson wrote, "This was a very relevant, even poignant, question. . . . I too was very eager to hear some words of wisdom and comfort." However:

> To my dismay, Brereton responded by advising the student to stick with her program undaunted. "If you have a Composition and Rhetoric doctorate," he told her, "you will find a job." Some in the audience murmured in disagreement. As for me, I was shocked at the complete ignorance of Brereton's response. It's not that I expected him to tell this student to choose another profession. Nor did I expect him to express the unmitigated job-market gloom that many graduate students and new PhDs know all too well. I expected, simply, the truth. Even a sugarcoated version of the truth would have been preferable to (let me just say it) an outright lie about rosy job prospects for Humanities graduates in any field.
>
> Was Brereton truly unaware of the labor crisis in the Humanities in general and in Composition in particular? . . . After all, the MLA had declared a job market crisis back in 1998, which is plenty of time for the news to trickle up to those who occupy even the loftiest towers of the academy. The shadow of contingency is everywhere.

Co-presenter Trimbur, she observed, far from correcting his colleague, remained silent, despite his established Marxist theoretical bent. "It seemed to me that Trimbur was annoyed to have to respond to a job-market question at all."

The outcome of this silence, writ large, among Marxist and non-Marxist faculty offices and conference halls across the country is that thousands of Ph.D.'s from every rank and status of program are left on their own without skills or training to confront a brutal job market in a collapsing academic economy. Thousands of Ph.D.'s left, in Ann Larson's words, "heartsick and furious." The fact that the academy's tenured idealists—all comfortably ensconced in secure positions with stable paychecks, abundant health insurance, and generous retirement plans—won't talk openly about the job search out of some commitment to "cultural critique," is in my view indefensible. No critique of the neoliberal academy should take place on the backs of its most vulnerable members.

My advice in this book is meant to fill this void, addressing every angle of professionalization from building a competitive record, to writing a job cover letter, CV, and teaching statement, to managing an interview, to negotiating an offer. It explains the unspoken cultural biases and judgments that govern tenure track hiring and demystifies the criteria upon which tenure track job seekers are actually judged. And it points to possibilities outside the academy for those job seekers who decide to move on and reinvent themselves for a post-academic career.

Let me pause here to make myself perfectly clear: Individual efforts alone cannot overcome systemic forces. My advice cannot counteract the wholesale contraction of the university economy, and this book cannot conjure jobs where there are none. Job seekers can and should make their very best efforts, but there are not enough jobs for everyone. Some—perhaps most—people reading this book will eventually have to move on to nonacademic career options.

What this book can do is reveal how the job market works, so that you can make educated choices about how to proceed in it. As a cultural anthropologist I am always alert to the ways that members of a group create boundaries of insider and outsider, get and keep power, operate within hierarchies and then challenge them, and impose unspoken norms of speech and behavior. In everything I write I disclose the taken-for-granted knowledge of the academy that is widely understood by insiders (tenured professors) but rarely spoken aloud to outsiders (you, the as-yet-unproven graduate student apprentices). I explain the systems of value by which academic records of productivity are judged, so that you can most efficiently devote your time to the productivity that counts on the job market. And so you can decide when the effort exceeds the return on investment, and when it's time to move on to another career.

Is it strange that I run a business helping others get into a career that I left? Some seem to think so, but I don't. I've been both happy and unhappy in the academic career. Not all campuses or departments are the same, and when you find a good match between your goals and a campus culture, the academic career can be delightful. I know what it means to enjoy an academic job, and I hope that a few lucky individuals still have the opportunity to do that.

For you, the tenure track job is probably still Plan A. You want the job because it's what you trained for and it is a job doing the things you most enjoy, particularly the research and teaching that you've mastered at such sacrifice and effort, over so many years. In this job you get to work with smart, like-minded colleagues. And in this job, once you get past tenure—and assuming that tenure continues to exist—you get unparalleled job security. Millions of graduate students pour their hearts and souls and dollars into graduate school training. The best thing you can do is to learn just how the tenure track job market works, how to plan for it from the first day of graduate school, how to perfect your applications for it, and how to decide when it's time to move on.

While I strongly believe in your ability to leave the academy and do other things (I devote the final part of the book to this topic), I know that you want to make your best effort to succeed in your Plan A. We don't know how much longer tenure track jobs will be around. But they're still around now in small numbers, so if you want to go after one, I support you.

THREE

··········

The Myths Grad Students Believe

Unfortunately, Ph.D. students are largely resistant to professionalization. It seems that many don't want to learn the truth of a
collapsing academic job market any more than many faculty want
to admit it. Far too many keep their heads firmly in the sand, pre-
ferring to fixate on the minutiae of immediate graduate school
requirements—the classes, papers, comprehensive exams, and dissertation. They rest all their hopes in the completed dissertation as
a magical talisman of scholarly success, unaware that it is scarcely
more than a union card—the bare minimum proof of eligibility
to apply for the rapidly disappearing jobs that allow for continued
scholarly work.

Certainly they are encouraged in this by faculty advisors, who,
when confronted with anxious reports from the job hunt, offer the
easy evasion "just focus on your dissertation," as far preferable (for
both advisors and advisees) to a hard conversation about an academy in crisis, on the one hand, or flaws in a student's record, on
the other.

But on a grander scale, graduate students (particularly in the humanities) are some of the most earnest and uncritical devotees of
the Work of the Mind myth. Indeed, they enter graduate school in
the belief that somehow the realm of the academic will be a grand
departure from the competitive rat race that prevails in the corporate sector. "How wonderful!" they can often be heard saying: "I

can get *paid* (a paltry teaching assistant stipend, but paid nonetheless) to *think* (about continental philosophy/medieval Buddhism/ethnic nationalism/transgender identity/et cetera)!"

Many graduate students resent the message that the point of graduate school might be to prepare for an actual career, because it is the realm of the career and its grasping, self-interested imperatives from which they are so often fleeing.

Consequently, graduate students cling mightily to a number of hoary myths about the academic job market. Here is a partial list:

- "I am judged on the brilliance of my ideas, not on the lines on my curriculum vitae."
- "I am a beloved teaching assistant and all of my years of TA experience will make me marketable."
- "I heard of a guy who got a job without any publications."
- "I'm not ambitious for a high-pressure job so I don't need a fancy CV."
- "I'll be happy if I can just get a teaching job, so I don't need a fancy CV."
- "My advisor's famous so I don't need to worry."
- "My discipline is doing fine."
- "My committee says our department has a great placement rate."
- "I didn't go into this for the money."
- "Those bad things happen to other people who aren't as brilliant as I am."
- "My passion sets me apart."
- "I'm the exception."

All culminating in a renewed doctrinal affirmation of the Work of the Mind: "The point of graduate school is not to prepare for a job, but to think great thoughts and contribute to human knowledge!"

As one grad student wrote in a review of a workshop I gave at one of the University of California campuses, "Dr. Kelsky's advice of thinking about graduate school as a means to a job was both helpful and disheartening. . . . While I do agree that thinking long term about how each thing you do in graduate school will shape your future, I also think that graduate school is much more than a means to a job. Graduate school is a place to explore, discover, and learn with others. It's a place to talk and debate with intellectuals, innovate, and challenge the limits of knowledge in your field."[1] She concluded, "The connections that you make in graduate school through getting involved, mentoring undergraduates, and teaching are invaluable. Although these may not show up as a line on your CV, they will shape who you are and help you during your job interview."

This reviewer is wrong, of course, that "getting involved, mentoring . . . and teaching" are going to "help you during your job interview." They are nice things, to be sure, indeed valuable things, and should be supported as general good practice. But make no mistake: They are not things that get a candidate short-listed.

It is understandable that graduate students would want to believe that dedication and passion get jobs. Passion is an important component of the graduate school enterprise—without it, how could someone finish a grueling years-long Ph.D. program? And in a different era—the high-growth 1950s and '60s, for example—passion and dedication may have been the key to success. However, in an era of Olympics-level competition for today's almost nonexistent tenure track slots, passion counts for the tenure track job market just as much as a passion for running gets a person to the Olympic gold medal podium. In short, it counts only as the motivator for a set of specific skills leading to a narrow set of quantifiable and mostly objective outcomes, in this case publications, grants, targeted teaching experience, and impressive references.

And while you may not be particularly concerned about the objective career imperative at twenty-five, when you are just starting out on your graduate school journey, by thirty-four, fatigued from years of deprivation and often with new household obligations, health expenses, or dependents, passion doesn't pay the bills. And neither, unfortunately, does teaching, if it's happening in the adjunct classroom.

One common tactic graduate students turn to in an effort to appear "realistic" while allowing denial to remain intact is a preemptive rhetorical reduction of career aspirations. This arises in statements such as:

- "I am not too ambitious."
- "I don't need much money."
- "I don't need a high-ranking position."
- "As long as I can teach at some small college, I'll be happy."

As if a lowered career bar renders the job seeker immune to market forces. This rhetorical move is usually combined with the previously mentioned overinvestment in the value of teaching. Former adjunct Nathaniel C. Oliver described this rationalization as it once influenced his early adjuncting days:

> I've always been frugal in my spending habits, so the low pay did not bother me much at first, assuming as I did that after a few years of apprenticing, I would be moved up to full-time, as long as my work continued to be acceptable to my superiors. At times, it was difficult to accept that I was teaching a full course load while making poverty-level wages, but again, I assumed that my diligence would be rewarded, not with riches, but simply with a comfortably middle-class job. Like all academics, I have always had big dreams for myself, but I felt that time had made my aspirations more modest and therefore, more attainable.[2]

There aren't many other words to describe this graduate student stance toward the academic job market than denial. Denial, and a willingly dependent and juvenile subject position. The graduate student in the rhet/comp event described in chapter 2, after all, turned to her professors for "hope." And the blogger Ann Larson wrote that she anxiously awaited words of "comfort." But why should tenured professors be repositories of hope or comfort? In fact, Brereton's message—stick with your program and you'll get a job—is precisely a message of hope and comfort. The students know that it is profoundly wrong ("the audience murmured in disagreement") but can't bring themselves to stop seeking the reassurance. It should be clear by now that asking professors for hope and comfort is seeking a false reassurance that professors can still, somehow, make everything turn out all right. It's asking for a bedtime story. It exposes a stance of childlike dependency, not a position of self-reliance.

In a *Chronicle of Higher Education* piece, William Pannapacker described the reactions of would-be graduate students to his writing on reasons to avoid graduate school in the humanities:

> The follow-up letters I receive . . . are often quite angry and incoherent; [the writers have] been praised their whole lives, and no one has ever told them that they may not become what they want to be, that higher education is a business that does not necessarily have their best interests at heart. Sometimes they accuse me of being threatened by their obvious talent. I assume they go on to find someone who will tell them what they want to hear: "Yes, my child, you are the one we've been waiting for all our lives."[3]

He, too, urged a prompt rejection of this childlike subject position: "It can be painful, but it is better that [those] considering graduate school in the humanities should know the truth now, instead of when they are 30 and unemployed, or worse, working as adjuncts at less than the minimum wage under the misguided belief that more teaching experience and more glowing recommendations will somehow open the door to a real position."

There is no "safe haven" for Ph.D.'s on the academic job market. Telling and hearing the truth requires quite the opposite of puerile messages of hope. To avoid the Ph.D.-adjunct-debt spiral, you must first face the truth of the collapsing academic economy yourself. You must choose, consciously, an approach that minimizes risk and maximizes return on your investment of time and money in the Ph.D. enterprise. And you must declare independence from any advisor who peddles false hope.

To do this, you must use every year in graduate school to produce a record oriented precisely to the demands of the tenure track market, while keeping an eye open to nonacademic options. This effort should start not in your final year in the program, but much earlier; it is possible to begin preparing for the academic and nonacademic job market even before you enter graduate school, and to deliberately adapt your strategy as you move through the program. In this way you take an autonomous, adult stance toward your own professional future, rather than putting it in the hands of in loco parentis advisors.

Never forget: Your advisor keeps drawing his paycheck whether you get hired or not. Your advisor pays his mortgage whether you can pay rent or not. Unhappy that your advisor doesn't have your back? Have your own back. Protect yourself.

PART II

GETTING YOUR HEAD IN THE GAME

FOUR

· · · · · · · · ·

The Tenure Track Job
Search Process Explained

Now that we've established all the obstacles to attaining the coveted tenure track position, let's roll up our sleeves and get down to the business of explaining how you can maximize your chances of doing so.

One of the demoralizing aspects of the tenure track job search is the black box feel of the whole process. To the job seeker it seems like ads appear, you apply, the application disappears into the maw of some mysterious "search committee," and weeks or months later your heart is broken on the jobs wiki. Or, wonder of wonder, you get a request for more information. But, what is actually happening out there in search committee land?

To answer this we actually have to start about a year earlier, with the creation of the job ad itself. In this chapter, I'm going to begin there, at the birth of a "line," and follow it all the way through a typical hiring process. It goes without saying that this is just a general model, and actual cases will vary in timing, organization, and institutional policies.

A Line Is Born

In fall of the year before the ad comes out, the dean of the college will ask all the departments in the college to submit their hiring requests for the coming year. The department will meet and discuss this over one or more faculty meetings, and vote on a ranked hiring priority list. The department chair will submit this to the dean.

The dean will consider all the hiring requests of all the departments in the college (keep in mind in a college of arts and sciences at a major R1 university this may number more than one hundred) and decide which hires will be authorized to move forward. In our current economic crisis only a small proportion get the coveted nod.

The hire that is authorized is called a "line." As in, "We've been authorized to fill the line in Japan anthropology." Or, much more rarely these days, "We've gotten approval for a *new* line in Japan anthropology!"

An Ad Is Written

With that authorization, the department head convenes a hiring committee to construct the job ad for the line. For the purposes of our model, I will posit that this committee is made up of five members—four faculty members and one graduate student. This committee's work will start in the spring, and will be devoted to administrative details such as outlining the process, setting deadlines, and defining the search priorities: For example, "We are particularly interested in candidates with specialization in gender and sexuality and/or the environment." These priorities will reflect the interests of the hiring committee members as well as, to some degree, the stated priorities and plans of the department as a whole. The department will vote on the final ad, and in late spring, the ad will be submitted to the relevant disciplinary newsletters, the *Chronicle of Higher Education,* and other venues, to go out in the August or September issues.

It is an interesting fact that the fanciest schools will place the most impossibly general ads—"Princeton is seeking a cultural anthropologist"—while lesser schools will be more specific: "University of X is seeking a cultural anthropologist of Japan, with a specialization in gender. Additional expertise in the environment and/or ethnicity preferred."

Why? Fancy schools operate in the belief that they will consider only "the best of the best," and having no need to justify their choices, they tend to leave themselves the largest pool to choose from. And then the egos at play may prevent any agreement on an area of specialization.

Other schools will be operating within search parameters more rigidly dictated by current budgetary limitations and currently or temporarily available "pots" of money. So their searches tend to be specific.

Federal affirmative action policies require that the candidates short-listed for a position actually fulfill the listed qualifications of the position. Be aware, however, that this adherence to the letter of the law is not universal. It is more common at public institutions where records are public. I am not a lawyer and not versed in the ins and outs of employment law, but it seems there is a good bit of latitude for interpretation regarding how the successful candidate meets the qualifications, particularly at private institutions. Thus, candidates should apply for jobs for which they are basically qualified, even if they don't meet every single qualification listed in the ad.

A Review Is Conducted

Once the deadline has passed, all of the complete applications will be collected for initial review. Incomplete applications will typically be discarded, although if a candidate looks particularly promising and is missing a recommendation letter, the search committee may take the step of contacting that candidate to let her know (note that, as I discuss in chapter 41, this courtesy is increasingly rare).

At this point, the search committee commences the grueling process of compiling the long short list. The long short list is the list of candidates who may be asked for more information or invited to a conference or Skype interview. While all searches differ, for our purposes we will say that the long short list contains twenty-five names.

The search committee at this point will be dealing with perhaps 300 to 1,000 applications, and they need to jettison approximately 275 to 975 applications as quickly as possible to get to this manageable list.

Each member of the search committee will evaluate the files, reject the vast majority, and generate a list of twenty-five names. They will then meet as a group and discuss these names. If any of these candidates reflect a particular area of expertise shared by a faculty member not on the search committee, that faculty member's special opinion may be solicited. At the meeting, the names that make the top twenty-five lists of all five members of the search committee will instantly be "passed" onto the long short list. Little discussion will be devoted to them because they are so obviously strong. Similarly, any names that appear on four of the five committee members' lists will probably make the long short list without debate. Discussion instead will be devoted to the remaining slots, and the candidates whose names appear on only three (or fewer) of the search committee members' lists. Search committee members will explain their choices and justify them by pointing to strengths in the record or connections to existing programs in the department or across campus. Eventually, all will come to a shared agreement about the final list.

Those top twenty-five—the long short list—will then enter the next stage of the search. They may have their references called at this point, and be asked for longer writing samples. In most cases they are also invited to a conference or Skype interview, a 20–40-minute interview with some or all of the members of the search committee.

The Short Short List Is Finalized

Based on the results of this review of additional information, which typically takes place in October, November, and December, and meeting the candidates personally at the conference or Skype interviews, the search committee will then meet to compile the short short list.

The short short list typically contains about five names. These five candidates' files will be made available to the faculty as a whole (which in large departments probably has not been involved in the actual search process up to this point), for review.

The short short list must be ranked in a faculty vote. Things often get heated here. Some departments have a kind of decentralized ethos in which the faculty places a great deal of trust in the judgment of the search committee, and simply rubber-stamps the ranked short list, while other departments will view this as a battle royal, with egos flying and long-simmering resentments, alliances, and agendas emerging into open conflict. When this debate concludes the top three, or as many as the department can afford, will be invited for campus visits. Often the pleasant duty of inviting the candidates to visit will move away from the search committee to the department head, reflecting the fact that in some departments the search committee will be dissolved at this point, and all further deliberations will take place among the whole faculty.

In many searches the invitations will go out just before winter break, with visits scheduled for January and February. It is worth noting that with the increasingly frenzied state of the market, sometimes this pace is accelerated, and campus visits will be scheduled for December with an offer made before winter break. These early offers can result in much consternation for the recipients, who then have to weigh accepting a perhaps lesser offer early, or turning it down to wait for the results of other campus visits at better schools later. It's a dilemma.

Campus Visits Take Place

In any case, the candidates come to campus for their visits. A two-day visit is common, although small, resource-poor campuses may restrict visits to one day. Administrative assistants will be in charge of arranging details of lodging and flights with the candidates. On any campus visit, the schedule typically begins with the pickup at the airport, and concludes with the drop-off for the return flight. In the interim will be a packed schedule of meals, short meetings with individual faculty members, a formal sit-down meeting with the search committee, the job talk or teaching demo or both, meetings with the department head and dean, and a campus tour that includes visits to the library, special collections, or centers or programs particularly relevant to the candidate.

Shortly after the final candidate is dropped off at the airport to go home, the final decision-making process begins. In some departments this will continue to involve the search committee as a deliberative unit, while at others, where the committee was previously dissolved, it will occur among the whole faculty. Here there may arise a new battle royal. And now that the candidates are flesh-and-blood humans, emotions can run high.

A Decision Is Made

The debate will typically focus on the candidates' performance in their job talk and Q and A, on their demonstrated ability to fill the research and teaching needs as advertised (that is, the fit), and their likability and/or collegiality: Is this a person whom we can tolerate seeing in the hallways and at faculty meetings for the next five or ten years?

After some hours or days of debate, the faculty votes on the ranking of the candidates. The candidates will be ranked not just first, second, or third, but also "acceptable" and "unacceptable."

At that point, if all three top candidates are viewed as unacceptable, the alternates will be invited to visit. Similarly, if the top candidate is voted as acceptable and the other two unacceptable, and the top candidate turns down the job, then the alternates will be invited.

If all available candidates are unacceptable, or all acceptable candidates are unavailable, then the search "fails." Nobody is hired, and the department will have to start the process of requesting a reauthorization of the same line the next year.

But if one of the acceptable candidates is offered the job, and accepts it, then the search comes to a successful close. The offer is made and negotiated. The elements of the offer will likely be dictated mostly at the dean's level. Contents of offer letters vary widely in level of detail and specificity, but will usually include the teaching load, salary, start-up funds, moving funds, junior sabbatical or leave, general insurance and retirement benefits, and other basic elements. Some other elements of the offer, such as annual conference travel funding, may be arranged through an email agreement with the department head but not listed in the contract. This will vary widely by institution.

Once the contract is signed, it is all finished. The candidate—no longer a candidate now, but the "new hire"—will, we hope, receive warm welcome emails from his or her future colleagues, and will start packing up his or her apartment to move sometime over the summer.

FIVE

Stop Acting Like a Grad Student!

The biggest challenge for the tenure track job seeker is not finishing the dissertation, churning out publications, or cultivating fancy recommenders. It is transitioning from the peon mentality of graduate school to the peer mentality of the job market. The inability to make this transition is one of the core causes of failure on the job market, and it is one about which most job seekers remain utterly unaware. Approaching the job market from the peon subject position means that almost every word of the job application materials will have a wheedling, pathetic, desperate tone that will render them distasteful to every reader. Substituting emotionalism and pandering—interspersed with overcompensating moments of wild grandiosity—for actual facts and evidence of the academic record renders the application materials worthless for the purposes of securing a job. The candidate is rejected again and again, and has no idea why. She has no conception that it is her entire presentation of self in terms of ethos and meta-message that is systematically sabotaging her chances with each and every application.

The irony of graduate training is this: The better a grad student you are the worse job candidate you make, because a properly socialized graduate student is one who has internalized a subject position of subordination to the will of the faculty. While in the realm of ideas, faculty will allow for—maybe even encourage—a certain amount of independence in their graduate students, in the larger interpersonal "frame" of graduate training, they expect obsequiousness and deference. This is, of course, never expressed by faculty members and would likely be vehemently denied. Because the hierarchy is thus disavowed, graduate students have little means of recognizing how marked they are by their place in it. Consequently they are unlikely to recognize the ingrained patterns of deference and humility that characterize their written and spoken self-presentation, let alone overcome them.

The problem is, you write and speak like a graduate student. And the problem is, search committees aren't looking for a graduate student; they are looking for a faculty colleague. They want not a peon but a peer. A collegial, pleasant, and courteous peer, to be sure. But a peer.

This identity misapprehension is just as likely to afflict the Ivy Leaguers as those from other programs. It is the biggest problem that job seekers have.

Here, I sketch the most common ways that you act like a grad student, and sabotage yourself in your job search.

1. You Drone On and On About Your Dissertation

Please stop talking about your dissertation. Nobody really wants to hear about your dissertation. We do not care about your dissertation. By which I mean, the dissertation that you wrote in graduate school. What we care about is what you produce from the dissertation that translates into CV lines.

Remember: Search committees don't want to know about your dissertation beyond proof that you wrote one and that it's (soon to be) finished and defended. What they want to know is how that dissertation accomplishes specific goals that serve the hiring department: that is, how it produces refereed publications, intervenes in a major scholarly debate, wins grants and awards, translates into dynamic teaching, transforms quickly into a book (if you're in a book field), and inspires a viable second project.

In interview situations, learn to talk about your dissertation in short, punchy bursts, no more than a few sentences at a time. This gives your interlocutor the chance to say, "How interesting! Tell us more about that." To which you respond in another short, punchy burst. Please recall that interviews are dialogues. They are not monologues. Think of a tennis match. They lob the ball, you lob the ball back. Relate all elements of the dissertation to specific elements of productivity, such as participation in debates in the field, publications, grants, and so on.

2. You Think People Are Out to Get You in Your Department

Beware paranoia, which is endemic to graduate student life.

With very rare exceptions, faculty barely even think about the graduate students in their departments, beyond asking, once a year, whether any of them will just finish already so the dean can get off their back about their pitiful completion rate. The people in the department want you to finish. Period. Whatever that takes, that's what they want you to do. So just do that, OK?

Paranoia is unattractive, and a major red flag signaling an immature candidate. You may think that your dark insinuations of how your project really offended some people in your department make you look mysterious and misunderstood, but actually they make you look tiresome. Regardless of how you were treated in your department, say nothing but collegial things about it on the market. Because how you talk about your Ph.D. department suggests how you will talk about your future department. And your future department wants a colleague who has a positive attitude.

3. You Think People Are Out to Get You in Your Discipline

You're sure that your "radical" perspective/argument/position/ stance has earned you powerful enemies in the field. It likely has not. Likely few people are even thinking about you. If you're getting negative responses to your work, it's likely not because your argument single-handedly overturns the foundational orthodoxy of your field and has inspired widespread jealousy and resentment. It's because the work is not yet good enough. As irritating as many academics are, they generally do respect sound argumentation backed up with compelling evidence. Provide those, and chances are your "radical" perspective will get a hearing. I'm not saying you won't have to fight for your perspective. But it has a good chance of being a fair fight, not a case of your total persecution by the powers that be in your field.

Tales of victimization, such as how your "argument really pissed off some people," at the last conference, will not make you look desirable. They will make you look like a drama queen. And one thing no search committee wants? A drama queen.

4. You Constantly Repeat Your Main Point

Graduate students are insecure. This is understandable, because their status is insecure. One outcome of the insecurity is that you tend to pile on examples that "prove" that your topic is a legitimate one. It's the classic dissertation disease of seeing your topic in every single thing in the world. Everyone suffers this to some degree when they are at your stage. Further clues to this issue are phrases in your writing such as, "This is evidence that my topic is an important one," or "thus demonstrating the urgency of research such as mine."

A myopic obsession with your dissertation topic, the overuse of examples to prove its significance, and the pleading insistence on its importance are all hallmarks of immaturity as a scholar and potential colleague. Search committees are looking for a colleague who might be fun to talk to. What that means is someone who is confident that their topic is sound, who gives a reasonable amount of evidence for the topic, and who can show its importance to major debates in the scholarly field. And then who can talk about something else that is actually interesting.

5. You Make Excuses for Yourself

This is the one that if I had superpowers, I would reach through the pages of this book, grab you by your collar, and shake out of you. Right now.

Graduate students are so conditioned to dealing with intimidating advisors that they're like the Pavlov's dogs of excuses.

Professor: Hi. How are you?

Grad student: I'm sorry I didn't get that chapter in to you! I got sick over the weekend, but I'll have it done this week, I promise!

Professor: You were sick? Oh, no! How are you feeling now?

Grad student: I have a 102 fever but it's OK—I spent the morning in the library, and as soon as I get through teaching my three sections, I plan to skip dinner and make up for the writing I didn't get done over the weekend!

Professor: Wow, take care of yourself.

Grad student: It's OK! I can write through the delirium!

Stop that! Stop it now!

Excuses are what you make when you start from the default of what you haven't done, or have not yet read. I call this the grad student default to the negative, and I'll return to it later in the book.

For now, when someone on the search committee asks, "How would you teach our intro course?" you do not answer in any of the following ways:

- "I haven't really had a chance to teach a big course before, so I'm not sure how I'd do it."
- "I'm not sure how your department likes it to be done, so I'd definitely follow your lead on that."
- "I taught it last year but it didn't really go all that well, so I'd want to make a lot of changes."

No, those are excuses. Instead, you answer in one of these ways:

- "I enjoy teaching large courses because I get to reach a new set of undergraduates and show them all the things our field can do."
- "I will use X textbook because I find that to be the best one, and I will augment it with some unconventional materials like Y and Z."
- "I will take a balanced approach that introduces the X perspective and the Y perspective. Obviously my own work falls more in the X camp, but it's important in an intro class that the full scope of the field is well represented."

You are the expert. You are in command. Perhaps you haven't taught the intro course before—that matters not. You prepare, so that you can speak about how you will. When speaking of your research, reject the temptation to harp on what you "still need to address." Focus exclusively on what it does achieve. Embrace the positive.

6. You Wait for Permission

I could build a new wing on my house if I had a nickel for every client who explained their lack of publications by saying "My advisor never told me to publish." Or who told me they lost a year on the job market because their advisor said they "weren't ready." Or who never went to a conference because their advisor never suggested they should.

If your advisor doesn't do these things, then you have to do them for yourself as best you can. And make no mistake: Ultimately, responsibility for your job market preparation is on you.

Nobody told you to publish? Really? You really never once grasped after eight years in a graduate program, reading hundreds of refereed journal articles a year, that publishing a refereed journal article on the subject of your dissertation might be a thing you'd need to do?

"Nobody encouraged me to go to the national meetings"? Well, why did you wait to be encouraged? You know they're there! They happen every year! Surely you heard that the faculty were going? And some of your friends?

In a similar vein, don't ask for permission to apply for jobs. Many candidates are tempted to contact the department or search committee to anxiously explain their record and ask whether they make an appropriate candidate. This is a pointless exercise. If you are eligible to apply for the job, apply for the job. Don't wait to be given permission by the department. No summary of your qualifications in an email or phone call is a substitute for a comprehensive presentation of your record. And one person's opinion about your record is not a substitute for the deliberation of the committee as a whole.

The fact is, searches are unpredictable. While the ad may list several specializations, those are not necessarily the specializations that will come to govern the ultimate decision. This may arise from something as simple as the fact that the faculty member who insisted the ad prioritize X, back in the previous spring, is on unexpected research leave this fall. The rest of the search committee, now freed of the imperative to prioritize X, can focus on Y or Z, as they had hoped to all along. Or perhaps colleague Jones, the department's specialist on China, got an unexpected job offer and abruptly left campus over the summer. Suddenly China looms large as a priority of the department, even though it is nowhere listed in the ad. The combination of possible circumstances is endless. The point is, you don't know them.

So don't querulously ask for permission to apply. If you meet the minimum conditions of the job, apply for the job. And don't wait to be told to prepare for the job market. I hope that your department and advisor are assisting, but ultimately, that is on you.

7. You're Submissive

Graduate students tend to display the classic signs of submission—tilted head (ref: your puppy), bowed shoulders, tightly crossed legs, weak and vague hand gestures, a tentative, questioning tone. You have a wimpy, cold fish handshake. You avoid direct eye contact. You mumble and mutter and talk too fast, and, above all, you ramble in an unfocused and evasive way. You will often either smile and laugh too much, or conversely be grimly humorless (a sense of humor being one of the first casualties of the graduate school experience).

Few people have all of these traits, to be sure. But most grad students have some of them.

You must square your shoulders, straighten your back, lift your chin, and loosen your elbows. Take up all the space in the chair. You can do this even if you are a small woman because it's in the body language. See Amy Cuddy's influential TED talk for tips on how to do this and why it matters.[1] As she famously says, "Our bodies change our minds, our minds change our behavior, and our behavior changes our outcomes."

Make direct eye contact. Do not, under any circumstances, fuss with your hair, clothes, or jewelry. Speak in a firm, level tone. Women, speak in a lower register if you can—for better or worse, lower tones are the tones of authority. Smile in a friendly way at the beginning and end, but not too much while you're talking about your work. If a joke arises naturally in the conversation, of course run with it. Search committees love a sense of humor, when it's displayed in the course of smart collegial repartee. But in general your work is important and deserves a serious delivery.

Beware of mumbling, rambling, and trailing off indistinctly. Your listeners need to know when you have finished speaking, so that they can respond and a dialogue can ensue.

And, lastly, attend to your handshake. If you do nothing else from this chapter, please, I beg you, do this. Get up from your chair, go find a human, and shake their hand. Shake it firmly. Really squeeze! Outstretch your arm, grip their hand with all your fingers and thumb, look them firmly in the eye, smile in a friendly, open way, and give that hand a nice, firm shake. Repeat. Do this until it's second nature. If it doesn't feel right or you aren't sure if you're doing it right, find an alpha male in your department, and ask him to teach you.

Banish the wet noodle handshake.

Seriously, grad students, butch it up.

SIX

·····

The Attributes of a Competitive Tenure Track Candidate

Over my years of working with Ph.D. job seekers, I've identified six attributes that characterize the effective tenure track job candidate. This doesn't mean that these six attributes guarantee anyone a job. It does mean that anyone who does score a tenure track job will possess all or nearly all of them.

The attributes are productivity, professionalism, autonomy, self-promotion, collegiality, and a (five-year) plan.

Let's take these in turn. I will return to these elements multiple times throughout this book. Indeed, I have built in a degree of re-petitiveness intentionally so that readers using this book as a reference guide will encounter the same information no matter which chapter they read.

Productivity

You will have a record of professional accomplishments beyond the requirements of your graduate program. These will include major publications such as a signed book contract (if you're in a book field), and/or refereed journal articles, national and international grants, high-profile yearly conference activity, invited off-campus talks, substantive solo-teaching experience, and illustrious scholars writing your recommendations.

Professionalism

You will grasp that the best record cannot get you a job if it is not properly and professionally presented. This encompasses the wording and organization of your job documents, your verbal self-presentation, your body language, your appearance, and your grasp of the cultural norms of behavior and status in the academy.

Autonomy

You will behave as a full-fledged autonomous adult member of the scholarly community and not a second-class subordinate of your advisor or any other scholar, living or dead.

Self-Promotion

You will create connections with scholars in your field, beyond your dissertation committee. You will make yourself known as an up-and-coming scholar in your field, and ideally have a reference letter from a well-known scholar located outside your Ph.D. institution.

Collegiality

You will have the ability to connect on a human level with other humans, make appropriate eye contact, show an understanding of and interest in the department and its members, and have an ability to converse on topics other than your dissertation.

A Plan

You will have a five-year plan that demonstrates your ability to maintain your productivity—in publishing, conferences, grants, and self-promotion—through the arc of tenure, into a second major post-dissertation project.

The five-year plan can be a confusing and intimidating exercise for many graduate students, so let me elaborate on how to do it.

The five-year plan is a month-by-month grid that includes:

- Specific writing projects with deadlines for completion, submission, and revision
- Graduate program deadlines for exams, proposals, and defense
- Major conferences with deadlines for submission of abstracts and proposals
- Job market deadlines
- Major funding deadlines, including both small grants to support short research trips, and large grants to fund dissertation fieldwork
- Networking goals, including reminders to get in touch with editors about publishing, or to meet up with people at conferences
- Teaching timelines
- Submission dates for awards and honors

When you are in the quest for a tenure track job, the plan helps you to continually look up, evaluate, and adjust. Spend too much time looking down, at the minutiae of your classes or dissertation, and you'll find that critical opportunities have passed you by—opportunities to publish, get funding, attend meetings, and make connections. As one client remarked, "Once I began drafting my plan, I realized how vague and perhaps unrealistic my goals have been; I only wish I had thought to map out the next few years sooner!"

Here I want to share a plan inspired by those produced many years ago by my first Ph.D. student, who is now a tenured professor of anthropology at an R1 institution.[1]

This student was the rock star of five-year plans. She first began working with me as an undergraduate student on an independent study, and then proceeded on to graduate school as my advisee. She finished her Ph.D. in seven years, and this included lost time from a switch of institutions when I moved to take my second job. From her earliest days in graduate school, she had a five-year plan. She updated it annually and always shared it with me.

In this hypothetical plan, the first year shows a series of deadlines for submission to the major conferences in two fields—the Association for Asian Studies and the American Anthropological Association. June of the following year shows the deadline for a dissertation fieldwork fellowship. July shows the preliminary exams, and August includes the proposal defense and move to Japan for fieldwork. September of that year shows writing-up fellowship deadlines. The first two years also show the due dates for a committed book chapter (draft to editor, then requested revisions, and last, the final copyedited draft). Year three shows a planned date for the completion of the first dissertation chapter in June; other chapter completion dates follow.

You will note that years four and five are mostly empty except for continuing major conference submission deadlines, and an anticipated defense date. As these years draw closer they would be filled in.

The student who inspired this five-year plan example obtained, in total, some $200,000 of research funding in graduate school (in cultural anthropology—a field that does not have large grants), in addition to her basic TA funding package. She had more than one publication before finishing, and secured a tenure track position at an R1 institution in her first year on the market. As I said, she's now tenured.

Many of my readers tell me they are intimidated by the five-year plan. They feel frightened to think so far ahead, or anticipate major life goals. But as you can see from the example, the plan is as much about staying on top of deadlines as achieving major goals.

But let there be no mistake: Staying on top of deadlines is exactly what allows a person to achieve major life goals. The person who succeeds in getting into the national conference is, first and foremost,

EXAMPLE OF A FIVE-YEAR PLAN

	Jan	Feb	March	April	May	June	July	August	Sep	Oct	Nov	Dec
'14			12 Book Ch. due	15 AAA Paper Abstract		24 Fulbright-Hayes		7 AAS Paper Abstract		22 Conf. Travel Grant		3-7 AAA 31 JPN: Race 1st
'15	Revise Book Ch.	3 Univ. Travel Grant	1 Diss F'ship 15 AAA Paper Abstract 26-29 AAS			29 JPN: Race Revisions	1-3 Quals	6 AAS Abstract due 15 Oral 25 Move to JPN	1 Wen-Gren Diss. F'ship 20 Guggenheim	30 Book Ch. (final)	18-22 AAA	
'16	Start Ch.1	10 Leave JPN	4 JPN: Race Publish 31 AAS	1-3 AAS		1 Ch. 1 Done	31 AAS Panel Proposal	1 Book Chapter Publish		1 Ch. 2 Done	16-20 AAA	
'17	1 Ch. 3 Done	15 AAA Panel Abstract	16-19 AAS		1 Ch. 4 Done				1 Revise Diss		29-30 AAA	1-3 AAA Send Diss to readers!
'18			15 ACLS Public Fellows 22-25: AAS		1 Hunt Post-Doc	Diss. Defense!					14-18 AAA	

the person who actually remembers to submit the proposal to the national conference, by the deadline, properly formatted.

One of the most important outcomes of the five-year plan is that you never miss a submission deadline for a conference or a funding opportunity. As you learn of new conferences and funding opportunities, you simply add them in, without losing track of the other deadlines. You also plan out a publication schedule, and put your own deadlines for submission to journals right there in the plan. The money racks up, the publications rack up, and the networks rack up, and voilà, the cumulative effect five years later is an impressive CV that gets you short-listed.

Some of my clients have even included life events such as getting pregnant in their five-year plans and while I admire their determination, I am skeptical. You can't plan for everything, nor should you try. But plan for your career, because in that way you take control of it. The five-year plan allows you to be the master of your own process, and not passively leave it in the hands of your advisor, your department, or "fate." You decide when you'll write, when you'll defend, when you'll publish, and so on. While you can't control outcomes, these are all your decisions to make.

SEVEN

Building a Competitive Record

From the first moment the Ph.D. emerges as a thought in your mind, you can begin building a competitive record for the tenure track job market. These are the tasks to plan for as you construct your five-year plan for graduate school and beyond. Every decision you make—including whether to go to graduate school at all, which program to go to, which advisor to choose, and how to conduct yourself while there—can and should be made with an eye to the job you wish to have at the end. Many of these themes will be addressed in more detail in later chapters, but here is a checklist to copy and tape to your wall.

Before Graduate School

Ask yourself what job you want and whether an advanced degree is actually necessary for it.

Choose your graduate program based on both its focus on your scholarly interests and its tenure track placement rate. If it doesn't keep careful records of its placement rate, or does not have an impressive record of placing its Ph.D.'s in tenure track positions, do not consider attending that program, regardless of how appealing it may look.

Choose your advisor the same way. Before committing to an

advisor, find out as well as you can how many Ph.D.'s that potential
mentor has placed in tenure track positions in recent years. While
there is no foolproof way to do this, your best bet is to schedule
a visit to the campus and arrange to meet with current advanced
ABDs. They are usually the best-informed members of a department about recent placement rates. By contrast, early graduate students and faculty may well be united in denial, disinformation, and
false hope.

Go to the highest ranked graduate department you can get
into—so long as it funds you fully. That is not entirely because of
the "snob factor" of the names themselves (although this does represent serious cultural capital), but also because of the financial resources of leading departments. They are likely to offer funding
packages that come closer to approximating actual local cost of living. They have more scholars with national reputations to serve as
your mentors and letter writers, and they maintain lively brown-bag
and seminar series that bring in major visiting scholars with whom
you can network. Never assume, however, that Ivy League departments are the highest ranked or have the best placement rates.
Some of the worst-prepared job candidates with whom I've worked
have been from humanities departments at Yale, Harvard, and
Princeton. Do not be dazzled by abstract institutional reputations.
Ask steely-eyed questions about individual advisors and their actual
(not illusory) placement rates in recent years.

Do be aware, however, that the placement history of a top program tends to produce its own momentum, so that departments
around the country with faculty members from that program will
then look kindly on new applications from its latest Ph.D.'s. That,
my friends, is how privilege reproduces itself. It may be distasteful,
but you deny or ignore it at your peril.

Do not attend graduate school unless you are fully supported
by—at minimum—a multiyear teaching assistantship that provides
a tuition waiver, a stipend, and health insurance. Do not take out
new debt to attend graduate school. Because the tenure track job
market is so bleak, graduate school is a serious financial risk; a generous graduate stipend for all your years in the program is the requisite condition for pursuing it. The humanities and social science

fields are particular risks because the teaching assistant/graduate assistant stipends they offer have fallen far further behind the actual cost of living, overall, compared to those in the sciences. While some social science graduate programs offer a livable TA wage, this is rare among humanities and social science graduate programs. Make a budget for yourself to weigh your real living expenses (including your health care, child care, and other expenses) against the stipend offered. Use online cost of living calculators and information gleaned from actual graduate students in the program to ensure your figures are accurate. Do not consider attending any program that does not guarantee full coverage of these expenses for at least five years.

Do not be misled, however, by any institution's own use of the term "full funding." "Full funding" refers to the department's maximum stipend. That stipend is virtually never tied to actual living expenses in the geographical location. Institutions set a cap on stipends that arises from internal institutional calculations and negotiations, not the needs of real human beings residing in the area. Therefore, you must calculate the dollar amount you are offered against the real cost of living associated with the place, for the size and needs of your household. Realize that the majority of humanities respondents to a Ph.D. Debt Survey that I conducted in 2013 who have debt of $50,000 to $200,000 had what their institutions referred to as "full funding" packages for their Ph.D.'s.[1] Typical humanities stipends of some $14,000 to $18,000 a year are inadequate to cover actual living expenses, especially for those with dependents. When these are augmented with even small loans, the end result after a seven- to ten-year course of study is five- to six-figure debt. The department will not disclose this information. It is your responsibility to make these calculations.

Apply to six to ten graduate programs. If you are admitted with funding to more than one, leverage the offers to get the best possible package at your top choice (yes, you can negotiate).

Meet, or at least correspond, with every potential advisor so that you understand whether he or she has a hands-on approach to professionalization training and will be personally invested in your success.

Be entrepreneurial before even entering graduate school to locate and apply for multiple sources of financial support. Thoroughly investigate department, campus, regional, and national
funding options, as well as funding from special interest groups.
Do not forget the law of increasing returns: Success breeds success
and large follows small. A $500 book scholarship makes you more
competitive for a $1,000 conference grant, which situates you for a
$3,000 summer research fellowship, which puts you in the running
for a $10,000 fieldwork grant, which then makes you competitive
for a $30,000 dissertation writing grant.

Early in Graduate School

Never forget this primary rule: Graduate school is not your job;
graduate school is a means to the job you want. Do not settle in to
your graduate department like a little hamster burrowing in the
wood shavings. Stay alert with your eye always poised for the next
opportunity, whatever it is: to present a paper, attend a conference,
meet a scholar in your field, forge a connection, gain a professional
skill.

In year one and every year thereafter, read the job ads in your
field, and track the predominant and emerging emphases of the
listed jobs. Ask yourself how you can incorporate those into your
own project, directly or indirectly. You don't have to slavishly follow
trends, but you have to be familiar with them and be prepared to
relate your own work to them in some way.

Have a beautifully organized and professional CV starting in
your first year and in every subsequent year. Keep your eye out for
opportunities that add lines to your CV at a brisk pace.

Make strong connections with your advisor and other faculty
members in your department, and in affiliated departments. Interact with them as a young professional, confidently. Eschew excessive humility; it inspires contempt. Do not forget the letters of
recommendation that you will one day need them to write.

Minimize your work as a TA. Your first year will be grueling, but
learn the efficiency techniques of teaching as fast as you can, and

make absolutely, categorically, sure that you do not volunteer your labor beyond the hours paid. Believe me, resisting will take vigilance. But do it. You are paid for X hours of work; do not exceed them. You are not a volunteer and the university is not a charity. Teach well, but do not make teaching the core of your identity.

Be aware that faculty members in a variety of departments will be able to direct you to different grant sources, which, over time, will help you to continue paying for your studies without accruing debt. Not all faculty members are familiar with the same grant sources, so breadth is important.

Seek mentors widely. Assemble a team to support you in all of your needs—academic, but also emotional, logistical, financial, and so forth. Your advisor is but one member of your team. Other committee members, other faculty you meet in classes, administrators you encounter—all can assist. In my own graduate training in cultural anthropology, I leaned heavily on two English professors, my department head (an archaeologist), a historian who was the husband of my then-husband's advisor, and the dean of the graduate school, whom I had met early on in mandated National Science Foundation award meetings. All of these relationships came into play during my rough final year in the program, when I needed help extracting myself from a difficult advisor situation.

Strategize your writing projects in your courses, theses, and dissertation, to form the basis of potentially publishable papers. If offered the option of writing a master's thesis, seriously consider taking it, as it can form the core of your first refereed journal article. Plan out a publishing trajectory to ensure that you have at least one single-authored refereed journal article, and preferably more, before you defend your dissertation. While I can't tell you how many publications you need (this is field-dependent), I can tell you that the leap from zero to one is the most important. I call it The Power of One. A candidate with one peer-reviewed journal article is exponentially more credible than a candidate with none.

Attend every job talk in your department and affiliated departments religiously. It matters not if those talks are in your field or subfield. Go to them all. Job talks and other job-search opportunities such as attending a lunch with a candidate, serving on a search committee, or simply examining an applicant's CV and file are the best training you can provide yourself on the real operations of the tenure track job market, as opposed to your private and often delusional assumptions.

Beware of collective grad student paranoia. Other graduate students can be valuable as friends and allies, but don't become enmeshed in drama, and don't make the mistake of turning to them for professional advice. That is called the blind leading the blind.

Attend national conferences annually. It's fine to also go to local and regional conferences, but they must never take the place of your national conference, which provides irreplaceable insight into trends in your field, the ethos and habitus of your discipline, and the behavioral norms of professional scholars. It also presents the opportunity to network and to attend seminars dedicated to professional skills such as writing grant proposals or journal articles.

Strategize how to travel to conferences, and work with your cohort to make a habit of driving together to major national conferences and lodging together.

Apply indiscriminately for money, and master the fine art of tailoring your work to meet a grant agency's mission. You'll be surprised by how much the act of transforming your project to meet a new mission reveals to you hitherto unrecognized potentialities and insights into the work itself. Applying for a wide range of grants is one of the best intellectual exercises in which you can engage.

Take every opportunity available to present your work publicly. While I emphasized the importance of national conferences for reputation purposes, actively pursue every possible local and regional opportunity for experience purposes. Public speaking is one of the core skills of an academic career. Make your mistakes in graduate school, where the stakes are low, so that you are a master of the podium when the stakes are high.

In Your Final Years of Graduate School

Avoid like the plague offers of publication in edited collections, which is where good publications go to die. If you have a piece of work that can pass muster as a publication, make sure that it goes into a refereed journal, the best one you can reasonably manage. Don't ever throw it away on conference proceedings or the like. (This applies to the humanities and most social sciences; some conference proceedings in the sciences are legitimate publication venues. Know your field.) Following your conference presentations, do not be seduced by expressions of interest from editors of collections or third-tier journals or mystery "academic" presses. The opportunity may seem easy but you will pay the price later when the collection is delayed for years or the publication is too low in status to help you on the market.

By your third year or so, apply annually to present a paper at your national conference. If you are in the humanities, do not waste time participating in poster sessions. If you are in the hard sciences or experimental social sciences, check with a trusted advisor about the value of posters.

In the year before you go on the job market, propose and organize a high-profile panel for your national conference that is made up of up-and-coming assistant professors. Ask a well-known scholar to serve as discussant. Make efforts to have the panel respond to, or engage with, a trending topic in your field and/or one that is identified as the primary theme of that year's national meetings. This panel is your "coming out" party, and makes you visible on a national stage, framed and contextualized by the more established scholars who already have reputations on the panel's topic. (For more on the specifics of organizing a panel, please see chapter 19.) At the conference, do not forget to organize a lunch (or dinner or coffee) for the panelists to get to know them better and lay the groundwork for future collaborations and possibly letters of recommendation.

Cultivate a letter writer who is not from your Ph.D.-granting institution. Having all your recommendation letters come from your own committee or department is a sign of a relatively immature candidate. It is not a death knell in your first or second years on the market, but be aware that the strongest and most successful candidates will have a recommendation from an influential senior scholar from outside their home department who can speak to their standing in the field (and not simply to their performance as a graduate student).

Write your dissertation with an eye to the publications that it will become. As I have said, you need at least one refereed journal article while you are still ABD. At the same time, be aware that publications that date from before you accept your tenure track job do not typically count toward tenure. So the balance is delicate indeed. You must publish enough to get a job without prematurely exhausting the supply of material you will need for tenure. That is why I recommend writing a master's thesis, which will give you material for a publication without cutting into your dissertation material.

If you are in a book field, you need a plan for your book, even if you are still finishing the dissertation. Have a timeline for the production and submission of a book proposal to several presses for an advance contract. Note that you are permitted to submit multiple book proposals as long as you disclose you are doing so in the accompanying cover letter.

Be aware that presses will not look kindly at a book proposal in which more than half of the material has already been published in articles. Therefore, in a typical five-chapter dissertation, you want no more than two chapters to be put out as refereed journal articles. While writing the dissertation, have a publishing plan in place. You may write one chapter, for example, with an eye to fast publication while you are ABD. Set aside other material for refereed journal articles while you're on the tenure track. Meanwhile, write the dissertation itself as much like a book as your committee will allow. If your committee insists on methodology and literature review chapters, write them with the full knowledge that they will most likely be removed from the ultimate book manuscript.

Remember that the best dissertation is a finished dissertation. Your dissertation must satisfy a committee, while your book must satisfy a set of reviewers and an editor who operate nationally and internationally. Do what it takes to satisfy your committee and finish. Leave the Sturm und Drang for when you are revising the manuscript into the book or articles that will become the real mark of your scholarly reputation.

Be the sole instructor of at least one course but not more than three (if you can help it). After about three courses, teaching delivers diminishing returns and becomes a distraction from the real capital-producing work necessary for the tenure track job market, which (unless you're applying to community colleges) is publication and conference activity. If your department does not offer ABDs the opportunity to teach their own courses, then carefully seek an opportunity from another college in the area. Do a good job, but do not allow your teaching to derail you from the writing, publishing, grant writing, and conferences that are the core elements of the tenure track search. TA experience is not an adequate substitute for teaching a course of your own.

Go on the market while ABD, because you want to make your worst mistakes while you still have a year of financial support from your home department. Most people who prevail on the market need several years to do so.

Cultivate a professional persona as a young scholar. That persona is separate from your previous identity as a graduate student and is, instead, confident, assertive, sophisticated, and outspoken. Devote as much time as it takes to writing out brief—and I do mean brief—summaries of your dissertation research, teaching techniques and philosophy, and future publication plans. Practice delivering those brief summaries until they become second nature.

Make your application materials absolutely flawless. Take your ego out of the process and ask everyone you know to ruthlessly critique your CV, letter, teaching statement, and research statement. Prioritize the advice you receive from young faculty members who have recently been on the market, and from senior professors who have recently chaired search committees. Above all, read my blog!

Some graduate students will rush to follow these rules, some will panic and view the task as impossible, and others will indignantly reject their "careerist" and "neoliberal" ethos. The choice is entirely yours. But be aware that the best and most competitive candidates—the ones whom I have watched and assisted as they sailed through the job market into tenure track offers—had every one of these elements on their record.

EIGHT

....

Your Campaign Platform

Overburdened search committee members don't want to know about every last little thing you've ever done or thought. They want to know you, rather, as a neat, legible, and memorable package of skills that meets their needs for the job advertised. All of the search committee members should be able to walk away from every stage of evaluation with consistent understandings of your profile in terms of research, publishing, teaching, and future research plans. If one member says "he's the guy who does X," they should all know exactly who she means.

In my first job market workshops, when I was still a graduate student myself, I used to say, cynically, that you should transform yourself into a "commodity." Nowadays, while I don't think that's wrong, I find it more helpful to suggest that you think of yourself as a political candidate with a campaign platform.

Think back to Barack Obama's first presidential campaign. Before he ran, he and his team of advisors hashed out his platform—where he stood on all the major questions of the domestic economy, security, immigration, and so on. This platform became his bible—he never deviated from it, although he would, of course, spin it differently depending on whether he was speaking to millionaire Democratic donors or Detroit autoworkers. But no matter whom he was addressing, you'd instantly know that this was Barack Obama, Democratic candidate for president of the United States. There was no mistaking him for Mitt Romney, or an independent, or some other Democrat.

That needs to be you, campaigning for your job. You need to stand for things, and those commitments need to be consistent across the board, and instantly recognizable as yours. Of course, you can adapt them depending on the type or area of job to which you're applying, especially if you can apply across disciplines. But for each type of job, hammer out the planks of your platform on all the major questions related to undergraduate and graduate teaching, current research, future research, publication plans, service, administration, and collaborations. For each job to which you apply, particularly when you reach the stage of interviews and campus visits, make sure you deliver a clear, legible, plausible, and consistent message across the board, to all who ask. You don't win over hearts and minds by being mealy mouthed and noncommittal, but by articulating a platform that meets the needs of your "electorate."

How do you create your platform? I suggest you think of it as containing something like eight planks. Those planks relate to the elements of a faculty profile mentioned above. Notice I said "faculty" profile, not scholarly. Your platform must extend beyond your research to encompass your broader subject position (even praxis, if you will) as a faculty colleague. And there needs to be an identifiable commonality tying together your commitments regarding teaching, research, service, and so forth. "Make yourself into a little package with a bow on top!" I used to tell job seekers wryly back in my first workshops. By which I mean, make all your parts fit together.

An example will help, and for the sake of accuracy, I'll use my own early career case.

My platform coming out of graduate school in cultural anthropology in the mid-1990s contained the following elements:

- Area focus: Japan—contemporary, "postmodern," and transnational Japan; not the Japan of villages and tradition.
- Topical focus: gender, transnationalism, and critical race studies; this derived from but moved well beyond my dissertation focus on internationalized urban career women seeking jobs and partners abroad.

- Disciplinary identity/commitment: humanistic anthropologist with strong investment in critical theory and literary analysis (many of my sources were textual), but always grounded in extended ethnographic fieldwork.
- Research program: targeting cultural studies–inflected journals (*Public Culture*, *Cultural Anthropology*, and so forth); planning a book with a major university press; planning a second project on transgender identity in Japan, a project I'd been developing for several years.
- Pedagogical commitments, Japan/Asia: Japan is little understood beyond stereotypes; commitment to teaching about Japan as transnational, fully "(post)modern." Able to teach East Asia in general in similar vein, and grow Asian studies to meet student fascination with J-pop, anime, manga, and so forth.
- Pedagogical commitments, anthropology: enthusiastic proponent of the reflexive turn, critical anthropology, and mixing standard approaches with new attention to race, gender, and sexuality; particular enthusiasm for intro-level, undergrad teaching; anthropology is essential in teaching the urgent topics of globalization, multiculturalism, and diversity.
- Campus/interdisciplinary orientation: trained in a four-field department and committed to four-field training (a big issue in anthropology); committed to interdisciplinary collaborations with English, comp lit, East Asian literature, cinema studies, and sociology; enthusiastic participant in cross-campus humanities center–types of venues; interested in bringing an anthropological voice into cross-campus dialogues.
- Service commitments: strong orientation to professionalization training for graduate students especially, and also undergrad career preparation.

As you can see, most of these are a statement of this, not that. And the planks stand in a loose organic kinship with one another: You can see a prevailing orientation toward fluidity, border crossing, and change—research on transnational actors, teaching students operating in multicultural environments, engaging in conversations across disciplines, putting Japan in dialogue with critical theory.

I certainly adapted the planks of this platform to different disciplines, since I applied for jobs in Japan studies, anthropology, and gender studies. I also adjusted it for particular departments. For more conservative anthropology departments, I emphasized the four-field commitment and empirical fieldwork, and downplayed the critical theory. When speaking to the Asian studies side of a joint Asian studies and anthropology position, I prioritized evidence of my ability to teach specific courses on Japan, China, and Korea. But in all adjustments, I remained consistent to my basic identity as outlined above.

Let me hasten to add that you will never incorporate these platform statements as such in your job documents. That would be "telling, not showing" (you'll learn more about why this is bad in later chapters). These are just internal rubrics that you can use to organize your identity as a candidate. When you articulate your identity in documents and interviews, by contrast, you instead *show* the ways your research and teaching outcomes demonstrate these commitments.

"But what if that's not what they want?" I can hear you asking. There are two ways to answer that. The first is, it's true—it may not be what they want, and you may get passed over for the job. However, that outcome is less likely than this alternative: that they find themselves edified and inspired by your clarity of vision and your strongly held convictions, and adjust their own thinking because of them. "We thought we only wanted X, but having read this application, it seems important to expand our thinking to include Y." That is what strength of conviction can do. It is persuasive and inspiring. I believe that it opens more doors than it closes, as long as it's presented not with dogmatism or judgment, but collegially, as the start, rather than end, of the conversation.

NINE

....

Why They Want to Reject You

So, you've eradicated self-defeating grad student habits, you've made your five-year plan, you've written your dissertation, you've scheduled your defense, you've established your platform, and you're heading out on the market. You've done everything Dr. Karen has said, and it's going to be a breeze! Right?

Wrong.

Why?

Because, in a nutshell, the search committee wants to reject you. They don't love you. They aren't excited to see your application come in. On the contrary, they dread dealing with it. But it's not personal. It's not *you* they dread, per se. It's the search itself. The whole exercise of sifting through applications, evaluating, discussing, interviewing, inviting, and offering in this demoralized and downsized industry.

Let me explain. You probably never thought about this before, but one of the consequences of the evaporation of tenure lines and tenure track faculty is an intensified service burden on those full-time faculty that remain. Their teaching may or may not have increased—that depends on the dependence of their department on adjunct substitutes. But adjunct population notwithstanding, there are things that only full-time tenure line faculty can do, and most forms of administrative service are among them. Fewer faculty are handling more administrative tasks, and teaching under less desirable conditions, and seeing their incomes fall further behind the cost of living . . . and they are not a happy lot.

Here's something else you probably never thought about. When and under what conditions do those overburdened faculty members actually read your files? Are they sipping cocktails on a breezy veranda, poring excitedly over the brilliance emanating from each and every page? Actually, no. Here is the average day of the faculty member who is reading your file:

She wakes up at seven a.m. to get two kids up and fed, teeth brushed, and out the door to school. Runs from school to the office, and preps for her large intro class (enrollment three hundred). Teaches class. Comes back to seventy-five emails from large intro class complaining about grading of recent midterm. Meets with teaching assistants who handled the grading and are now at the center of a mass undergrad class mutiny. Handles crying TA. Rushes out to lunch meeting. Rushes back for office hours. Meets with fifteen unhappy students, several of whom threaten to speak to the dean about her class. Works on paperwork for recertification of large intro class for gen ed requirements in the college. Realizes data are needed but office administrator, now shared with two other departments, is unavailable to provide data. Walks to an office across campus to find someone who can provide data. Pores over impenetrable enrollment figures. Comes back late for faculty meeting. At faculty meeting department head explains further 18 percent budget cut to be absorbed in the coming semester, reductions in TA lines, and increasing enrollments in all courses. Leaves faculty meeting early under the judgmental glares of childless colleagues, rushes to pick up kids from after-school care. Hustles kids home for piano lessons and soccer. Throws dinner on the table at six-thirty. Cleans up kitchen. Argues with partner over unwashed dishes from breakfast. Helps kids with homework. Bathes kids and puts them to bed. Folds clean laundry left over from night before. At nine-thirty sits down to computer to log in . . . and groans to discover there are 349 viable applications. Lecture for next day's class still not finished.

Is this search committee member excited? Eager? Enthusiastic? No, my friend. She is exhausted. Dare I say enervated. What she wants, what she wants more than anything in the world at that moment, is to be able to reject 324 of those applications so that she can get to the long short list she needs for the next day's meeting, shut down the computer, and go to bed.

How much time is she going to give to each application in this initial rejection round review? A minute or two; five if you're lucky. The letter gets skimmed, and the CV gets glanced at. And voilà—93 percent of the files are summarily dispatched to the reject folder so that she does not have to look at them or think about them or worry about them for one more second.

Overwork, exhaustion, irritability, second shift, increasing service, and ballooning numbers of applications—this all comes together into that moment when your file is opened and gets its first look. It's not pretty. They don't love you. What they want, with all their hearts, is to reject you.

So what do you do? You deliver an undeniable record in a small number of flawless pages. You give them exactly the information they need, and not one word more.

A two-page job letter, a one-page teaching statement, a two-ish-page research statement (this is variable, as I explain in chapter 27), and let's say (just as an example, not a prescription!) a five-page CV . . . on those ten slender pages rest your hopes for permanent, secure employment, health insurance, benefits for you and your family, and the opportunity to work in your chosen profession. There are no ten pages that you'll write that carry a greater weight, and that are worth more money.

And yet candidate after candidate throws these documents together in a day or two, believing that somehow—by magic perhaps—all the years of work will simply automatically translate into the outcomes they desire, with no sustained critical effort on their part to do the translation of it in language the search committee will respect and respond to.

Needless to say, this belief is incorrect. A set of job documents requires hours and hours of painstaking, exhausting, excruciating work. The stakes will never be higher, and the odds are as far from being in your favor as odds can be. This is the time that you understand just what you're up against, and just how far you need to reach within yourself to find the words to translate years and years of work into perfect, polished, factual, unemotional, honest, non-manipulative prose that articulates, without hysteria, desperation, pandering, or flattery, the match between your record and the advertised job.

Some dismiss this attention to the writing as an anal, obsessive-compulsive preoccupation with meaningless detail. It isn't. The space of translation between the record and the outcome is a space of tremendous creativity and meaning—it is a kind of self making—and it deserves deep care and attention.

TEN

······

When to Go on the Market
and How Long to Try

Some job seekers sail out on the market, get short-listed, get a campus visit, and get an offer, all in their first year. It does happen. But it's the exception. For most job seekers, the coveted tenure track job offer comes only after years of searching and many rejections.

That is undoubtedly why the question I'm asked most often by readers is "When should I go on the market and how long should I keep trying?"

The first question is easy to answer. You should go on the market as early as you can, ideally as an ABD. I know that not everyone will agree with this advice, but I give it for two reasons. The first is that it is my strong belief that only after large quantities of painfully humiliating failures on the job market will you gain the skills to succeed. This may not be true for others, but it was most definitely true for me. My first year on the market, as an ABD, was a bloodbath. If I had not had that year while still safely affiliated with my graduate institution, I would never have learned what I needed to prevail on the market the following year.

The second reason is simply logistical. If you wait until you've finished the Ph.D.—indeed, even if you wait until you've defended the dissertation—you are probably too late in the job cycle to score anything for the coming year. And with the dissertation defended and the degree finished, you have nowhere to go, nothing to do, no affiliation, and probably no income. And that is a terrible place to be, both financially and professionally.

Let me review the timing of the job market cycle from chapter 4: The majority of good jobs are advertised in late summer and fall, with interviews in winter and offers in spring. Therefore, in the pursuit of unbroken affiliation/income after the Ph.D., you must apply for jobs in fall term of the year you plan to defend, and then ideally get offered a job in March or April, defend in May, submit in June (or August, although that is not preferred), and start your new position in the fall. To do otherwise leaves you empty-handed. Do not believe any advisor who tells you otherwise.

In short: Go on the market as an ABD. If you have the elements of a competitive record that I describe throughout this book, you'll be a competitive candidate.

ABDs, of course, have special challenges in overcoming the graduate student identity. Here I give a list of ten things to attend to:

1. You must have your dissertation substantially finished, and have a rigorous writing schedule and *a firm defense date*. This defense date must be stated clearly in your cover letter, in the first paragraph. You must not deviate from this writing schedule.

2. You must have *at least one publication, and preferably more, in a refereed journal.* You will not be competitive without this.

3. You must have a *compelling dissertation topic,* however that is defined in your field. It must be timely enough that search committees are motivated to grab you now rather than later.

4. You must have *a vibrant conference record* at the leading national conferences in your field, for papers on your dissertation topic.

5. Your ABD year, you must *organize a major panel* for the leading conference in your field. You must gather leading young scholars (not other ABDs and graduate students!) to speak on the panel. You must score an important senior scholar in your field to serve as the discussant. Ideally, you acquire for

your panel whatever "special" status your national conference confers, such as invited status.

6. You must have a recommender from a high-status institution
   outside your Ph.D.-granting institution. The presence of *a
   third recommender from an outside institution* proves that you are
   far beyond the normal run of ABDs and are, in fact, a dynamic young scholar soon to be launched.

7. You must be able to *see beyond your dissertation* to the book/se-
   ries of articles that it will eventually become, and articulate
   that publication plan clearly.

8. You *must not make querulous excuses* about the state of the dissertation ("I am still working on chapter four," "I know I need
   to add more discussion of race," "I need to revisit the archive
   to gather more material for my second case study," and so
   on). This is graduate student talk, not job candidate talk.

9. You must be able to *speak about teaching as a professor, not a
   TA.* You must have your own original courses developed, as
   well as ideas for basic intro courses and core seminars in your
   field.

10. You must be able to *articulate the import of your dissertation in
    advancing disciplinary boundaries* and forging new knowledge
    and connections in your field(s). Nobody wants to hear about
    what your dissertation is. They want to hear about what your
    dissertation *does.*

You must, of course, also have an impeccable CV, a flawless cover
letter, and a dynamic teaching statement. You must know how to de-
code a job ad. You must know how to dress and speak in interviews.
As an ABD, you may have a harder time jettisoning graduate student verbal habits, but it's by no means impossible.

Now, turning to the question of how long to keep trying on the
market after one or more unsuccessful years: Unfortunately, on
that front, I cannot offer absolute recommendations, because everyone's circumstances differ. I hear many stories of those who had
to search for that first job for five years, adjuncting the whole time.
I've heard some say it took them seven years.

Your decision will hinge on your personal circumstances. You

have to evaluate your level of debt, sources of income from family or other work, and your stomach for rejection and uncertainty.
You must balance the need to earn sufficient income to prevent further debt, while keeping enough time to remain active in publishing, conferences, and so on. Give yourself a clear end date. In the
current economy, I would question continuing as an adjunct longer
than about three years. Adjuncting is inherently exploitative and
should be used strategically and instrumentally by job seekers only
insofar as it serves their needs and goals. Adjuncting for seven years
while searching for a tenure track job might make sense if you have
a spouse or family member who can make sure you're not living in
poverty for all those years. But if you don't have that support, such
a plan could well be financially and psychologically ruinous.

Adjuncting itself does not spell death to your tenure track
chances, as long as you frame it correctly in your job letters. If you
tell a desperate and emotional story about an adjuncting or nonacademic employment "gap," the gap will loom large in your record.
If you tell a factual story about your academic output, the gap will
appear minimal and/or irrelevant.

Too many adjuncts inadvertently write job letters that communicate an identity as an adjunct rather than a potential tenure track
hire. This is a mistake. An understandable mistake, to be sure, but
still a mistake, because of one simple fact: The department running a tenure track search is not seeking to hire an adjunct. Just as
you don't emphasize your graduate school past in your job documents, you also don't tell a story that foregrounds an adjunct identity. This is—let me be perfectly clear—not because I believe search
committees have a bias against adjuncts, or that I believe adjuncting is shameful. It is because a chronological account of one-off
courses taught on a range of different campuses cannot stand in for
a systematic account of a unitary overarching teaching profile that
is portable to the new institution.

The typical tendency is to tell a chronological tale of how you
taught as an adjunct here and an adjunct there, and taught this
class at the U of X in fall 2014 and this other class at Y College
in spring 2015, and then taught this other new class at the U of
Z in fall 2015. Resist that temptation. While you believe it shows

the depth and breadth of your teaching experience, this particular phrasing actually ends up foregrounding all of those campuses, and the traveling you did between them, rather than a cohesive and unitary teaching profile. Search committees don't want a chronological narrative of when and where you taught so much as they want an ahistorical demonstration of what and how you teach. The basic rule when it comes to teaching is not when and where but what and how. In short, the historical story of prior adjunct classes tethers you both to the past and to other campuses, rather than foregrounding the pedagogical methods that you will be bringing to the new campus in the future.

Moving between these two approaches usually requires only a few tweaks of tense and detail in the teaching paragraph of the cover letter. Teaching paragraphs will ideally articulate courses you are prepared to teach, specific courses you have taught or can teach, and, most important, how you teach them, using distinctive and memorable methods. Don't be afraid to use the present tense for all teaching verbiage. You can easily translate the previous courses you taught as an adjunct into non-geographically-tethered descriptions of the classes themselves, teachable anywhere. An example will help. Rather than writing, "Last spring I was offered the opportunity to teach Introduction to Cultural Anthropology at Carleton College, and in that course I had students conduct mini-ethnographies of the town of Northfield," you will write "In my Introduction to Cultural Anthropology I always assign mini-ethnography projects in the local community." See the difference? The universities in South Carolina or Arizona, and so forth, to which you're applying don't need—or want—to know about Carleton or Northfield. They need to know how you will teach, for them. Search committees need to be easily able to imagine you as a faculty member in their departments. Invoking the names of other universities and colleges is an obstacle to that.

Then there is the issue of campus status. If you name other campuses, and those other colleges and universities are of lesser status than the job being applied for, it has the effect of making you look less than qualified for the tenure track position. Conversely, if they are of much higher status, their continual mention will potentially alienate. Imagine a search committee at Middle Tennessee State, for example, reading a letter that proclaims, "While at Princeton I taught X. Later at Princeton I developed a new course in Y. Then as a visiting assistant professor at Dartmouth I taught Z." It's not verbiage that will warm the MTSU professor's heart, and it doesn't reassure the professor that you'll be suited to teaching MTSU students.

Regardless of how long and where you adjunct, make sure you're protecting yourself and your financial and emotional interests as well as you can. Do not sacrifice your health and well-being indefinitely at the altar of tenure track aspirations. When choosing among several options, make sure to go for the one that advances your personal cause the best. Weigh your immediate need to build a competitive record for the purposes of the job search against your long-term financial and mental health.

ELEVEN

·············

Where Are the Jobs?
Institution Types and Ranks

As you gird your loins for the job market, you need to have an accurate understanding of the types of jobs to which you might apply, and the match between those jobs and your particular profile and platform. In my work at The Professor Is In, I've come to recognize what I call the "R1 candidate." This is a candidate who typically comes from an elite program, has received major fellowships, attends national conferences, has published in major refereed journals, and has at least one influential referee on her reference list. When I see a client like this (and I see a lot of them), I know immediately the type of job she'll be prioritizing and the type of job documents she'll be producing. That doesn't mean her documents are in good shape. Usually, they're a train wreck. But I can see what the documents are going to look like when we're done, and where they're going to be sent, and how they're likely to be received.

Not all candidates are R1 candidates, nor do they have to be. There are many ranks and types of tenure track jobs available. But in this era of job market compression, there is no longer a clear distinction between those R1 candidates who apply for R1 and other elite jobs, and other candidates who apply for lower ranking jobs. Because jobs of any kind are so few and far between, R1 candidates routinely apply for, and are grateful to get, any jobs at all, including those at regional teaching colleges in far-flung parts of the country, where the teaching loads are high and the pay minimal. As a result, these formerly humble teaching colleges have grown greedy for more competitive types of candidates than they could previously attract, and expectant of higher levels of research productivity than they actually support.

But I get ahead of myself. For now, let me clarify the various types and ranks of institutions that advertise tenure track positions. Please note that what follows are thumbnail sketches only, and individual institutions will vary widely. You can discover the rank and type of any institution by searching in the database of the Carnegie Foundation's Classification of Institutions of Higher Education.[1]

At the top are the Ivy Leagues. These are usually the "best" jobs in terms of teaching load (lowest) and salary and benefits (highest), but these perks come at a price: extremely high research productivity expectations and an often cutthroat competitive atmosphere. Not all Ivy League departments will necessarily tenure their assistant professors, so the job, while excellent, may well also be temporary. On the other hand, anyone leaving an Ivy assistant professor position tends to land on their feet in an excellent second job, not least because the prestige and connections they gained during the years at the Ivy provide all manner of cultural, academic, and actual capital to exploit.

Ranked next are what throughout this book I call the R1s, although that old Carnegie classification has been replaced by RU/VH (research university/very high research activity) for research institutions that maintain a comprehensive slate of Ph.D. programs and very high expectations for research. This clumsy neologism slides off the tongue not nearly so smoothly as R1, which I still prefer and use in this book. R1s are the major public institutions such as the University of Wisconsin, Penn State University, Ohio State University, and the University of Washington, and private institutions such as Duke, Emory, and Tufts. These also encompass some but not all of the campuses of such behemoth systems as the University of California, including Berkeley, Los Angeles, Irvine, Davis, and so on. R1 positions offer low teaching loads and relatively high salaries, but these will vary widely based on the geographical location of the institution and its current financial status, particularly among the public universities.

A major gap has emerged between public and private R1 faculty compensation in recent years. State legislatures have drastically cut funding to public higher education institutions, causing salaries there to stagnate. At the full professor level, R1 faculty lagged behind private R1 faculty by 24 percent in 2013, increasing from 18 percent in 2004.[2] But this has not happened evenly across institutions or states, and individual programs and colleges will also vary widely due to differing levels of endowment and fund-raising success. As one example: A finance department in a rich college of business on a poor campus will likely offer much higher salaries than a comparative literature department in a poor college of arts and sciences, even if it's on a wealthier campus. Because of this variability, it is almost impossible to predict exactly the financial conditions you'll find at your public R1 position, but in all cases there will be high research expectations paired with substantial research support.

Next on the list comes the elite small liberal arts college, or SLAC. The SLAC is a category that encompasses a wide range of institutions. At the elite level are private, liberal arts colleges such as Williams and Amherst in the East, Pomona and Claremont McKenna in the West, Macalester in the Midwest, and Davidson in the South. These colleges, which usually enjoy large endowments, offer high salaries and research support, while maintaining a focus on undergraduate teaching. Positions at colleges like this will likely bring the perks of an R1 or Ivy position, but without the opportunity to teach graduate students. While institutions like this publicize their focus on the student experience and the centrality of teaching to their mission, job seekers should be aware that their research expectations for both hiring and tenure may be virtually the same as an R1's.

Next come R2s, or, in the newer Carnegie parlance, research university/high research activity (RU/H), such as Auburn, Loyola, and Northern Illinois. These campuses will sometimes be secondary or tertiary campuses in a state system, and will maintain master's programs (with some Ph.D. programs scattered in), and a relatively higher teaching load.

Let me pause to explain teaching load. In broad-strokes generalization, while the standard teaching load in the humanities at an Ivy League might be 2/1, and at an R1 something like 2/2, at an R2 institution it will be more like 2/3 or 3/3. These figures refer to the expected number of classes taught by each faculty member per term; for example, 2/2 means that the average faculty member is expected to teach two courses in the fall semester and two courses in the spring semester, barring any special course releases or administrative leave, or so forth. Humanities faculty always teach more—as a category—than science or business faculty, reflecting their lower economic clout and higher service burden on the corporatized campus.

Thus the primary difference in positions at an R1 and an R2 will be in the expected teaching load. There is, or should be, an indirect relationship between teaching load and research productivity expectations: The higher the teaching load, the lower the productivity expected for tenure. In theory.

Middle-ranked SLACs such as Grinnell, or Franklin and Marshall will likely have a similar teaching load to an R2, somewhere around 2/3 or 3/3, depending on the college and department. These schools recruit both students and faculty from a national pool, and salaries and benefits will be good but not lavish. There will be a commensurate balancing of faculty focus between research and teaching demands.

Low-ranked SLACs such as Susquehanna or Monmouth are what I typically refer to in this book as regional teaching colleges. They draw their student body primarily from a regional community. Their teaching loads are very high—4/4 is not uncommon—and salaries are low. It is here that we see the greatest transformation in the competitiveness of the search pool. In the old days, elite R1 candidates rarely sought these positions. Those days are gone. Now even an Ivy-trained Ph.D. may well be thrilled with a tenure track offer at a small regional teaching college. As a result, expectations for applications, and for tenure, are in flux. Don't assume that research should be marginalized in your profile when you apply to these institutions. They are learning that they can expect significant research productivity from their faculty, without necessarily providing the web of support that is taken for granted at R1s, R2s, elite SLACs, and Ivy Leagues.

One guest poster wrote an account on my blog of a search at his regional teaching college: "I work at the sort of school that most of us, when we entered graduate school, thought we would only consider working at if we couldn't get a job anywhere else. The teaching load is heavy. The location is not ideal for most academics. The institutional culture can, at times, seem more like the DMV than an institution of higher learning."

When the search reached a stalemate between older faculty who wanted to hire good teachers, and brand-new faculty who wanted to hire researchers, the administration weighed in on the side of research-centrism. "Apparently, this boosts the campus's standing with the state, which brings more money in, which makes administrators happy." Expectations for tenure on that campus similarly rose.

Small regional colleges with current religious affiliation, such as Saint Mary's in California or Hope College in Michigan, maintain a strong religious foundation governing issues of faith and morality, and you may sometimes (although not always) have to make a faith-related commitment as a requirement of employment. Institutions like this frequently prioritize a campus culture oriented around this shared religious identity, and administratively, may be very insular and lack transparency. Colleges with a former religious affiliation, such as Nazareth College in New York (much in the news in 2013 for the famous "W" case discussed in chapter 50), share some of the qualities of these campuses even when they are no longer explicitly affiliated with a denomination. Teaching loads are high (4/5 or 5/5), and salaries are usually quite low.

Finally, there is the community college. Community colleges are typically two-year institutions in which teaching is the preeminent criterion for hiring and tenure, and teaching loads are very heavy (5/5 or higher). Community colleges serve a widely diverse population of students, including adult students, returning students, and those still developing their skills for college-level work. Consequently classes may be less rigorous, and may meet in the evenings and on weekends. Community colleges are not my area of expertise, and I refer readers to the writings of Rob Jenkins, a tenured professor of English at a southern community college who writes a regular column for the *Chronicle of Higher Education*. What I do know is that salaries at community colleges are often quite competitive, and may be equivalent to those at R2s and mid-tier liberal arts colleges. And many Ph.D.'s who find themselves at community colleges discover that with practice and effort, they can combine the heavy teaching load with research productivity. Many find life at these colleges unexpectedly rewarding. As historian John Ball wrote in a recent essay on his work at a community college: "I have found a great deal of freedom in the classroom, institutional backing for maintaining my scholarly connections, and interesting and supportive colleagues. Perhaps most important of all, I have found students who have challenged me to rethink how I look at history. And in the end, isn't that the best thing one can find in one's classes?"[3]

As you contemplate these different ranks and types of institutions, make sure you do not delude yourself with the idea that since you "aren't really ambitious" and "don't really want a cutthroat kind of environment," you can ignore the elements of the competitive record I describe in this book. As I hope I've made clear, community colleges and other small colleges are in no way a low-stress alternative for slacker Ph.D.'s who don't want to work too hard. The competition is intense at every single level of institution, and every institution maintains high standards and expectations for its hires. It is, in all ways and on all campuses, a buyer's market.

TWELVE

• • • • • • • • • • •

Where and How to Find Reliable Advice

If you're reading this book, you're getting good advice. But a book can only go so far. At some point you're going to need personalized advice by people who have taken the time to know your record and your career goals. Where do you find this? There are five places to look: your advisor, your other professors and academic mentors, career services on campus, online resources such as *Chronicle Vitae* and *Inside Higher Ed,* and paid services such as The Professor Is In. I'll discuss each of these in turn.

All Ph.D. students turn initially to their advisors for job market advice. Advisors are a mixed bag: Some are great, some are good, some are mediocre, and some are downright awful. There are advisors who extend themselves in every possible way to support their advisees, and there are advisors who extend themselves in a range of surprising ways to undermine and sabotage them. More than active sabotage, however, a kind of benign neglect, at least as regards job market preparation, is typical.

I can't tell you what kind of advisor you have, but I can tell you this: Don't ever accept anything your advisor tells you about the job market without getting a second opinion. I am not speaking here about your scholarly project and the dissertation itself. I have no opinion about those. Well, I do—make sure your research is original, valid, up-to-date, well written, and finished. But beyond that, the intellectual project is not my concern. I am talking about your competitive record for purposes of the job search. Do not assume that your advisor either a) understands the components of a competitive job market profile at this point in time; or b) is able and/or willing to advise you on how to achieve it.

You certainly want to ask your advisor for advice. And I hope that what you receive is good. But once you get it, check it against the advice that you find in this book, on my blog and other online resources, and against the advice you get from other academic mentors, especially junior faculty who have recently prevailed on the job market.

Beware of any advice like the following:

- "You don't need to publish."
- "You're not ready to publish."
- "Just finish your dissertation and don't worry about anything else."
- "You'll have no problem getting a job once you've finished the dissertation."
- "Everyone in our discipline/field gets good jobs."
- "Our department has an excellent placement rate so you don't need to worry."
- "Don't seek out teaching experience; it will only distract you."
- "Focus on your teaching; it's the key to getting a job."
- "Don't go to conferences."
- "Go to all the conferences, regardless of expense."
- "Working on [advisor's pet project] will look great on your CV."
- "You're not qualified to apply for [major research grant/writing fellowship/postdoc]."
- "You're not qualified for any jobs."
- "You're only qualified to apply for postdocs, not jobs."
- "Only apply to a few, select jobs; the rest are beneath you."

Nobody knows why so many advisors give advice like the above, but they do, and it is dangerous.

Your search for second opinions will take you to your other

professors and academic mentors. These you can find anywhere. Start with your committee and other faculty in your department, and extend outward to mentors across campus and at different campuses around the country. There is no limit on the number of these mentors you can cultivate. As I said in an earlier chapter, cultivate a team.

Of course you'll want to be vigilant to disciplinary boundaries. For example, your mentor in cinema studies may not know much about the four-field tension in anthropology, but he knows a great deal about judging institutional status. Or, he can't tell you if the content of your proposed ethnographic methods class is up to date, but he can tell you if your suit sleeves need to be hemmed. No one mentor is an expert on everything, so be proactive in seeking information from many, always prioritizing those who have fresh-lived experience of the job market. It's valuable to cull advice from different locations and combine it.

Many grad students, not knowing how to find help from advisors, or having sought it unsuccessfully, turn in desperation to career services on their campus. This is generally a mistake. While career services seem to be making an effort to improve their offerings for graduate students in recent years, it is still an office on campus whose primary purpose is to serve undergraduates. They understand entry-level job searches, and how to make a business résumé and cover letter. They are not typically well versed in the intricacies and oddities of the academic job market. There are exceptions to this rule, and if you have evidence that your career services staff are indeed well informed about the tenure track search, then by all means use them. But if you're not, approach cautiously, if at all. I don't doubt that they are sincere. I don't doubt that they take their jobs very seriously. But anyone who has not been responsible for the awful task of evaluating several hundred CVs for a single scholarly position is not qualified to opine on the fine points of CV organization and content.

This is because it is not just the information on the CV that is at issue; it is the ethos or rhetoric of the CV—the aura of the CV that communicates that you, the candidate, are the genuine article, an insider. If tenure track hiring is now the equivalent of the

Olympics, then mistakes within the .001 realm in your job documents are enough to keep you from even being short-listed. Career services staff typically don't grasp distinctions at this fine a level, although there are exceptions.

Fortunately, the Internet has transformed the state of career advising for would-be academics. The career advice pages of *Inside Higher Ed*, the *Chronicle of Higher Education*, and *Chronicle Vitae* are now filled to the brim with hands-on information on writing a CV, composing a cover letter, planning a publishing trajectory, interviewing, teaching, getting writing done, evaluating service, and so on. Hapless job seekers without live advisors to hand are no longer operating in an information vacuum.

As with any subject, though, approach this with the research skills you've perfected in your years in graduate school.

It's sad that many graduate students bring their intellectual A-game to their research, but approach professionalization as a shameful, furtive afterthought. It is understandable, given the hostile environment that often prevails toward these efforts. But in establishing your autonomous stance to your career, bring the intellectual heft that you use for your dissertation to this work as well. I don't care who you are; if you're finishing a Ph.D., you are an accomplished researcher and can find, evaluate, and catalog useful advice for the job market. Don't accept advice at face value. The same rule applies here as above: Cross-check it against other opinions, and draw your own conclusions.

Finally, you can consider using paid services. This is a relatively new development, and The Professor Is In is among the first and only businesses offering assistance on job documents and interview techniques. Other coaches and consultants are available to assist with writing projects, overcoming writer's block, and even finding work-life balance. Paying for advising is often dismissed by professors as further evidence of the neoliberal downfall of the academy, and you might encounter resistance from your advisors when they discover you've done it. Their mixed feelings are not altogether surprising: Your turn to paid help reveals the lack of assistance in the department, and commodifies what is imagined to be a fundamentally non-commodifiable advisor-advisee relationship. Remember that you don't have to tell your advisor that you are seeking this help.

On the other hand, some advisors direct their advisees to The Professor Is In's blog and services as a part of their professionalization training. In 2013 I received an email from an R1 full professor in a STEM field:

> You have literally changed my life in terms of how I mentor my students. I have been a terrible mentor (the nice guy), and I'm growing with every interaction I make, based on every post you post. Yes I know it is . . . mentoring that I should be able to do, but I have very much to learn.

It is my view that if you would seek an athletic trainer to help you get in shape, or a ceramics teacher to help you learn to throw a pot, then you can consider an academic consultant or coach to help you gain the academic career skills you want. Obviously I am not a neutral party in this question. Nevertheless, I believe paid experts have a valuable place in providing specialized training when it is desperately needed and not otherwise available. When evaluating paid consultants, be sure to examine their academic records closely—to be effective, an academic consultant should have years of experience in the academy, with a successful record in publishing, conferences, and tenure. And beware the bitterness trap. All too many former academics harbor enormous feelings of resentment toward the academy. Any paid advisor, whether in the academic or post-academic realm, should have a positive attitude about all possible career options, and should be able to support you with a combination of unvarnished realism and genuine enthusiasm.

THIRTEEN

........·........

Why "Yourself" Is the Last Person You Should Be

A number of years ago, I was working with a client whom I'll call Margaret, a full professor and department head in the social sciences in an East Coast R1, who had contacted me for assistance in refining the letters of recommendation she was writing for the increasingly desperate job-seeking Ph.D.'s and adjuncts under her care. Margaret was sincere, earnest, and generous of spirit. She was committed to the welfare of these candidates. She had no idea how unusual she is.

Toward the end of our conversation, she asked if I had any final thoughts on how to advise people to prepare for interviews and campus visits. She said, "Of course, I always tell them to just be themselves. I mean, that's always the best advice, isn't it?"

I involuntarily guffawed. "Oh good God, Margaret!" I burst out. "Are you kidding me? *That's* what you tell them?"

A startled silence, followed by a sheepish laugh. "Really? That's not good advice? Why?"

Why indeed. Because if you are fresh from the hazing of Ph.D. training, you are insecure, defensive, paranoid, beset by feelings of inadequacy, pretentious, self-involved, communicatively challenged, and fixated on minutiae. You aren't all of these things, of course. But you're likely some combination of them. Consequently, here's how you act under the pressure of the job market: rambling, obscure, petrified, subservient, cringing, disorganized, braggy, verbose, grandiose, tedious, emotionally overamped, off-point, self-absorbed, and fixated on minutiae.

The exchange took me back to the day oh so many years ago, when I asked my own advisor for some advice for an upcoming campus visit. She said: "Oh, just be yourself." And not knowing any better, I heeded that advice. And went out and made an utter fool of myself.

The fact is, "yourself" is the very last person you want to be.

Here's what actually needs to happen: You have to jettison "yourself." In its place, you have to create a professional persona. That persona is a full-fledged adult who demonstrates a tightly organized research program, a calm confidence in a research contribution to a field or discipline, a clear and specific trajectory of publications, innovative but concise, unemotional plans for teaching at all levels of the curriculum, a nondefensive openness to the exchange of ideas, and, most important, a steely-eyed grasp of the real (as opposed to fantasy) needs of actual hiring departments, which ultimately revolve, in the current market, around money. Let me take each of these characteristics of the "non-yourself" professional persona in turn.

A Tightly Organized Research Program. You will articulate your dissertation project/current project in approximately five sentences that sketch the topic, its data, text or objects of study, its methods, its approach, and its core argument. I will use my own long-ago dissertation for an example:

1. My dissertation is on the subject of Japanese women's internationalization. 2. Looking at women's trajectories abroad through study of English, study abroad, work at foreign firms, work abroad, and relationships with foreign men, I examined women's own narratives explaining and justifying a turn away from Japan and toward the West. 3. I argue that women use the West as a means of critique of patriarchy in Japan, both in the form of a narrative trope, and also as an imagined and idealized alternative site of work and marriage.

4. I also consider these narratives through the lens of critical race theory, in order to examine the place of whiteness in them as an object of desire. 5. In the end, I conclude that women's narratives, while oppositional in Japan, often end up colluding in or reinforcing heremonic Western discourses of white, Western male superiority and desirability, discourses which are circulated globally through American popular culture.

A Calm Confidence in a Research Contribution to a Field or Discipline. You will be able to articulate, in one or two sentences, the orthodoxy-challenging intervention of your dissertation in a field or fields. This will not be simply "additive" ("People have looked at X but nobody has yet looked at Y"; "I am building on the work of X and Y"), but will articulate your work as distinctive, individual, and poised to challenge previous understandings. ("In contrast to common views in the field of X, my research shows that instead the core variable is Y. This shifts how we view A and B.") If you cannot articulate this, you are not ready for the job market.

Beware in particular of the word "extends." Search committees don't want to hear that your research extends other work, and they certainly don't want to hear that your next project extends your first project. Why would the hiring department spend good money to get someone whose work is basically derivative or predictable? Your work may well have been influenced by other work—everyone's is. This is not newsworthy! In a job document your dissertation work must be depicted as original, distinctive, and, above all, autonomous. Your second project can, of course, grow organically out of the concerns of the dissertation project. But, again, it must be on a clearly new topic. Nobody wants a one-trick pony.

A Clear and Specific Trajectory of Publications. You will map an "arc" of publications that links past, present, and future. You will say something like, "As you saw from my CV, I have two refereed journal articles published on this body of work in the *Journal of X* and *Journal of Y*. I have another in revise-and-resubmit stage at the *Journal of Z*. Beyond that, I am finalizing my book manuscript, and am speaking with editors at Duke and Chicago about a contract. I expect that to be complete in spring of next year, and after that I am planning two more articles based on material that didn't make it into the book. Those publications will complete the publishing arc of this work, and I will then move on to my second major project." You will have this answer prepared for all interviews regardless of rank of the institution.

Innovative but Concise, Unemotional Plans for Teaching at All Levels of the Curriculum. You will speak to specific courses, both intro level and more advanced, and both those already on the department's books and new ones you anticipate developing. You will describe them in a brief and organized manner that gives the course title, the takeaway points, the primary themes, the texts or readings, and one innovative assignment that ideally incorporates digital resources or social media. And then you will stop. You do not endlessly list course names, numbers, ideas, readings, or lecture topics. You also do not wax emotional about the "thrill" of teaching and the selfless efforts you dedicate to it. That says: adjunct.

A Nondefensive Openness to the Exchange of Ideas. When an interviewer says something like, "I notice you don't really address gender in much detail in the dissertation. Do you have plans to develop that?" you do not respond, "Oh my gosh, yes, it's true. I didn't really get to include gender. I really *wanted* to, but, uh, you know, I just ran out of time, and that's a total lack in the dissertation, I *know,* and I'm totally going to focus on correcting that." You do respond: "Yes, thanks for raising that point. In fact, as I worked deeper into my analysis I discovered that gender was not the primary variable, and that a focus on X allowed me to keep my emphasis on Y." This is the nondefensive part. You can then, if appropriate, follow with, "I am increasingly intrigued by the role of gender, and am working up a manuscript that addresses it from the perspective of Z to submit to the *Journal of Q.* I'd look forward to talking to you more about that." That is the open part.

A Steely-Eyed Grasp of the Real (as Opposed to Fantasy) Needs of Actual Hiring Departments. Departments do not care about what makes you tick. They do not care about how you came to be who you are, or how you "feel" about the "privilege" of teaching and the "honor" of research. They are investing time and money into the addition of a new research and teaching resource to their department, and they need to know if you will be that resource. They are under the gun, from the dean's if not the chancellor's office, to increase enrollments, grow class sizes, bring in grant money, increase faculty productivity, improve student retention, eradicate "underperforming" small courses/programs, and reduce lines. Here's what is not prioritized: the scholarly minutiae of your research. Here is what is prioritized: your ability to demonstrate, with evidence, quickly, that you publish a lot in high-ranking journals, bring in grant money, thrive in large classes, harness digital resources to do more with less money, can work across disciplines, and teach well enough to avoid lawsuits.

Developing these elements of the professional persona is exceedingly difficult, and requires enormous levels of practice. For many candidates, writing out versions of these responses and practicing them—in the shower, in front of the mirror, with your significant other, and in mock interviews with peers and professors in your department—is the only way that they become second nature. Over time, practicing these responses allows some of this persona to feel more natural, and, indeed, legitimate. But to a degree, it may never feel that way. And that is fine. In the privacy of your own mind, you can continue to be beset by insecurities, anxieties, and self-doubt, and the victim of rambling, disorganized thinking and an obsession with minutiae. But when you go out on the job market? That self needs to stay firmly out of sight, while your persona takes center stage.

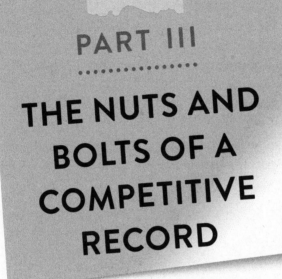

PART III
················

THE NUTS AND
BOLTS OF A
COMPETITIVE
RECORD

FOURTEEN

·················

Take Control of Your CV

The CV is not a passive document that you mostly ignore, and up-
date only grudgingly. Your CV is your "mini-me"; put another
way, it is your standard-bearer on the job market front. It is an extension of yourself, and it needs ongoing, active attention.

When I was a young assistant professor, a respected senior colleague gave me some advice about CVs. That colleague was a model
of productivity, and she liked me and wanted to see me succeed.
This piece of advice was not a trick for organizing the CV but rather
a trick for thinking about it. She told me, early in my first year in
the department, "Make sure that each month you add another line
to your CV."

Each month add another line to my CV? Really? That sounded
impossible. But she did it, sure enough, and her CV was a thing to
behold.

She reassured me. "This is not going to be hard for you," she
said. And she was right. By the time I added on the national conferences I attended every year, and the talks on campus, and my new
classes, and small and large grants, and article manuscripts, and
local and national committees, and the reviewing I did for journals
and presses, I did have nine new items a year (we didn't count sum-
mers). Sometimes I had a lot more than nine new items a year. It
wasn't that hard.

The key was to keep my CV prominently in mind. When I had

to make choices about how to spend my time, which requests to accept, and when to say no, I thought about my CV. Did I want the line? Did I need the line? Was it a good line? Was there a better line? It was an amazingly clarifying exercise.

Sure, I did things to be collegial—things that didn't translate into CV lines. I helped out colleagues. I went the extra mile for students some of the time. I was a good department citizen. But I was focused. I knew what my goal was, even when my life became more complicated with the arrival of two children. And that goal was tenure. And tenure required a certain number and type of lines on my CV.

As my career went on, I had the opportunity to see many CVs of students and peers from my own and other institutions. I realized that many of them had not received this kind of advice. They had not been adding a CV line each month, and had not been taught how to weigh different kinds of lines. And a lot of them were struggling. They weren't getting the jobs they wanted. They weren't getting the grants. They weren't getting tenure.

They didn't seem to put two and two together.

CVs are not just passive records of things that you happen to do. They are records that you actively, consciously, and conscientiously build. You watch your CV, you think about it, you develop it. You ask, "Is it where it should be right now, this month, related to the goals I want to reach this year?" If not, take action that very day to change it. Finish that half-done article. Submit for a grant. Apply to a conference. Get yourself invited for a talk.

If you are still in graduate school, or still seeking your first tenure track job, the one-line-a-month pace might be hard to achieve, and that's OK. I offer it not to put impossible stress on your already stressed-out life, but to communicate that you can hold yourself to plans and benchmarks. The CV is a document that you grow with intention and deliberate effort.

However, a warning: Don't let your desperation to add lines to your CV cause you to choose cheap, low-status accomplishments. That is a common error, especially among inexperienced junior academics. Not all CV lines are created equal. Never believe that a book review will aid your tenure track job search. Never believe that organizing your advisor's symposium will catapult you onto short lists, despite what he may have told you.

Everybody has done it—accepted an offer to publish or present a paper because it was handed to you, possibly by a friend or ally, without any particular effort on your part. "It'll be quick!" you say to yourself. "I'll get an easy line on the CV out of it!" Who knows, you might even congratulate yourself on your career savvy.

The quick and easy sale items of the academic career leave you with a CV that looks like the stockpile of an extreme couponer—a collection of stuff that you'll never use and that doesn't sustain you. Put in academic terms, the CV becomes a repository of quasi-achievements that don't actually bring you visibility and job offers.

A reader once wrote to explain:

During my years as a tenure track assistant professor, I went about publishing and doing research the way I do the grocery shopping: concentrating on the sale items like conferences, book reviews, on-line collaborations, i.e., all things that seemed "affordable." As a result I stock up on unnecessary items and find myself too tired to focus on the important things, those items that do not go on sale, but that are the building block of a good kitchen: articles and books. Although I have managed to publish quite a bit, I have squandered a lot of time and energy, because I did not have a clearly elaborated research plan.

One high-risk, high-cost item—a book proposal successfully written and pitched to the leading press in your field, or a journal manuscript dragged through the excruciating review process of the top journal in your area—is worth ten cheap alternatives such as book reviews.

If you are an extreme couponer of the academic marketplace, don't be misled by the rapidly growing length of your CV. If the content is not rich and meaningful, the quantity counts for little.

So what should be on the CV as you head out on the market? While I discuss all of the elements more thoroughly in subsequent chapters, here is a quick checklist. Your record will be viewed holistically, and should show a balance of all of these elements.

Publishing

Competitive tenure track candidates will leave their Ph.D. programs with one or more published articles under their belt. The actual expected number will vary based on field. In some fields, such as history, graduate students may be likely to finish with just one peer-reviewed article. In other fields in the humanities and social sciences, the expectation may be closer to two or three. In the experimental social sciences, quantity reigns and numbers may be higher. I cannot give any specific number for any specific field. Just make sure that you have published according to the expectations of your discipline.

Peer-reviewed journal articles are the gold standard, and should be prioritized. Expect to turn one of your dissertation chapters into a peer-reviewed journal article. Do not be seduced by invitations to submit your research into edited collections. Aim for the best journal you can manage. I elaborate in chapter 16.

You may have the opportunity to publish predoctoral work such as your master's research. Go for it. Undergraduate work, or nonacademic writing, however, will not count in most cases.

Grants

Pursue all the grants that you can, small to large. Small grants on your CV strengthen it for the purposes of larger grant competitions. But don't languish at small grants; consider them stepping-stones to larger applications, and by the end of your program, do your best to have at least one major national or international grant on your record. I elaborate in chapter 17.

Conferences

Get in the habit of going to your major national disciplinary conference. If your work spans more than one field, then go to the conferences of the two major disciplines in which you expect to be competitive for jobs. Don't spread yourself across three or four different disciplinary conferences, however, as it's expensive and makes you look scattered. In my own case as a cultural anthropologist of Japan, I faithfully attended both the annual meeting of the American Anthropological Association and the Association for Asian Studies. Smaller, regional conferences are often a pleasure to attend because they offer the chance for deeper intellectual exchange. That is great for intellectual stimulation and networking, but keep in mind they are not the equivalent of the national conference in terms of CV line. Graduate student conferences count for even less; they may be fun and fulfilling, but accurately weigh their relatively minimal value on the CV. I elaborate in chapters 19 and 20.

Teaching

Get solo-teaching experience before you go on the market if you can. If your department doesn't offer Ph.D. students the chance to teach their own courses, then seek an adjunct opportunity at a local college. Understand that your years of TA experience count for little on your record. TA experience doesn't demonstrate ability to handle your own courses. I elaborate in chapter 15.

Service

Service doesn't get people jobs. Two things follow from this fact: Don't do too much service, and don't overemphasize the service that you do in your applications. The fact that you selflessly give of yourself for the greater good is not a strength on today's market. Service is not in itself a bad thing, of course, but it will hurt you if it appears to stand in place of peer-reviewed publications, major grants, and conference activity. The most valuable kinds of service for the job market are diversity-related initiatives—because increasing numbers of job applications ask for diversity experience—and experience on search committees. I strongly recommend that all graduate students gain experience on a search committee in their department. It gives you the inside view of how a job search is run, and how candidates are discussed and evaluated. I don't have a chapter on service; my advice on service can be summarized in the line with which I started: Don't do too much of it, and don't devote much space to it in your job documents.

FIFTEEN

· · · · · · · · · · · ·

Getting Teaching Experience

One of the hard truths of the job market is that TA experience counts very little as teaching experience for the purposes of the job hunt. There is an unbridgeable chasm between the work of a TA and the work of a sole instructor, and when search committees review files, they are prioritizing experience as a sole instructor. Now, before you raise your voice in protest against the blatant unfairness of it all ("How can I get my first teaching job if I have to have teaching experience to get it?"), rest assured that search committees by and large do understand that everybody has to start somewhere, and new Ph.D.'s and ABDs may still be desirable hires even without much (or any) record of teaching. However, to strengthen your record for the purposes of the job hunt, you will want to have solo-teaching experience if you can get it. This chapter addresses how.

Start with your own department. Many departments offer their advanced ABDs the opportunity to teach their own courses, precisely for the reasons outlined above. If your department offers this option, take it, and maximize it to teach a course that is either a) closely tied to your own research interests, or b) one of the bread-and-butter intro, theory, or methods courses that every department across the land is always seeking to staff. When you go out on the job market, you will most often be asked about your ability to teach both of these types of classes.

If your department is one of those that uses the term "TA" even when a graduate student is the sole instructor, be vigilant to clarify your actual status as sole instructor in all of your job documents.

Now, if your own department does not provide these opportunities, then you must search elsewhere. Start on your own campus, and see if related departments or campus centers might have openings, or offer competitive awards that include developing and teaching your own course. On one of my former campuses, the gender studies program ran an annual competition for an award that allowed a graduate student to propose, create, and teach an original class (and get paid decently for teaching it).

Once you've exhausted the options on your campus, look outside. Cast your net widely to encompass any and all higher education institutions in your area, from elite universities to community colleges. Any solo-teaching experience is better than no solo-teaching experience, even if it is at a low-ranking local college. Get your name on the adjunct/instructor lists for all departments even tangentially related to your area of expertise, on all campuses that you can reasonably reach. Don't hesitate to call or email the heads of these departments to inquire about possible openings, and don't forget to inquire again just before the start of each semester. When I was a department head, I was amazed at how often I found myself without a warm body to put in front of a scheduled course, just a few weeks before the semester's start. On at least one occasion an opportune phone call from a local Ph.D. at the right time proved the solution to my problem.

Of course, you'll also be perusing the job pages of all colleges and universities in your area.

Beware the grad student–ish tendency to assume that you can't teach courses outside your area of expertise, department, or discipline. You may feel unqualified to pose as an expert about anything other than your dissertation topic, but when it comes to undergraduate teaching, the fact is, if you can read it, you can probably teach it.

By virtue of your years in graduate school, you have the ability to read and assimilate information quickly, a knack for grasping key points and arguments, a basic understanding of how to organize a course, and the will to pontificate for hours on end. Ergo, you have all the skills you need to teach virtually any course that is within a wide throwing distance of your field. Can a cultural anthropologist teach biology? Probably not. But depending on her research specializations, she can plausibly consider teaching in sociology, linguistics, religious studies, women's and gender studies, ethnic studies, international studies, area studies, and perhaps even as far afield as cinema studies, economics, communications, or comparative literature. The classic advice to new university teachers is stay one week ahead of the students. And indeed, many courses have been taught on less. As long as you read ahead of your students, you can handle the class. And don't forget, Google is your friend. Don't be afraid to search widely for other courses on those topics, and "borrow" abundantly from your predecessors' readings and assignments. Don't worry, you'll pay it forward later.

What about online teaching? Some online teaching experience is good to have, and if that is all you have available to you, then pursue it. Indeed, increasing numbers of campuses are seeking some online teaching experience for their regular faculty hires. However, online teaching is never the equivalent of face-to-face teaching experience for most tenure track job searches.

What about high school teaching? In most cases outside of the field of education, this will not assist your job search. High school teaching just doesn't count as university teaching experience, and you can't really mine it for credibility in a tenure track job search. One possible exception might be teaching at elite prep schools where the Ph.D. is a required qualification. This still would not substitute for college or university level teaching, but it might carry some weight on your record.

If you are on the market without solo-teaching experience, all is not lost. You'll want to develop syllabi or course descriptions for courses you could teach—both basic introductory, theory, and methods courses, as well as several specialized classes based on your work. Many graduate programs make the creation of a course syllabus an element of their comprehensive or qualifying exams. This is an excellent practice. Even if yours doesn't have this formal requirement, you can use your exams as foundations for courses.

Just be sure that the syllabus you create is a teachable, manageable one for students, and not a stealth effort to show off your command of a literature. Search committees don't need a recitation of all you've read. They need to know that you can teach a viable class.

SIXTEEN

·············

Publish This, Not That

One of the things that faculty know and grad students don't is the hierarchy of status among types of publications. Experienced faculty members understand with perfect clarity that only some types of publications will serve them in their quest for merit raises and promotion to full professor. Yet, somehow, this common-sense cultural knowledge is almost never shared with their advisees. As a result, far too many graduate students waste their best material and squander the best years of their academic lives on worthless (for the purposes of the job market) publications such as book reviews, conference proceedings, and chapters in edited collections that a) never see the light of day, b) take endless years to get published, or c) get published but only in obscure hardcovers that even university libraries don't buy.

Let me explain to you what counts and what doesn't as an academic publication for the purpose of the job hunt. I speak here primarily from my experiences in the humanities and social sciences, so readers in the experimental social sciences and hard sciences should consult with experts in their own fields to determine whether and how conventions on conference proceedings and co-authorship depart from what I describe here.

Peer-reviewed, or refereed, journal articles are the gold standard. The journal should be the highest status you can manage. I am constantly asked, "How does one know the status of journals?" I cannot help but respond, "After five to ten years reading articles in your graduate seminars, reading and collecting articles for your qualifying exams, and reading for the literature review of your dissertation, how do you not know the status of the journals in your field?" During these years it is incumbent upon you to notice which journals are most influential, which ones routinely publish the top scholars, which ones are most often cited.

I can't tell you the status of journals in your field. What I can tell you is that the status is finely distinguished to some extent by abstract ranking, but also calibrated based on the type and topic of work you do. Thus, for me, as a highly humanistic cultural anthropology Ph.D. student, the journal *Cultural Anthropology* was an excellent journal for me, while *American Anthropologist,* the then generally higher ranked flagship journal, was at the time (early 1990s) too quantitative for my work. For another cultural anthropologist working in a more empirical or quantitative vein, however, *AA* would have been the better choice. This is the type of deliberation that every grad student should master well before they go out on the job market.

It goes without saying that the highest ranking journals have the lowest acceptance rates, so there is risk involved. The candidate must weigh a variety of factors, including the likelihood of rejection, timing of decisions, and timeline to publication. Obviously you need acceptance on a timeline that serves the job search. A journal that holds your manuscript without a decision for eighteen months can derail one to two years of your job search. You need either an acceptance in time for your applications, or a rejection in time to resubmit to another journal before all job market hope is lost. It is wise to seek the counsel of experienced faculty in your publishing niche about hidden practices of journals with regard to response times. If a journal has held your manuscript for many months without a decision, cut bait and withdraw it.

A few other rules:

Do not put your material into chapters for somebody else's edited collection. This goes double for vanity publications and Festschrift.

Do not for a moment, if you are in the humanities or social

sciences, consider conference proceedings as a "publication." I don't even know why those exist, outside of the sciences.

Book reviews count for little on your CV. Many graduate students mistakenly view the book review as a legitimate publication in the prominent journal hosting it, and they get caught up in the ego gratification of publicly passing judgment on major scholarly works in the field. Yet the book review, regardless of the status of the journal soliciting it, is not peer-reviewed. It is solicited, and then it is more or less rubber-stamped, so long as it abides by basic reviewing ethics and conventions.

A book review does show that you are considered legitimate enough to review a significant book for an established journal—that is, that you have some degree of reputation and visibility in your field. So it will not harm your record, as long as it is accompanied by peer-reviewed publications, and as long as you don't have more than about three. Be aware of opportunity cost—ask yourself if time spent on a book review is distracting you from writing the peer-reviewed publication that will actually count. Be aware that a preponderance of book reviews on the record of a junior candidate (say, more than five or so) will cast doubt on your understanding of publishing for tenure.

What about coauthorship? Many people deal with the inevitable insecurities attendant upon the academic career by snuggling up to friends and colleagues to hold hands and write things together. If you are in the humanities and soft social sciences, don't coauthor until you're tenured. In these fields, coauthored pieces count for only about half the value of a solo-authored piece, and they also obscure the amount of research and writing you were actually responsible for. That complicates the process of evaluation. If you're in the hard sciences or experimental social sciences, coauthorship may be the norm, but author order may be contested. Speak with a trusted expert in your field as you plan out that element of your publishing trajectory.

If you're in a book field, it goes without saying that you need a plan for the book from your first days on the job market. You might still be ABD and not even finished with your dissertation, but you need a publication plan for a book, a timeline, and ideas about presses. If you're about one year beyond the Ph.D., you'll want to actually have a proposal under way, and two or more years beyond the dissertation, you want to have the proposal submitted to a press for an advance contract.

You need to do this whether you've scored the tenure track job offer or not. After a few years on the market, the book ceases to be the linchpin of your tenure case; instead it becomes the thing necessary to get your foot in the door for a tenure track offer. How many years does this take? Well, there's no hard and fast rule, of course. But if you're four or more years out from the Ph.D. and still without a tenure line job, you're going to need to get that book under contract and in production to stay fresh.

Let me step back and revisit the basic calculations that go into publishing for the job market and for tenure. (These apply to the humanities and the social sciences; STEM fields are altogether different.)

Most likely your early publications will derive from your dissertation project. Which is fine, except for one dilemma: You also have to draw from that body of research for your tenure publications.

If you're at an R1, you'll likely need something along the lines of five articles and a book for tenure (always confirm your own tenure expectations for your department and institution). Your tenure review committee will likely hope to see about three articles on the dissertation project, and then perhaps two others on a second major project. And the only publications that typically count for tenure are the ones produced or published after the start of your tenure track contract. Therefore, you must move carefully. Don't overpublish from your dissertation and exhaust its material before getting a job, or you'll have nothing left for the tenure track. Another factor to keep in mind: As I mentioned earlier, publishers will not look kindly on a proposal for a book if more than half of its material has already been published as articles. If you have a five-chapter book, two chapters can be previously published as articles, but when you get to three, things get a bit sticky. If you have material from a master's project or a side project—or some dissertation material that didn't make it into the dissertation or book—use that intelligently to flesh out your publication record while maintaining sufficient new material for the tenure track.

If you gain a tenure track job on the basis of having a book out, then what will you have to submit for your tenure file? Well, if you're at an R1, the answer is likely a second book. And that's hard, because once you're employed, you'll never have the abundant time for reading, conceptualizing a project, research, and writing that you had as a graduate student.

I know what you're probably thinking: "I had no time as a graduate student!" Well, actually, compared to the life of a tenure track faculty member, graduate school is more or less a trip to the beach. As a professor, you'll be encountering new administrative and service demands, plus the increased expectations of undergraduate (and perhaps graduate) students for your attention and time. You also may have new obligations on the home front. It's intense on a whole new level.

If you have published the book prior to getting a job, then when you get the tenure track offer, you'll do three things. The first: Attempt to negotiate for some of your previous publications to count toward your tenure case. The second: Hit the ground running as fast as you can on a viable, plausible major second project, one you can manage while teaching mostly full-time. The third: Begin applying for research leave right away, so you can get year two, three, or four off to complete significant work on that second project. That way it can be published as articles and/or a book manuscript by year five.

None of this is easy, by any means, and it all takes careful planning. You know that I advocate having a five-year plan as described in an earlier chapter, and this type of delicate calculation is the primary reason why.

Some folks hope to substitute an edited collection for a solo-authored monograph. The edited collection will stand in as a "book" for purposes of job or tenure at a lower-ranked teaching institution, but it will not at any R1 or elite SLAC, which require a solo-authored manuscript. Therefore, it is risky to invest your precious post-Ph.D., pre-tenure-track years in this endeavor.

Please hear me when I tell you an edited collection is not

equivalent to a solo-authored monograph. I know that you want to demur, and that you will offer me a host of reasons why. To save time, I will summarize our conversation below:

Ph.D. student: Should I do an edited collection?

Me: No.

You: But it's the papers from a conference panel. Is it OK then?

Me: No.

You: But I'm coediting it, so I don't have to do all the work. Is it OK then?

Me: No. And, please, coediting? Are you kidding me?

You: But all I have to do is collect and edit the papers and write an intro. Is it OK then?

Me: No. And you're doing all this and don't even have a chapter in it? Are you kidding me?

You: But I'll have a book for tenure.

Me: No, you won't. Edited collections don't count at R1s and such.

You: But it'll get me a job.

Me: You want to know what'll get you a job? A refereed journal article in the top journal in your field. Write that! Write two of them! Heck, you can write a whole monograph in the time you are going to waste fighting with your contributors, waiting for the external reviewers, arguing with your press, agonizing over the copyediting, and trying to market the book because your press doesn't spend a dime in advertising.

You: Really?

Me: Yes.

You: An editor from a really great press I never heard of actually got in touch with me! And asked me to do it! Is it OK then?

Me: No, and never, ever, ever accept an offer of publication from someone from a press you've never heard of. Or even a press you have heard of, if they come chasing after you.

It's the prom, sweetheart. Don't go with the first person who asks you (unless they're the dream date you've been waiting for). Do the work and get yourself into position to get the date you really want.

You: But I am already committed.

Me: Get out of the commitment.

You: But it's my friends.

Me: Have drinks with your friends. Go to Vegas with your friends. Do not waste your precious writing and research time gathering up and, God forbid, editing, your friends' questionable essays, and volunteering unpaid, uncredited time to get your friends a publication. And by the way, their chapter in your edited collection is barely going to do them any good, either.

The conversation, of course, ends like this:

You: But I'm going to go ahead and do this edited collection.

Me: It's your funeral.

But it doesn't have to. Save yourself. Just say no to the edited collection.

I am aware that my advice about publishing runs counter to the scholarly ideal of sharing and collaboration and probably makes you unhappy. You may respond that you got into academia for the intellectual exchange and have no desire to stay in the field without it. You may be heard to mutter darkly about "cold-blooded calculations" and "neoliberalism."

What can I say? I understand your feelings, I really do. But if you want a job, you need to know how your record is being read. Collaborative endeavors, in the humanities and social sciences, count for less.

In this as in other things, the things you enjoy are not necessarily the things that count. Just because it is meaningful to you doesn't mean it's going to help you get a job. Choose the path that you believe in, but do so in full knowledge of the risks.

SEVENTEEN

·····················

Why You Want and Need Grants

Grants are an essential element of a competitive record, for two reasons: They are excellent lines on your CV, and you need the money to do the work and stay out of debt. No other element of your record represents such a perfect combination of both symbolic and actual capital. I mean, how much money did you make from your last journal article? Therefore, grants should be prioritized at every stage of your career, from your earliest days in the master's program to the job search, life as an adjunct, assistant professorship, and beyond.

Upshot: Apply early and often.

In part VIII I will address the nuts and bolts of grant applications, and give you my Foolproof Grant Template. But here I want to discuss how to think about grants as a required element of your competitive record.

Too many job seekers consider grants as kind of an afterthought, like, "It would be nice to have the money but it's not going to make a major difference either way." The lackadaisical attitude that results is evident in your grant proposals. In my years of working with students, I saw endless grant applications for awards both large and small that had clearly been thrown together at the last minute.

Students generally took what I call an "aggrieved stance" to the work of writing for money. While no grad student worth her salt would ever expect to write a dissertation chapter in a week, the twenty-five-page grant application necessary to acquire the generous funding to actually write the dissertation gets a few grudging days, resented as an "intrusion" in the schedule of "important" writing.

When I encounter the aggrieved stance, I can only ask, "How is funding an intrusion?" How are you going to write your dissertation or book, and write it well, if you don't have the wherewithal to free yourself from excessive teaching burdens and constant anxiety over making ends meet?

Think of it this way. Suppose you're applying for a two-year postdoc. The postdoc pays $50,000 a year, with $10,000 in research support, and full benefits, plus conference travel funding. Added together, the package is valued at $85,000 a year, or $170,000 in total. Now imagine that you devote two hours a day to the proposal, over the course of one entire month. Does that seem ridiculous? Are you thinking, nobody has time to spend two hours a day for a full month on one application? Well, let's add it up: Sixty hours of work for this postdoc amounts to $2,833 per hour of work. How ridiculous does it look now?

I was a pretty good grant writer in graduate school, and enjoyed full funding through my entire program, fieldwork, and writing. It eased my path in countless ways, and made graduate school a real pleasure. It also enabled me to indulge my curiosity in ways that directly served my intellectual growth. How? you ask. Well, my book started out as but a faint glimmer in my eye when I went down to Waikiki to surf each evening as a new graduate student at the University of Hawai'i, and I began to ponder the odd pickup scene among young Japanese female tourists and local guys there. If I hadn't had the leisure to take up surfing my first year of graduate school, I would never have spotted this "hidden in plain sight" phenomenon that everybody on the beach was talking about and nobody understood. It started as an entertaining fieldwork project for my first methods class in the master's program. That evolved into my master's thesis. I kept getting funding for this project, as it developed into a wider examination of motivations for Japanese women's internationalizing impulses. The funding kept coming, mostly because it struck everyone as a fascinating, counterintuitive topic.

But at the end of my program, when I applied for a national research grant to do additional fieldwork in Japan, I struck out. I was shocked. Everyone loved my project! How could they reject me?

A few months later, picking myself up from my disappointment, I went back to the application and studied it with fresh eyes. And I saw immediately what I'd done wrong. I had assumed that funders would consider the topic fascinating because I did, as did "everyone else" from my graduate program. I didn't bother to explain my project's significance or context; I merely announced the new research, expecting them to fund it.

Looked at with new eyes, the application was arrogant. It was self-involved. My years of grant writing success had made me complacent. "Of course you'll fund me," the application implied. "How could you not?"

That was my wake-up call to stop leaning on any inherent appeal of the project, and start doing the work necessary to establish its intellectual merit. I rethought my approach, reapplied, and was successful. And that was when I got the first inklings of what grant writing is really all about.

Eventually I would develop the Foolproof Grant Template and its Hero Narrative, which I introduce in chapter 51. This is a robust template for demonstrating efficiently the legitimacy, urgency, and viability of a project for the purposes of funding. It rests on a simple formula: Topic X is an important phenomenon, and scholars A and B have examined it. However, nobody to date has yet addressed Y—and without Y we remain ill-informed about a side of X that is essential to our intellectual/disciplinary/social well-being.

Over time, I learned to appreciate grant writing, not just for the money it brought my way to keep satisfying my curiosity and supporting my projects, but for the new angles that it constantly opened onto the projects themselves. This is another virtue of grant writing that is lost in the aggrieved stance. Writing for different funders with different agendas forces you to approach your topic from different angles. It's not so much that you change your project as you discover new realms of significance arising from it.

An example might be useful: In the same year, as a new assistant professor, I won major fellowships from both the National

Endowment for the Humanities and the Japan Society for the Promotion of Science. The agendas of these two organizations could not have been more different—the first was firmly in the camp of the humanities, the second firmly in the camp of a quantitative social science. With thought and reflection, I made my project on Japanese women's internationalization speak to both. In the former case, I emphasized women's narratives of selfhood and identity—the stories they told to make sense of a complex positionality and compromised agency on the border between Japanese and Western places and imaginaries; in the latter case, I emphasized demographics—the statistics showing changing patterns of study abroad and residence abroad accompanying Japan's postindustrial transformation. Both of these were genuine interests, and they both illuminated the project.

Grants play another role. They establish your credibility within a field or area of study. Thus, they also help on the job market. To continue my own example, the NEH supported my identity as a humanistic anthropologist, while the JSPS reassured anxious biological anthropologists and archaeologists in four-field anthropology departments that I was a cultural anthropologist who actually made sense.

In the end, learning to sell your project to various constituencies with different agendas is tremendously valuable to your career. You don't know whom you'll encounter at conferences, on campus visits, or in your new department, but you do know they'll come from different disciplinary locations and have a variety of agendas. Grant writing is one of the best techniques you can use to explore your topic from different angles and find ways to frame it that compel and intrigue all of these potential collaborators.

EIGHTEEN

Cultivating Your References

One thing I advise all clients to do, but particularly those who are still ABD, is to start cultivating a third or fourth recommendation letter writer who is not from your Ph.D.-granting institution.

As I have explained at several points, having all of your letters come from faculty from your Ph.D. committee is a sign of a relatively inexperienced job candidate. Don't panic. It isn't a complete deal-breaker, particularly if you are blessed with faculty members from your department who are influential. Similarly, if you are an early ABD, the absence of an external letter writer is not damning.

But the strongest competitors for the jobs you're applying for will have cultivated influential references in their field from outside of their campus. This becomes quite urgent if you are more than a few years beyond your Ph.D. Then the reliance on your Ph.D. department faculty for your recommendations quickly begins to stand out, and eventually will damage your candidacy and destroy your chances for tenure track jobs.

Why is this the case?

We have established that tenure track search committees are seeking to hire colleagues, not graduate students. But the faculty from your Ph.D. program know you as a graduate student. They may think highly of you, but ultimately they will likely speak about you in terms of your performance in their classes, your work as a

TA, and your writing in the dissertation. Search committees don't care about how you did in Professor X's class; they are looking for national and international reputation and achievements as a professional scholar.

Ultimately, the letter writers who can best speak to your reputation and achievements at this level may well be scholars outside of your graduate program with whom you have collaborated, as a (junior) peer, on conference panels, professional symposia, and various publications. If you can dig in and cultivate a letter writer out in the discipline—one who knows you from one of these collaborations—that person will write about you as a young colleague and peer. The reason you want the external letter writer to be well known is simple: Her letter will carry more weight. For that same reason, you want her to come from a high-ranking institution; academia is hierarchical, and a letter writer from an obscure institution will do little to help your case.

This doesn't mean you need to replace your Ph.D. advisor; in general, your advisor can safely write for you for about five years, and some people have their advisors write for much longer than that. Your new letter writer will instead replace one of the other Ph.D.-committee members.

I think I hear wails of despair, in the vein of "How can I possibly *do* this?"

It is not difficult, but it takes time. First of all, you need to put yourself into contexts where you will meet senior scholars. You need to actually attend national conferences, as well as brown bag talks, workshops, and symposia on your campus. You have to pursue publication opportunities as they arise, and above all, in your debut year on the market, organize a high-profile panel for your national conference. These are the occasions in which you begin to meet and mingle with scholars from other parts.

If there are scholars whose work has been particularly influential on your own, make the effort to meet them at a conference, as I describe in chapter 20. Ask for even just fifteen minutes of their time, if they are very busy. It is possible they might have time for coffee. Whatever it takes, get a conversation started.

After an acquaintanceship has been made, stay in touch. Send an email thanking them for their time. Ask your department if they can be invited to campus. Invite them to serve as a discussant on another panel that you are organizing.

If they agree to serve as a discussant, send them your paper well in advance, and ask politely for early comments to help your writing of the final draft. They might not have time. But they might do it. If they do, engage meaningfully with their comments. Then interact with them actively at the panel itself, and continue the conversation afterward, over drinks.

As the acquaintance grows, ask for their advice on smallish matters such as a publication venue for a manuscript or a grant opportunity.

Now, there is one primary rule of cultivating supporters/letter writers, and that is this: Do. Not. Impose. Also, do not send long, dreary emails about your struggles in your department and suffering at the hands of your wretched advisor. Nobody wants to hear it. They will, however, often lend a hand, as long as they are not imposed upon, to assist a junior scholar. (As one of my early supporters told me when I used to endlessly complain about my advisor: "Karen, we're happy to help you, but nobody needs to think you were badly trained.")

When time has passed, ask your acquaintance if he or she would have time to read a chapter of your dissertation and send feedback. Give them plenty of time; do not impose a deadline. If they agree, that's a good sign that they support your work and development. Incorporate some of their suggestions, engage in dialogue about their comments, and be sure to thank them warmly for their time.

And now, when you have established a working relationship, you may broach the question of their serving as one of your letter writers. Be aware that they may have their own Ph.D.'s on the market, who are competing against you for the same jobs. It is possible that even if they like and support you, they will not be willing to write a letter. Don't take it personally; it is a legitimate choice on their part.

But they might. And once they do, you will have the perspective not of someone who was basically paid to take care of you in their capacity as one of the graduate faculty in your department, but rather an impartial, independent agent, who can evaluate you vis-à-vis your field as a whole. Their letter provides evidence of your participation on a national level, and signals your early preparedness for your ultimate tenure case down the line.

By contrast, the Ph.D. in her fourth year on the market who is still relying on a letter from a graduate faculty member that says things such as "Jennifer produced an A paper for my seminar!" or "She was the best TA in the program," or "She wrote a very comprehensive and impressive dissertation," is trailing the ghostly aura of her graduate student self behind her, signaling that she is, still, not really tenure track material.

While we're on the subject of references, if you have scored a teaching position off-campus, you will want to request a letter from the chair of that department or, failing that, from a senior colleague in that department. These colleagues can speak of you as a colleague, and speak to your teaching. Be proactive about getting that person into your classroom to observe you. Make sure she sees your syllabus and assignments, and copies of your evaluations (assuming they're good, that is). The letter from your current institution serves as assurance to the hiring committee that you are a legitimate colleague, that you show up for classes, that you're collegial and pleasant to be around, that all in all you're a good, solid department citizen. Nobody from your Ph.D. committee can provide that information, and neither can your other scholarly references.

In the end, a balanced roster of letters at about three years out will include your advisor, a well-known person who knows you as a colleague or collaborator, a senior colleague from a teaching position who will provide a detailed teaching reference, and—assuming you have space for four letters—one of your other Ph.D. committee members who has stayed up-to-date on your post-grad-school life. Make sure that all of your referees are given updated CVs, and are informed of your latest grants, awards, conference talks, and publications.

NINETEEN

·················

Applying to Conferences

I have explained that conferences are an essential element of any competitive job market record. But which conferences? And why?

As with publishing, there is a hierarchy of status among conferences. National disciplinary conferences are at the top, then subdisciplinary or topical (but still national) conferences, then regional conferences. At the bottom are graduate student conferences. These give you experience in presenting a paper, but count for little as a line on the CV. Grad student conferences can have other advantages, of course. As a tenured colleague at a public R1 that hosts an annual graduate student conference told me, they are invaluable for meeting graduate students from other universities, networking with the keynote speaker, learning to give and receive feedback, and providing a place to focus on intellectual exchange rather than status jockeying.[1] These are indeed all valuable skills.

Just don't forget that in general there is an inverse relationship between the status of the conference and the quality of the collegial exchange—the large national conference is high status but may well be alienating and depressing; the small conference is intellectually fulfilling but lower status. In addition to being places for intellectual exchange and collegial conversations, conferences teach you how things work. At the national conference you will see how various academics in your field talk, ask questions, argue, pitch books to editors, schmooze, network, plan collaborations, preen, work a room, and so on. The key is to achieve balance; weigh these competing goals as you choose how to spend your limited conference dollars, and make sure that any graduate conference never replaces a larger one.

Once you've decided on a national conference, you have to choose how you'll seek to get on the program. You often have a choice of poster, paper, panel submission, or invited panel submission. If you're ABD or beyond in the humanities or soft social sciences, avoid posters. Hard sciences may differ in this; know your field. For academics in the humanities and humanistic social sciences, however, posters are like the kids' table of the conference. If you have something to say, say it in a paper. It is the paper that gives you visibility and access to a group of panel-mates, the attention of a discussant, and exposure to a real audience. It is the paper that gives you experience in speaking in front of a group, and handling the terror of an open Q and A period.

It is not hard to submit a paper for a conference, but organizing a panel is more challenging. While all disciplinary associations will differ in their requirements, I can sketch out the process as I encountered it in my fields of anthropology and Asian studies. Be sure to confer with experts in your field, and study your disciplinary association instructions.

Note the deadline, and start work about two to three months before the submission deadline. You need to start early because you are a person with little social or academic capital. To grab participants for your panel, you must act early and quickly. The first thing you do is check the conference theme, if there is one. Is there a way to relate your scholarly project, in a broad sense, to that theme? If you can, that helps your chances of acceptance.

Think of a panel topic. This should derive organically from your dissertation research, but be bigger and broader than the research itself—an "umbrella" concept that can hold both your dissertation research, as well as three or four other related papers. It should not be so broad as to be entirely dull ("Gender and Asia," for example). But it should not be so detailed as to be impossibly narrow ("Japanese Women Who Study Abroad and Marry Foreign Men"). It has to hit the sweet spot of a topic broad enough to appeal to a sizeable audience, while being specific enough that it reflects your particular and memorable scholarly profile. Let's say "Women and Globalization in Japan," or "Gendered Transnationalism in Japan," or, stepping a bit wider, "Gendered Transnationalism in Asia." The first would get the smallest audience, the second a slightly larger one, and the third larger still.

Many conferences have a special kind of status for some panels: for example, an "invited panel" or some such. Those are typically reviewed by subdisciplinary units, and have earlier deadlines. If you feel your work fits beautifully into such a subdisciplinary unit, then try to make the earlier deadline. It is a smaller review pool and your panel will get more attention.

Once your theme is decided, you choose a title, and write a panel proposal abstract. This will follow the instructions for panel proposals given on your meeting website. A basic template for proposals is this: Start with a broad topic of general interest, refer briskly to the existence of scholarship on this topic, note a gap in the scholarship, observe sternly the scholarly stakes of such a gap, declare the theme of the panel addressing the gap, sketch the papers on the panel, and end with a gesture to the wider contribution and significance of these projects and the panel theme writ large.

Now, armed with the title and panel abstract, you solicit participants. This can happen in several ways. First, you can ask friends and colleagues. Second, you can send out a call for papers to your disciplinary Listservs, discussion boards, and the like. Third, you can find people around the country whose work you like and admire, and email them to ask. All of these are legitimate means of acquiring participants, bur for graduate students the first should generally be avoided.

This is because the most important thing is that you do not ask other graduate students. The point of this exercise is to launch you on the year that you first hit the job market. Huddling around the fire of an obscure little panel on Wednesday night or Sunday afternoon with a group of other unknown graduate students is going to do nothing to achieve this goal. The "graduate student panel" can be a kiss of death, audience-wise. Conference goers can usually sniff out a grad student panel by instinct on the program, usually because they don't recognize any of the names, everyone is from the same department, or the paper titles have a feel of naïveté or trying too hard. Thus the audience is small, and you will get a bad time slot. And then you're stuck in a giant ballroom with four people in the audience, and three of them are panelists' best friends . . . and that is demoralizing, for you and for the audience.

So, focus your efforts on young assistant professors. More senior people will probably already have panels lined up with old friends, but some young assistant professors will still be up for grabs, and getting increasingly anxious as the submission deadline nears.

Make sure that you maintain a good topical range (for example, if the panel is on an Asia theme, don't have all the participants working on Japan). Get provisional titles from your participants, as well as paper abstracts as early as you can.

Once you have collected your participants, you need to find a discussant (again, check your disciplinary norms). You will scan the national horizon for well-known tenured professors working on themes similar to the panel's. You will compile a list of candidates and perhaps ask your participants for their recommendations. You want a well-known discussant because that discussant will draw an audience to your panel that you—unknown graduate student that you are—cannot draw, and lend credibility to the whole project.

You will then take your package of material—the panel abstract, list of participants, and paper abstracts—and you will send an email of inquiry to the first Dr. Famous Professor on the list, inquiring politely but not obsequiously if she will serve as your discussant. She may say no, and you may need to move through three or four discussant candidates before you find one who is not already engaged. Don't take this personally. They are very busy.

In choosing both panel participants and the discussant, attend to the institutional location. Don't choose a set of participants all from a single institution. Frightened graduate students will often organize a panel with three other graduate students from their own department, and then ask a professor from the same department to serve as discussant. Don't do this. (If you are a professor and you are asked to serve as discussant for a graduate student panel that is comprised entirely of students from your home department, be a mentor and tell them "no," and tell them why: because they need to buck up and find a discussant whom they don't already know.)

Once you have collected all the participants and the discussant, you can then submit the whole package to the conference review committee. By the way, you might tweak your earlier panel abstract after you have solicited and received all of your participant submissions, as you'll undoubtedly get new insights and inspiration from them. You may have to solve small organizational problems such as deciding who will serve as chair of the panel. As organizer, you will likely want to serve as chair, as long as it does not prevent you from delivering a paper.

Et voilà, you have organized a panel. If the panel is accepted, you hope that you will be given a decent time slot.

Once the panel is accepted, you have the task of setting a deadline for your participants to submit their papers to you, which must be early enough to give the discussant plenty of time to read and think on prior to the date of the panel. You do not want an angry or alienated Dr. Famous Professor on your hands. Be respectful of her time, and send the papers early.

As panel organizer you also get to plan the panel get-together. This can be breakfast, lunch, dinner, or even just drinks, but as the organizer you can bring your little group together, with Dr. Famous Professor, for a little socializing at the conference. The timing of this event is always arranged around the convenience of the most famous and busiest person on the panel. The panel get-together is good, very good. You get to know the young assistant professors, and they get to know you, and you all get to know the famous professor. This is how reputations are built and careers made.

TWENTY

....

How to Work the Conference

Aside from doing their own paper or panel, few junior scholars actually know how to work a conference. That is, to use the five or so days of the conference period to maximize opportunities for networking, self-promotion, and building a public intellectual identity.

This is truly one of the secret skills of the successful academic career. While enlightened departments sometimes offer job market preparation seminars, mock job talks, teaching instruction, and guidance on grant writing, rare is the department that has ever held a workshop on "effective conferencing."

Unless a graduate student enjoys a happy combination of a naturally ebullient personality, tremendous intellectual confidence, a generous mentor who allows her to tag along, a large cohort of conference-going fellow graduate students, and fierce political instincts, chances are she will spend much of the early part of her conference-going career a) wandering forlornly through the hallways of the conference hotel, b) lurking in corners pretending to read the conference program, and c) hiding in her hotel room.

It is perfectly natural to dread the national conference. They are monstrously large. And alienating. And lonely. And embarrassing. Certainly the idea of marching up to Dr. Famous Professor in some hotel hallway with outstretched hand and business card at the ready is distasteful to almost everyone. And far too many people think that this is what conference "networking" involves.

I am here to tell you that it isn't.

Let us begin by talking in general terms about why you are at the conference in the first place. Your status at the conference will be different based on where you are in your career.

If you are a relatively new graduate student, you will plan to attend the conference, and no more.

If you are a master's student, you will plan to give a poster presentation at the conference.

If you are a Ph.D. student, you will plan to give a paper at the conference.

If you are ABD, or a brand-new Ph.D., you will plan to organize a panel at the conference.

If you are a young assistant professor, you will plan to organize a panel at the conference and become involved with a specialized section of your professional organization.

If you are an advanced assistant professor, you will plan to give a paper at the conference and serve as a discussant on another panel, one organized perhaps by graduate students, and take a possible leadership role in a specialized section of your professional organization.

And so on.

Whatever you have planned, make sure that you attend the national conference of your discipline on a yearly basis, as long as you can afford it financially. In chapter 47 I offer suggestions for reducing costs. Participation at the national conference of your discipline signals that you are a serious scholar and a contender for jobs. It is scary, alienating, and overwhelming. Go anyway.

And having gone, push yourself the following year to go again, and do something new. If you have attended one year, then give a paper the next. If you've given a paper one year, then organize a panel the next. If you've organized a panel one year, then serve as a discussant the next. In this way you increase your knowledge of your discipline and its inner workings.

Once you are accepted into the conference program, then the real work begins. Not the work of writing the paper. That is the intellectual project and none of my concern. No, this is the work of "conferencing." That is, extracting all of the capital that you can out of the investment of time and money that you have made into the conference experience. You have five days in a hotel with many thousands of scholars in your field. What are you going to do with them?

First off, have business cards. Make sure they are university business cards, with the university logo. Include your department, status (ABD, Ph.D. student, visiting assistant professor, and so forth), email, website, and cell phone number. Always carry your business cards in a small case made for this purpose. Do not stuff them into your back pocket or have them knocking around the bottom of your purse. They should always be clean and pristine. Practice ahead of time reaching in and extracting one without fumbling.

Of course you are dressed correctly. Refer to chapter 46 for more on that.

Your department may host a cocktail party for current and former students. Check beforehand and plan to attend.

Attend the business meetings of subfield organizations that interest you. Participate in the workshops on publishing and the job market. Hang out at the open bars (that part may be less difficult). The workshops on turning your publication into a book, interviewing, or teaching at community colleges are valuable. They also require advance registration, so do that.

But mostly, you network. You can do this in several ways, and the best ones require advance planning. If you are very junior and have little or no social capital, then grabbing an influential senior scholar for a conversation or coffee or a meal, on the spot, is virtually impossible. Your only real chance is by inviting them ahead of time.

A month before the conference, compile a list of the scholars whom you'd most like to meet. Be clear in your mind about why you'd like to meet them. Do you just want to say hello? Then study the program and find out their panel and plan to attend it. You may approach them afterward to shake their hand, congratulate them on their paper, briefly tell them about yourself—no more than a few sentences—and give them your card. And then walk away. Walk. Away. Do not cling or drone on.

Do you want to ask them to serve as an external member of your committee? Then send them an email, in the briefest terms explaining who you are and why you'd like to meet them, and asking them if they are free for coffee. Understand that they will likely not have any mealtimes available for you. But you might, if you're lucky, get a twenty-minute coffee slot.

Do you want to cultivate them as a potential reference? Then do the same as above, but be careful about how you couch the invitation. Remember that you are, at this point, just getting to know them. You can't ambush a perfect stranger and ask her to be your reference. Contemplate substantive reasons for seeking their advice—for example, how to proceed with publishing your book, including recommendations for editors or presses, perhaps. Use your time wisely. Be brief and well rehearsed. Do not cling. At the end, give a firm handshake. And walk away.

You will notice the emphasis I place on not clinging. The status jockeying of conferences is a major element of the conference and is ignored at your peril. You must not look like a hanger-on or a sad sack who has nothing to do and nobody to meet, even if that's what you are. You must give the impression of being a busy and dynamic young scholar. How do you do this?

Claire Potter, in her "Tenured Radical" column in the *Chronicle of Higher Education*, wrote a wryly entertaining set of recommendations for the national meeting of the American Historical Association in 2011. Her advice is widely applicable to all academic conferences. The emphases are mine.

- *Greet your graduate mentors but do not cling to them.* In fact, it is best, when you see them, to look as though you have somewhere very important to be. Practice saying into the mirror: "Gosh, it's really great to run into you—I'm off to the Chapel Hill booth to meet up with a friend/an editor/someone on my panel. Have a *great* meeting!" Only break this rule if they happen to be with someone very important in your field, in which case, *keep a keen eye out for an introduction.* Count slowly to five in your head: If the introduction is not forthcoming, *skate out of there.*

- If there is someone you know, but are unsure whether to greet or not, casually pick up a book and leaf through it. If said person greets you, look very surprised and say, *"OmygodIcan'tbelieveIdidn't see you!"*
- *If you run into someone you just did a hotel room interview with, you don't have to act like you are employed by an escort service* and pretend you have never met them. Smile and nod; if you are close enough to speak, say hello and say you had a good time in the interview. Even if you didn't.[1]

Potter reminds you to have a repertoire of go-to conference phrases, including a one-line description of your dissertation project, and a just-to-be-polite question to senior scholars: *"Are you having a good meeting?"*

She makes the point that the operative conference principle is to leave any and everyone before they leave you. "If you see someone's eyes drifting over your shoulder, even slightly," she writes, "say warmly: 'I've really got to run—*so* nice to have had a chance to say hello,' and quickly exit."

If you hope to get yourself invited to a dinner, be at the right place at the right time. Business meetings or membership meetings of subfield units, which are often held from four to six p.m., are an excellent opportunity. If you find ways to participate in that meeting (most obviously by volunteering to take on one of the leadership roles, such as secretary or treasurer or award committee member), chances are, somebody in the unit may well invite you to dinner. These meetings are listed in the conference program. Unless they are listed as "private" or "board only," you are allowed to attend.

A client wrote to tell me of her experience with a business meeting after her disciplinary conference:

Before the meeting, I scrolled through the list of presenters and emailed the people with whom I wanted to meet for coffee. I did not cling to other graduate students, even if it meant walking around by myself from time to time. The payoff was huge—I met the biggest names at the conference, some of whom quickly became my advocates. Two senior scholars took me to the business meeting, where they introduced me to everyone, told them I was on the job market, and asked them if they were doing any hiring. After that meeting, I decided to go to the business luncheon. Instead of sitting in the back with the graduate students, I marched up to the front of the room. When I noticed there was an open seat at the table reserved for the most prestigious scholars, I asked if the seat was taken—it was not—and sat down. I tend to be shy, but I knew that I had to act like an equal, not as a submissive grad student.

Not only did she have a successful conference, but shortly afterward she was offered a temporary teaching job by one of her new acquaintances.

Other ways to manage dinner: If you have a cooperative advisor, arrange to meet him or her for a beer at the hotel bar at a pre-dinner time slot such as five-thirty p.m. At six, when his or her friends arrive for their dinner, you may well be invited to come along. If you inspire enthusiastic discussion at your panel and audience members mob you afterward, you can sometimes spontaneously plan to meet later for a meal as well.

Aside from mealtimes, you can also work the book exhibit. The book exhibit is one of the best places to see your academic heroes in a casual setting. This does not mean that you can necessarily accost them at will, but you can see what they do, what books they look at, and whom they talk to. And you can sometimes strike up a conversation.

You also get to see how senior people talk to editors. Editors are at meetings to cruise the panels and find good materials for future books. Between panels, they hang out at the book exhibit, and senior people may be seen pitching their next books to them. If you're standing there, you get to surreptitiously listen in. This is how I learned to sell a book, in fact. I used to haunt the book exhibits as a master's and Ph.D. student, and by the time I had a book manuscript of my own to peddle, I had a pretty good idea of how to go about it.

Finally, check the schedule for the wine and cheese receptions at the major presses, usually on Friday night, launching the major books of the season. The authors will be there, and you might get to shake their hands, although it'll be a mob scene. Either way, you get some free food and wine.

The last thing that I will say about conferences is this: They are often alienating places. Sometimes the overt politicking can be a depressing thing to observe, let alone participate in.

Although I did all of the methods that I advocate here, with plenty of success, I never really enjoyed my national conferences, until one thing changed. That was when I reached out to, and joined, the Society of Lesbian and Gay Anthropologists (now Association for Queer Anthropology). Participating in that small society within the American Anthropological Association was a pleasure. Its members were warm, welcoming, irreverent, and down to earth. Dinners and drinks flowed naturally from its awards ceremonies and business meetings, and yielded plenty of opportunities for professional development as well. This connection came too late in my career to last for long, since very shortly afterward I left academia entirely. But it certainly demonstrated the value of finding ways to make a large national conference feel a bit more like the small and intimate conferences that we all prefer.

PART IV

. . . .

JOB DOCUMENTS THAT WORK

TWENTY-ONE

....

The Academic Skepticism Principle

Two things are critical to success on the tenure track job market: having a competitive record and presenting that record in a competitive way. Until now we've focused on the former. Now we turn our attention to the latter. Your job documents—CV, cover letter, teaching statement, research statement—need and deserve the same level of care that you give to any of the writing you do in your career, including your dissertation and publications. Your many years of work in a Ph.D. program are difficult to describe concisely. It takes time and effort to learn how. So in your five-year plan, block out at least one month, and preferably two or three, to produce these documents.

Your first drafts, like all first drafts, will be heinous. You will need the ongoing critique of dedicated readers, and you will need multiple edits. If any faculty member tells you an early draft is "great," do not believe him. These documents are almost impossible to write well without intensive help. Don't stop until you get the help you need, wherever you can find it.

The most important principle of all job document writing is this: facts, not emotions. Job seekers are all more or less desperate. If you've been looking for a tenure track job without success for years, you're growing more anxious with every passing year. Even if you're just setting out on your first attempt on the market, the zeitgeist in which you and your friends operate makes for a kind of preemptive desperation.

When that desperation seeps into your job documents, it derails them.

Why?

First, because desperation causes excess, and excess is the opposite of editing. And editing is what you must do to target your applications to particular jobs.

This is a problem of quantity. Desperate candidates engage in a writing practice that I call desperate cramming. The desperate crammer sticks every single thing she's ever done into the letter that might, however tangentially, relate to academia. That results in a four-page letter in ten-point type that degenerates into undignified lists of topics studied, theories used, fields engaged with, methods mobilized, conference papers given, classes taught, et cetera, et cetera, et cetera. You not only have an article under review, but you were also invited to contribute a chapter for a project, and you wrote two encyclopedia entries, and you were chair and presenter last year and the year before that at your regional conference, and the editor from Press Y said in an email that your book sounds interesting, and you were invited to give a guest lecture in the undergraduate survey course on the satellite campus of your university, and you are the webmaster for your interest group in your national association, and you also pet-sat your department chair's cat when he was in Spain.

OK, maybe not the cat. But everything else is crammed into your letter, which, by the end, will appear to the totally overwhelmed search committee members like a bewildering blur. The distracted and tired reader is not going to sift through a laundry list of every single little thing you have done to figure out if there is any substance to you as a candidate. The reader is going to see you as a graduate student who is lacking a clear platform. In the paragraph above, only the article under review, the chapter, and the mild expression of interest from the editor are worthy of mention, and even those require care about wording.

Inevitably, clients like this panic when I begin to cut. "But they *need* to know that I did this, this, this, this, and this. And they *need* to know that I am capable of doing that, that, that, that, and that. And the job ad mentioned X, so I need to show that I'm willing to do X and also X(a) and X(b) and X(c). . . ."

Guess what? No, they don't. They won't read this copious, list-heavy verbiage—verbiage that drowns them in detail and obscures the actually relevant work in the sheer quantity of *stuff*.

Listing is the primary culprit here. This is a typical case (all examples are composites of anonymized client work):

> In sum, my dissertation uses interviews, surveys, textual analysis, and Internet research in order to explore the impact of Facebook, Twitter, and Instagram on the social networks, family connections, and romantic relationships among a range of undergraduate students at large universities, medium-sized universities, and small colleges, in order to analyze the differences in usage patterns by variables such as race, gender, sexuality, and age.

It's not that the content of the lists is bad, per se, in this case, but that the constant repetition of lists gives the passage a hypnotic, deadening feel that squelches reader attention.

In addition to stylistic issues, there are intellectual problems with listing. The list is the flabbiest form of a scholarly argument. It is additive instead of analytical, piling on new variables instead of doing the work of winnowing and ordering them to make a focused argument.

List addiction is epidemic among young scholars who are trying to please everyone instead of fighting the good fight of declaring an argument and seeing it through to its singular conclusion. Or who are trying to prove that they can do everything and have no gaps in the project. Or who are just imprecise writers.

Dyads are the most common form of listing.

> These findings *challenge and refine sociolinguistic and anthropological premises and principles* to encompass *multilingual and language contact* settings in both *Japan and China.*

Dyads have a particularly hypnotic effect.

My role as teacher is to enable students to develop their *philosophical vision and literacy* through an *informed and sustained* practice of *traditional and contemporary* philosophical *methodologies coupled with critical study* of philosophical *history and theory*. I see in the rigorous study of this *history and theory* an important tool for challenging *undergrad and graduate* students to go above and beyond the *constraints and parameters* of their initial understanding of *formal and conceptual* frameworks.

Generally, listing and dyads are combined; in other words, if you have lists you have dyads, and vice versa:

My research focuses on transnational Latin American *history and culture, comparative race and ethnicity, and critical geography*. At its core, my work is interested in *how cultural and economic* processes produce social inequality *and how* ordinary people *interpret, inhabit, and influence* these processes. I employ critical theories of *race and space* to investigate how *national and transnational* histories of *war, empire, labor, and migration* articulate through Latin American *social and cultural* practices. My research explores how these histories shape the formation of Latin American *identities and communities* in relation to the production of racialized landscapes.

Count the dyads (eight), and the lists (three). Note that dyads are also a factor in sentence structure: in the above case, "My work is interested in how . . . and how . . ."

The outcome is a dizzying and tedious jumble of words that skims over a massive set of variables instead of clarifying a project.

Some lists are necessary, of course. Sometimes you must list the texts you study, the methods you use, or the topics you cover. The litmus test is not the appearance of one or two lists or dyads, but a continual dependence on them. If you have lists in every sentence, and dyads as far as the eye can see, then that is list addiction. Want a quick diagnosis? Do a universal search for "and" in your document—if you have a case of list addiction, the document will light up.

In the fashion competition program *Project Runway*, contestant mentor Tim Gunn always says, "Edit!" Just because one ruffle is good doesn't mean ten ruffles are better. It's the one flawlessly placed ruffle that catches your eye and takes your breath away. So it is with your job documents. The perfect streamlined match between the ad and your record is what inspires the search committee. Trust your record, and trust the readers to get it. Give them the achievements relevant to *this job,* and no more.

Second, there is the issue of quality. Desperate job seekers write bad materials because these materials consistently substitute emotion for facts. "I am sincere in my commitment to"; "I delight in the work of"; "I am so excited to be part of"; "I consider it a remarkable honor and privilege to be able to"; and my pet peeve: "I am passionate about."

First of all, this language is painfully overused. It doesn't communicate some original and compelling truth about you. It functions as nothing but noise.

But it's bad not just because it's hackneyed. It's also bad because it's just plain ineffective. It is an affront to what I have come to call the Academic Skepticism Principle. What academic makes a scholarly deliberation or judgment based on the level of emotionalism with which it's presented? "But I *really, sincerely believe* that Milton was [insert claim here]. And so, you know, you should agree with me." Did that work in your grad seminars? Did that work at your conferences? So why do you think it's going to work in your job search? No academic, be she a chemist or a classicist, is going to accept a claim just because you hysterically insist on it. She accepts a claim if the evidence supports it.

Job documents should not make claims about your feelings or your wants or your beliefs ("I am passionate about teaching," "I want to do a project on declining whale populations," "I believe in the importance of hands-on learning"), because statements such as these are unsubstantiated and unverifiable. In other words, anyone can make them. And as such, they are empty verbiage and wasted space in your letter. If you are, in fact, passionate about teaching, then let your substantive descriptions of your courses and teaching methods illustrate that. In short, show. Do not tell.

If you fill your documents with sincerity, belief, commitment, resolution, earnestness, eagerness, enthusiasm, and—worst of all—passion, you impose on the reader. I mean, why should they believe *you*, just because you raise a fuss? They don't know you.

The dead giveaway of telling not showing is adjectives and adverbs. I am not referring here to adjectives that describe, in a substantive way, the research subject itself (for example, "This study identifies a population of professionally ambitious urban Japanese women who pursue study abroad"), but rather adjectives that are meant to pump up the intensity level of candidate claims.

Here is a partial list of the kinds of adjectives (and their related adverbs) to which I refer:

- Incredible (incredibly)
- Amazing (amazingly)
- Striking (strikingly)
- Serious (seriously)
- Intense (intensely)
- Remarkable (remarkably)
- Considerable (considerably)
- Very
- Really

Some of you may doubt that such floridity would ever show up in a job letter, but alas, your doubts would be misplaced. They turn up frequently. The typical culprit: "This assignment produces some incredible student work!" It should be obvious that the Academic Skepticism Principle applies equally to the exclamation point, which is even more distasteful in a professional document. Let us not write a sentence like "My results were unexpected!"

And then there are the adjectives that purport to describe not the research claims, but the candidate herself:

- Sincere
- Eager
- Earnest
- Delighted

- Excited
- Honored
- Thrilled

And, of course,
- Passionate

The fact is, tactics like these are cheap. They are a lazy effort to exaggerate the import or impact of the work, or the putative personal appeal of the individual. And they are weak, because they always imply a comparator (the outcome that is not incredible or amazing or remarkable, the competitive who is not passionate) that is left unstated or assumed.

What reviewers need is evidence. So give them the facts. If the facts show an energetic and dynamic record, then your enthusiasm, eagerness, and, yes, passion, will be perfectly clear. But they will not cloud the information that the search committee needs to proceed with its deliberations.

TWENTY-TWO

What's Wrong with Your Cover Letter

I am on a mission to get job candidates to stop sending out self-sabotaging cover letters.

As a professor I saw terrible letters from the students of my colleagues at institutions around the country, when I read them as a member or chair of a search committee. I served on over ten search committees over the course of my career, and each garnered about two hundred applications. Now at The Professor Is In I see wretched letters daily from clients at every institution across the land. As of 2015 I've read perhaps three thousand letters. Nearly all of them start out awful.

Here are a few basic rules that, if you follow them, will ensure that your letter is properly formatted and organized, includes appropriate information, and avoids the worst errors of tone.

Fix these problems, and your letter will work for you instead of against you on the market.

1. It Is Not on Letterhead

Your letter must be on letterhead if you have a current academic affiliation of any kind. This is the convention in the United States, although it is not in other countries. I understand that for some it raises the appropriateness of using the stationery of one job to apply for another. Nevertheless, it is conventional to use institutional letterhead.

I understand that some departments are denying their graduate students access to letterhead. This is unacceptable, and you should take whatever steps are necessary to acquire it. You may steal the letterhead. You may Photoshop the letterhead. Do what you must, but send out letters on the letterhead of the department with which you are affiliated. Note that CVs, teaching statements, and research statements do not require letterhead.

If you do not have an affiliation because you finished your Ph.D. and have no academic employment at all, including adjuncting, then you can create a sober and understated personal letterhead. You may not use letterhead to which you're not entitled. That is unethical, and it is also stupid, because your readers are smart, and they notice.

2. It Does Not Follow Norms of Business Correspondence Etiquette

Your letter must follow normal letter etiquette, which means that it will have the date written out in the upper left, just under the letterhead, then a line space, then the full snail mail address of the recipient just below the date, left justified, and then a line space, and then the salutation: "Dear Professor," or "Dear Members of the Search Committee." Then it will have another line space, and commence: "I am writing in application to the advertised position in X at the University of X."

Nothing in this heading material may be left out. Similarly, nothing beyond this may be added in, including any kind of memo heading or title such as "Re: position in X." Letters do not have titles or headings.

Do not begin the letter "Please accept this application . . ." You are not a supplicant.

3. It Is Too Long

Your letter must be two pages in length if you are a junior candidate seeking your first or second job. Do not argue with me. If you are arguing with me, you are wrong. It must be two pages long.

Do not attempt to game the length with type size or margins. Your text must be 11- or 12-point type (in one of the standard professional fonts such as Garamond, Verdana, Times New Roman, and the like), and the letter margins must be approximately one inch wide. White space on a page communicates expansiveness and confidence. Line upon line of minuscule type, crammed up to the edges of the paper, by contrast, communicates insecurity and desperation.

Your reviewers are probably over forty. They are certainly tired, distracted, and rushed. They will not squint, nor they will strain their eyes.

Do I hear you claiming that you can't possibly say all you need to in two pages? Yes, you can. Do you want a job or don't you? Do it.

4. You Are Telling, Not Showing

All academics in the world, by virtue of being academics, require evidence to accept a proposition. Even the most esoteric humanist has to be persuaded with some form of evidence that a claim is valid. This is the Academic Skepticism Principle at work.

Your letter must include evidence. Empty claims such as "I am passionate about teaching" or "I care deeply about students," or "I am an enthusiastic colleague" can be made by anyone, and provide no means of proof.

Show, don't tell: Instead of "I am passionate about teaching," write something like "I used new technologies to create innovative small group discussion opportunities in my large introductory classes, technologies that were later adopted by my colleagues in the department." Or "I worked one-on-one with students on individual research projects leading to published articles. Several students later nominated me for our campus's Best Undergraduate Teacher award, which I won in 2015."

Don't waste reviewers' time with unsubstantiated and unverifiable claims.

5. You Drone On and On About Your Dissertation

As I have strained to make clear, we actually don't care about your dissertation. Seriously, we don't. Your dissertation is in the past. It's in the past even if you're still writing it. It's what you did as a student, and we're not hiring a student. We're hiring a colleague. We want to know about your dissertation only as it relates to past, present, and future colleague achievements, including publications, conference talks, grants, teaching, and interventions in your discipline.

Package up your dissertation into an easily digestible paragraph. Then, in a brief follow-up paragraph, specify the major debates in your field(s) that the dissertation intervenes in and the nature of the intervention it makes. We care less about the details of the topic than we do its intellectual or disciplinary import and significance.

From this discussion, move quickly to the conference papers and publications that came out of it, and the current and future publication plans that are forthcoming from it. Include how it shapes and motivates your teaching.

6. Your Teaching Paragraph Is Weepy

We don't care that you "love" teaching. What we care about is that you are an effective teacher. We need evidence of that, so give us some. And more to the point, we want to know you are an innovative teacher. How do you show that? Again, with evidence. Don't talk about your feelings about teaching; talk about your methods of teaching. Name specific courses, and describe specific methods you use in them. If you have specific outcomes in terms of teaching awards, mention those. If you have excellent evaluations, you can briefly mention one or two quantitative averages, but please, for the love of God, don't quote flaccid student remarks like, "This was a really great class!" or "Professor X was well organized!"

If you've been fully funded without ever setting foot into a classroom (my own case, actually), seek out teaching opportunities at universities or colleges in your area, and start cranking out the guest lectures. Get help from experienced teachers to craft some proposed classes in your field.

7. You Present Yourself as a Student, Not a Colleague

Don't be humble, groveling, or a supplicant. Be firm, confident, and forceful. Write in short, declarative sentences. Don't make excuses. Write exclusively about what you have done, and in all things make yourself autonomous, not dependent on advisors, committee members, principal investigators, head instructors, or other scholars. You're an expert in your field. Act like one.

Don't refer to faculty in the department to which you're applying as "Professor So-and-So" or "Dr. So-and-So." What are you, a grad student? In your paragraph of tailoring, write something to the effect of, "I would look forward to collaborating with faculty such as Smith on the theme of X and Yamazaki on the theme of Y."

For more on the challenge of tailoring, refer to chapter 23.

8. You Don't Specify Publication Plans

Specify which publications are out, which ones are in press, which ones are in submission, and which ones are in manuscript stage and where you intend to submit them. Do not expect the committee to dig this information out of your CV.

If you're in a book field, mention the presses with whom you're in discussions about your book. If you're not in discussions with presses about your book, start that immediately. Set a timeline for the book, and an anticipated submission date for the proposal to presses, with an eye to publication of the book well in advance of spring of your fifth year in the job.

9. You Don't Have a Second Research Project

The second project is now required for a successful tenure case at many institutions. It may not have to be entirely published, but by the fifth year, when your file goes out to external reviewers, that second project has to be, at minimum, proposed, under way, funded, and have produced some high-profile conference talks, and ideally an article or two.

It doesn't matter if you're still dotting your i's on your dissertation, you still have to have a second major research/book project in sight. This second project should arise organically out of the first, showing both continuity of interest and specialization, but also vibrant new directions. This shows that you are the real deal, an assistant professor worthy of tenure. Not a one-hit wonder, but someone who is going to keep up the work schedule through tenure and beyond.

No department wants to hire someone only to turn them down for tenure six years later. Show them you've got what it takes.

10. You Didn't Do Your Homework

Show that you have researched the department, know the faculty, have read their work, appreciate their contributions, and can contribute to the specializations of their specific programs. If they specialize in gender studies, and your project relates to gender studies, make that explicit. Mention one or two faculty members by name as potential collaborators. Collaborators, mind you, not mentors. Name specific initiatives or programs in the department or on campus to which you'd substantively contribute.

11. You're Disorganized and Rambling

Here's how a research-focused job letter should read.

DATE

NAME OF RECIPIENT/SEARCH COMMITTEE

DEPARTMENT

COLLEGE/UNIVERSITY

ADDRESS

ADDRESS

DEAR NAME/CHAIR OF SEARCH COMMITTEE:

PARA 1: I am applying for job X in Department Y. My Ph.D. is in Z, from the University of Q, in the field of R ([YEAR]). I am currently S at the University of W. My work broadly speaking focuses on A and B.

PARA 2: Your primary research project; briefly what, where, and how. Also, major sources of support.

PARA 3: Your primary research project's large contributions to the field and discipline as a whole—how it pushes boundaries, engages in dynamic new debates, and enlarges the discipline. This is a maximum of two or three sentences in length.

PARA 4: Your publications and conference papers, past, present, and future, on this project.

PARA 5: Your second project, with mention of publications, conference papers, and grants you have under way or planned.

PARA 6: Your teaching, as it ties in with all of the above.

PARA 7: An optional second teaching paragraph.

PARA 8: Your specific interest in the job and department to which you are applying. [To write this paragraph, consult the chapters on tailoring; focus on specific programs, specializations, and faculty by name, which shows that you have done your research.]

PARA 9: I look forward to hearing from you soon. Thank you.

SINCERELY,

SIGNATURE

NAME

12. You Didn't Tailor

You don't have just one job letter template file. You have at least five. Let's take my own case as a new Ph.D.—a cultural anthropologist of Japan with a focus on gender. I had the following letter template files ready to go:

1. General anthropology job, research institution
2. General anthropology job, teaching institution
3. Japan area studies job, research institution
4. Japan area studies job, teaching institution
5. Gender studies job, research institution
6. Gender studies job, teaching institution

This list doesn't include the postdoc letters. And it doesn't include the tailoring for each individual job, which as I said above, must include mention of that department's specializations, programs, and faculty. Tailoring at that level is addressed in chapter 23.

Here are examples of how three variations of the basic template would differ, using my early career material as a model:

General Anthropology Research Job: "My work uses multi-sited transnational fieldwork to track the life choices and identity narratives of young, internationalized Japanese women who pursue work, study, and marriage abroad. . . . The research shows how narratives of self-making can both resist and reinforce globally circulating discourses of race and gender that depict white men as idealized rescuers of women of color. . . . I am prepared to teach basic courses such as Introduction to Cultural Anthropology, Social Theory, and Research Methods, as well as specialized courses such as Culture and Transnationalism."

Japan Area Studies Research Job: "My work examines Japanese women as transnational actors who use work, study, and marriage abroad as a means of critiquing gender relations in Japan. . . . The research shows that women in Japan use idealized images of the West and

Western men as a resource to effect change in their opportunities and status within both the Japanese family and workplace. . . . I am prepared to teach basic courses such as Introduction to Japanese Culture and Modern East Asia, as well as specialized courses such as Gender and Globalization in Japan."

Gender Studies Teaching Job: "My work examines Japanese women who use transnational mobility as a means to critique long-standing mechanisms of Japanese patriarchy in the home and work-place. . . . I show how women's agency can be partially co-opted by globally circulating hierarchies of value that position men of color as inferior to white men. . . . I am prepared to teach basic courses such as Introduction to Gender Studies and Gender and Globaliza-tion, as well as specialized courses such as Women in East Asia, and Transnational Feminisms. My teaching emphasizes the application of gender theory to students' lived experiences, and I incorporate hands-on activities that bring current popular culture and social media memes into our discussion of theoretical concepts. For ex-ample . . ."

In general, when you write a teaching-focused letter, you first want to make sure you've been accurate in evaluating that you really need one for the job at hand. Job seekers routinely overestimate the number and type of jobs that want teaching-focused letters. Many elite SLACs and midrange colleges and universities should get a research-focused letter; reserve the teaching-focused letter only for those institutions that categorically prioritize teaching over re-search. You can investigate this by studying the job ad closely (it should speak exclusively or almost exclusively about teaching du-ties), and examining the institution's website (it will focus exclu-sively or almost exclusively on student life, rather than on research initiatives by faculty).

When you write a teaching-focused letter, adjust the template to read like this:

DATE

NAME OF RECIPIENT/SEARCH COMMITTEE

DEPARTMENT

COLLEGE/UNIVERSITY

ADDRESS

ADDRESS

DEAR NAME/CHAIR OF SEARCH COMMITTEE:

PARA 1: I am applying for job X in Department Y. My Ph.D. is in Z, from the University of Q, in the field of R ([YEAR]). I am currently S at the University of W. My teaching specializations are A and B, with an additional expertise in C.

PARA 2: My teaching focuses on [your core teaching philosophy with key themes and goals relevant to your discipline and subfield, as appropriate]. For example, in X course, I use Y readings to help students understand Z, with the goal of increasing their awareness of Q. Similarly in Y course, I . . . [describe two or three courses in total; these will respond to the courses mentioned in the ad, or be the basic courses you are likely to be asked to teach]. I am also prepared to teach courses such as A, B, and C. [Do not tether any of your past teaching experiences or courses to the other campuses at which you taught; render your teaching capacities as general and portable.]

PARA 3: My success in the above efforts has led to X awards [no runner-up "almost" awards] and [describe increased responsibility]. My effectiveness in the classroom is attested by my quantitative evaluations. [Include quantitative averages, no cheesy student quotes.]

PARA 4: Additional areas of teaching/pedagogy focus [discipline specific], study abroad, directing a program, innovative curriculum, and so forth. Here address any additional pedagogical requirements mentioned in the ad.

PARA 5: Research description [if you have/if necessary for the job—not necessary for teaching-only instructor positions]. Approximately six sentences: your dissertation topic, its material/data/texts, its theoretical or conceptual approach, the questions/themes pursued, your core conclusion, its contribution to the field.

PARA 6: Publications [if you have/if necessary for the job—not necessary for teaching-only instructor positions].

PARA 7: X and Y make this job particularly appealing/your department particularly attractive. [To write this paragraph, consult the chapters on tailoring; focus on courses to develop, teaching synergies with current faculty, and program or curriculum potential.]

PARA 8: I look forward to hearing from you soon. Thank you.

SINCERELY,

SIGNATURE

NAME

Follow these rules, and you have a fighting chance of getting short-listed.

TWENTY-THREE

· ·

Tailoring with Dignity

The tailoring of the job letter is, for many, the hardest part. Job seekers often confuse tailoring with pandering, flattering, or begging. Proper tailoring is none of these things.

The basic goal of the tailoring paragraph is to identify programs, initiatives, centers, emphases, and specializations on the campus to which you are applying, in which you, the candidate, could productively participate.

You should, of course, always mention some specific faculty by name with whom you might collaborate or co-teach, but names alone do not constitute persuasive tailoring. This is not because you should be paranoid about "stepping on toes" or "offending someone" (such a tiresomely common expression of academic paranoia) but rather that names alone don't communicate the substance of collaborations you envision.

Tailoring, done correctly, is demonstrating your familiarity with real, substantive ongoing initiatives that already exist in the department and on campus, and signaling your enthusiasm for participating in them.

Tailoring can, of course, take place in the larger content of the letter. As I demonstrated in the previous chapter, you can shift the dissertation orientation or your next project to be one that aligns with the theme of the job at hand. The courses that you list in the teaching paragraph could easily be shifted to reflect the advertisement.

But beware the temptation to resort to desperate pleading: "I can teach/say/be *anything* you want. . . ."

By contrast, good tailoring will read something like this:

I would particularly look forward to participating in the Ethnicity, Race, and Nationalism interest group in the department, and envision developing an upper-level undergraduate course, Ethnic Nationalisms in Eastern Europe, as part of that dedicated curriculum. I can envision collaborating with Smith on projects related to Eastern European politics and economics, and with Nelson on work related to the post-socialist transition. I am also interested in the activities of the Center for Democracy Studies on campus, and would look forward to bringing an anthropological and Eastern European perspective into those cross-disciplinary conversations.

Why is this good? Because in addition to showing a real familiarity with both a departmental emphasis as well as a campus-wide program, this paragraph communicates that the candidate is a good potential colleague who is willing to adjust his teaching to the needs of the department, and to represent the department and its interests in cross-campus, interdisciplinary venues.

Note that this paragraph does not display abject eagerness, undignified flattery, or desperate pandering. Examples of these include the following:

"I would be happy to teach any of your introductory courses, including Anth 103, 105, 112, or 121." (Abject eagerness to fill adjunct-level teaching needs.)

"I would be thrilled to be a part of a department like yours with such a long and illustrious history in the field of Asian studies." (Undignified flattery.)

"It would be a great honor to join the dynamic faculty of the English department at the University of X, and I would strive to be a productive member." (Desperate pandering.)

Of these, flattery is the most common. Check your job letters for lines like these:

"Your department is an exciting and dynamic intellectual community."

"As one of the top-ranked programs in the country, your program is very exciting to me."

"Being home to one of finest student bodies in the country, your campus would be an ideal location for me to start my teaching career."

"The University of X's culture of teaching quality, commitment to institutional diversity, and unique partnership with the community are major strengths."

Flattery will not get you the job. It will just make you look desperate. Instead, demonstrate with substance that you see specific ways you can contribute to department and campus programs.

The department's long-standing strengths in Francophone cinema make this position a particularly appealing one for me. I would look forward to the opportunity to develop courses on emergent cinemas from West Africa and the Caribbean, and can also envision bringing material on those cinemas into introductory courses such as Introduction to World Cinema. I am familiar with the annual film festival hosted by the Center for Media Studies on campus, and I would enjoy collaborating with those organizers to increase the representation of Francophone cinema in that festival's offerings.

Why is this good? Because it shows the candidate is already thinking like a departmental colleague, asking how she can be instrumental in widening the department's geographical and cultural coverage. She is also demonstrating that she is an involved and generous campus citizen who will add to the visibility and prestige of the department by getting involved in one of the campus's most high-profile events, the annual film festival.

All tailoring must be specific. Remember that if your claim is so generic that it can be made about any school or department, then it is not tailoring.

Examples of generic nontailoring include the following:

"I am excited to develop my career in research and teaching at your department."

"This position appeals to me because of the excellent faculty and resources on campus."

"I would be interested to develop a range of undergraduate and graduate courses in the department."

"I am intrigued by the many possibilities for collaboration in the department."

"My specialization in X will be valuable for the graduate students in the department."

If a claim is so generic that anyone can make it, it's not an effective claim for your candidacy.

The difficulty that applicants have with tailoring goes to the heart of the dysfunction that is graduate training focused on the dissertation project at the expense of career preparation. The tailoring paragraph is where you demonstrate your potential for collegial engagement, yet too many graduate students go on the market without the faintest idea what that means.

A last note on tailoring: It is not an overt "fit" sentence. You know the one—it's the sentence that says "With my background in X and Y, I am the ideal candidate for your position in Z."

Sometimes the fit sentence says "My combination of experience in X and Y makes me an excellent fit for your position in Z."

Claims like these will only rile up the academic skepticism impulse in readers who will, consciously or unconsciously, respond, "I will be the judge of *that*!" Is a search committee member really going to take the candidate's word for their suitability for the position? If we're going to do that, why search at all? Why not just take the one who says he's "ideal"?

One former colleague of mine said of the fit sentence, "Was I born *yesterday*? Do they think I'm that *naïve*? Do they think I'll just *believe* them?" Another said, "Gosh and golly! How could I, seasoned professor that I am, have failed to noticed the so plainly obvious fact, until you pointed it out, that among all the eminently qualified candidates for this job, you, yes you alone among them, are the ideal candidate for the position? I stand humbled before you in all your awesome idealness."

One depressingly common version of the fit sentence is "I believe that my training in X makes me a qualified candidate for this position."

This is, if it's possible, even worse than "ideal." Qualified candidate? There are probably twenty-five "qualified candidates"! Your goal is not to prove you are "qualified," but to demonstrate the ways that you are exceptional.

No amount of telling your reader about your fit can replace a paragraph effectively showing it.

So show us the money, candidate. Remember, talk is cheap.

TWENTY-FOUR

....

Rules of the Academic CV

The CV genre permits a wide range of variation, and there is no consensus on the value or desirability of one particular style. It is not possible to account for all the variables in style and substance that derive from all academic fields. For the purposes of this chapter, I am going to present a list of basic expectations that will produce a highly readable, well-organized CV on the American academic model. These expectations, as always, lean toward humanities and social science conventions. Always check your CV with experts in your own field to ensure its appropriateness vis-à-vis disciplinary norms.

Candidates seeking work in the United Kingdom or Canada might want to consult with experts from those countries for opinions on whether this American model will work well in searches there. Note that I provide no CV example in this chapter; that is because CVs should preserve a feel of the individual; following instructions rather than a model will allow your CV to remain your own.

Without further ado: Dr. Karen's Rules of the CV.

1. General Formatting Rules
- One-inch margins on all four sides.
- 12-point type throughout.
- Single-spaced.

- Consistent type size throughout, except the candidate's name at top, which can be 14- or perhaps 16-point type.
- Headings in bold and all caps.
- Subheadings in bold only.
- No italics except for journal and book titles.
- One or two blank lines before each new heading.
- One blank line before each subheading.
- One blank line between each heading and its first entry.
- All elements left justified.
- No bullet points at all, ever, under any circumstances. This is not a résumé.
- No box or column formatting. This interferes with the constant adjustments a dynamic professional CV will undergo on a weekly/monthly basis.
- No "cont'd" headings at the tops of pages. Page breaks will constantly move as the CV grows.
- The year (but not month or day) of every entry in the CV is left justified, with tabs or indents separating the year from the substance of the entry. The year-to-the-left rule allows readers to quickly track the pace and timing of accomplishments. Candidates are evaluated by their productivity over time, and *when* you produced is as important as *what* you produced. Years should be visible, not buried in the entry itself.
- No narrative verbiage anywhere.
- No description of "duties" under "Teaching/Courses Taught."
- No paragraphs describing books or articles.
- No explanations of grants/fellowships ("This is a highly competitive fellowship.").
- No personal stories.
- No self-indulgent ruminations ("My work at the U of X is difficult to condense.").
- Optional dissertation abstract: Some advisors insist on a separate heading for "Dissertation" with a short one-paragraph abstract underneath it. One year or so beyond completion of the dissertation, it should be removed.

2. Heading Material

- Name at top, centered, in 14- or 16-point type.
- The words "Curriculum Vitae" immediately underneath or above the name, centered, in 12-point type, if appropriate to your field. This is a traditional practice in the humanities and social sciences, but is going out of style. Double-check with a trusted advisor.
- The date, immediately below, centered, is optional. Senior scholars always date their CVs.
- Below the date, your institutional and your home addresses, plus phone numbers, should be on the left and the right side of the page, respectively, parallel to one another.

3. Content

- **Education.** Always first. List by degree, not by institution. Do not spell out "Doctor of Philosophy," and the like; it's pretentious. List Ph.D., M.A., B.A. in descending order. Give department, institution, and year of completion. Do not give starting dates. You may include "Dissertation/Thesis Title," and perhaps "Dissertation/Thesis Advisor" if you are ABD or only one year or so from Ph.D. Remove this after that point. Do not include any other verbiage.
- **Professional Appointments.** ABD candidates may have no professional appointments, and in that case this heading can be skipped. These are contract positions only—tenure track positions, instructorships, visiting positions, and the like. Postdoctoral positions also go here. Give the institution, department, title, and dates (year only) of employment. Be sure to reflect joint appointments if you have one.

  Please note that ad hoc adjunct gigs do not go here; only contracted positions of one or more years in length. Teaching assistantships and so forth are also not listed under professional employment. Courses that you taught as an adjunct are not listed under professional employment. No courses are listed in this section; they are listed later, under "Teaching Experience."

- **Publications.** Use these subheadings, as appropriate for your field and record:

  Books

  Edited Volumes

  Refereed Journal Articles

  Book Chapters

  Conference Proceedings

  Encyclopedia Entries

  Book Reviews

  Manuscripts in Submission (Give journal title.)

  Manuscripts in Preparation

  Web-Based Publications

  Other Publications (This section can include nonacademic publications, within reason.)

  Note that forthcoming accepted publications are listed with published pieces if they are accepted without any further revisions; they are listed at the very top since their dates are furthest in the future. If they are in press, they can be listed here with "in press" in place of the year, or "forthcoming" if they are accepted but not yet in press.
- **Awards and Honors.** Give name of award and institutional location. Year at left. Always in reverse descending order. Listing dollar amounts appears to be field-specific; check with a trusted senior advisor.
- **Grants and Fellowships** (if you are in a field where these differ categorically from awards and honors). Give funder, institutional location in which received/used, and year. Listing dollar amounts appears to be field-specific; check with a trusted senior advisor.
- **Invited Talks.** These are talks to which you have been invited at other campuses, not your own. Give title, institutional location, and date (year only) at left. Month and day of talk go into entries.

- **Conference Activity/Participation.** Use these subheadings, as appropriate:

  Conferences/Symposia Organized

  Panels Organized

  Papers Presented

  Discussant

  These entries will include name of paper, name of conference, and date (year only) on left as noted above. Month and date range of conference goes in the entry itself (for example, March 22–25). No extra words such as "Paper title." Future conferences should be listed here, once you have had a paper officially accepted but not before. It is not the convention to use the term "forthcoming" for any conference activity. The dates will be future dates, and as such they will be the first dates listed.

- **Campus or Departmental Talks.** These are talks that you were asked to give in your own department or on your own campus. These do not rise to the level of an invited talk but still may be listed here. List as you would invited talks. Guest lectures in courses should not be listed here or anywhere on the CV unless you are a very green candidate with little other content. Otherwise, they are viewed as padding.

- **Teaching Experience.** Subdivide either by institutional location, area/field, graduate/undergraduate, or some combination of these as appropriate to your particular case.

  Format in this way: If you've taught at more than one institution, make subheadings for each institution. Then list the courses vertically down the left (in this case, do not use the year-to-the-left rule that applies everywhere else). To the right of each course, in parentheses, give the terms and years taught. This allows you to show the number of times you've taught a course without listing it over and over. Give course titles but don't give course numbers, as they do not translate meaningfully across campuses.

  If the number of courses taught exceeds approximately

fifteen, condense this section; it is not essential for an experienced teacher to scrupulously list every single course taught, every single time. Just cover your general range of competencies.

TA experience goes here. No narrative verbiage under any course title. No listing of "duties" or "responsibilities"—we all know how to teach a class. There is one exception: If your department is one that has its TAs design and solo-teach courses, then you can clarify that you were instructor of record.

- **Research Experience.** Research assistant experience goes here, as well as lab experience. This section is rarely needed for humanists. This is one location where slight elaboration is possible, if the research was a team effort on a complex, multiyear theme. One detailed sentence should suffice.

- **Service to Profession.** Include journal manuscript review work, with journal titles (manuscript review can be given its own separate heading if you do a lot of this work), leadership of professional organizations, and so forth. Some fields put conference panel organizing under service; check conventions in your field. It is not typical to highlight the timing of service work, so the convention is that the entry itself is often left justified, with the year in the entry, deviating from the year-to-the-left rule.

- **Departmental/University Service.** Include search committees and other committee work, appointments to faculty senate, and so on. As above, it is not typical to highlight the timing of service work so the convention is that the title or committee is left justified, with the year in the entry, deviating from the year-to-the-left rule.

- **Extra Training** (optional). This is common among UK- and European-trained candidates. Include professional skills seminars, short programs, and the like.

- **Community Involvement/Outreach** (optional). This includes work with libraries and schools, public lectures, and the like.

- **Media Coverage** (optional). Coverage of your work by the media. Do not include blurbs or quotes from reviews. These are not movie trailers.

- **Related Professional Skills** (optional). Can include training in geographic information systems and other technical skills relevant to the discipline. More common in professional schools and science fields; uncommon in humanities.
- **Nonacademic Work** (optional). Include only if relevant to your overall academic qualifications. More common in business, engineering, and the sciences. Editorial and publishing work possibly relevant in English and the humanities.
- **Teaching Areas/Courses Prepared to Teach** (optional). You can give a brief list of course titles (titles only) that represent your areas of teaching preparation. No more than about eight courses should be listed here.
- **Languages.** List all languages vertically, with proficiency in reading, speaking, and writing clearly demarcated using terms such as "native," "fluent," "excellent," "conversational," "good," "can read with dictionary," and so on.
- **Professional Memberships or Affiliations.** List vertically all professional organizations of which you are a member. Include years of joining when you are more senior and those years recede into the past—it demonstrates a length of commitment to a field.
- **References.** List references vertically. Give name and full title. Do not list references as "Dr. X," or "Professor X." Give full snail mail contact information along with telephone and email. Do not give narrative verbiage or explanation of these references ("Ph.D. committee member," and so forth). The only exception is a single reference that may be identified as "Teaching Reference." This would be the fourth of four references.

When applying for teaching-centric jobs, you may move teaching content higher up in the order, to follow immediately after Education. Never remove research content, however. Remember that many teaching-centric campuses increasingly want to see evidence of your research productivity.

The central organizing principle of the CV is the Principle of Peer Review. Things that are peer-reviewed and competitive take precedence over things that are not. Publications are highly competitive, with peer-reviewed publications taking place of honor. Awards and honors reveal high levels of competition, as do fellowships and grants. Invited talks suggest a higher level of individual recognition and honor than a volunteered paper to a conference—this is reflected in the order. Campus talks are not as competitive, and come later. Teaching of courses, in and of itself, is not competitive. Extra training you seek yourself, voluntarily, is fundamentally noncompetitive. Once your CV has been hammered into shape in this way, it becomes easy to judge the value of any potential new line.

TWENTY-FIVE

······················

Just Say No to the Weepy Teaching Statement

Teaching statements are without a doubt the hardest of all job documents to write. The genre is rarely explained, the expectations are unclear, the expected content at first blush seems obvious and rote, and feelings about teaching are often intense and hard to articulate in academic prose. Because of these challenges, teaching statements are often appallingly bad, and they are bad in consistent ways.

Here are the major problems with the typical teaching statement first draft:

1. It Is Too Long

A teaching statement should be no longer than one page. A teaching statement is always subsidiary to the job letter and CV. As I've explained, search committee members are fatigued and distracted. While some dedicated individuals might enjoy reading multiple pages on teaching, the vast majority will not. A short teaching statement is easy to digest. Everything you need to say can be easily said in one page. Of course I mean one page with legible 11- or 12-point type and one-inch margins.

You know how when you get ready for a long backpacking trip, and they tell you to pack your backpack with everything you think you need, walk around the block with it, come back, and take half out? Well, when you write a professional job document, write everything you think need to say, then go back and take half out. Always write less than you think you need.

2. You Tell a Story Instead of Making Statements Supported by Evidence

This is the most common pitfall of the teaching statement. Candidates think the genre requires the "story of my teaching life." For example:

> I always like to use multimedia materials in the classroom. I first discovered the value of these when I taught Introduction to Cultural Anthropology at East Tennessee State last spring. In that class I had the opportunity to use a wide range of videos and online materials. Students told me that they really loved these, and I came to feel that these are excellent methods for promoting in-class discussions. I plan to use them in future classes as well.

Some of you probably think that the above is fine, but it isn't. It rambles and tells instead of shows. We don't want the Story of Teaching. We want principles of teaching, and evidence that you exemplify these principles in specific classroom goals and practices.

Remember that this piece of writing is sometimes called a Teaching Philosophy. I dislike that term, because I think it encourages writers to make the errors of emotionalism and navel-gazing rumination. However, it does clarify that the statement has to articulate a wide general good that can be achieved through university pedagogy at its broadest level. Then the writer demonstrates, in concrete and specific terms, how this good is manifested in specific teaching strategies, with examples. Then evidence is provided to show it was done effectively. Then there is a conclusion. And the essay is finished.

To repeat: wide general good—>teaching strategies that manifest this good—>examples from specific classes—>evidence that the strategies were effective—>conclusion.

3. You Express Sentiments That Are Saccharine, Obvious, and Indistinguishable from Countless Other Applicants'

All too often, the "wide general good" that writers fall back on is some tired blahdeddy blah about "encouraging discussion" and "supporting a variety of viewpoints" and "hands-on learning" and "promoting critical thinking" and "creating engaged learners" and . . . oh, sorry, I fell asleep.

Please recall that the search committee is reading something like 300 of these. Of those 300, approximately 285 are going to say that the writer "cares passionately about teaching," "uses a variety of multimedia materials," "promotes discussion," and "strives to educate students to be critical thinkers."

The sentiments you express in your statement cannot be saccharine or hackneyed or obvious. Your teaching motivations need to arise from a sharp and incisive understanding of your discipline and its contributions to the greater good. Then you need to give actual examples from classes that you have taught, examples that are not painfully obvious ("I use small group discussions!") but rather vivid and memorable ("I assigned mini-ethnographies of the local meatpacking district and then students shared these in a student symposium in the last week of term"). Ideally your teaching method will be memorable enough that reviewers will be able to say later, "She's that one who does those mini-ethnographies of the meatpackers, right?"

4. You Misread Your Audience

You may well have to write two teaching statements, one for a teaching-oriented SLAC, and one for a research institution. These won't be wildly different, but they may differ to a degree. Your readers want evidence that your teaching goals are consistent with the mission of the institution. If it is a SLAC, then you'll want to emphasize your methods for and successes in teaching small, intimate classes, and incorporating undergraduates in your research, for example. If it is a giant land-grant college, then you'll be best served by describing your success in using innovative methods and technologies to teach lecture courses of hundreds of students.

5. You Are Excessively Humble, Especially If You Are Female

Lines such as

"I was honored to have the opportunity to be entrusted with the core seminar in X,"

"I was fortunate to be selected for the award in X,"

"I hope that my methods will encourage students to . . . ," or

"I am always striving to improve my skills and seek training in new methods"

may seem charming and engaged, but are actually overly submissive and self-sabotaging. It is not an "honor" and a "privilege" to teach—it is a basic responsibility of a scholarly job. Speak of it as such.

6. You Are Excessively Emotional, Especially If You Are Female

Lines such as

"I am delighted when students tell me . . . ,"

"I would be thrilled to teach your course in X,"

"I am so excited to use new materials,"

"It would be a great pleasure to create new courses,"

"I would love to be a part of . . . ," or

"I can't say enough about how much I enjoy . . ."

may seem friendly and engaged, but are actually overly emotional and highly feminized in ways that sabotage your chances by substituting emotion for facts.

Women in particular must beware of their tendency to overinvest in this type of verbiage. Teaching at the tenure track level is not about being nice. The more efforts you make to sound nice, the more you sound like a perennial replacement adjunct.

Those who are competitive in the tenure track market articulate a teaching persona that is consistent with their researcher persona: serious, rigorous, disciplinarily cutting-edge, demanding, and with high standards and expectations. Of course it is important to show your collegiality, but that happens later, during the interviews and campus visit.

7. You Fail to Link Your Research and Teaching into a Single Consistent Whole

The teaching statement is not meant to suddenly depart from your scholarly persona to tell a random new story about how nice you are and how much you care about students. The teaching statement is meant to demonstrate that you are as self-directed, resourceful, and innovative in the classroom as you are in your research and writing. The connections between these personae should be seamless. If you are dedicated to new approaches to medieval manuscripts in your research, then show us how you use medieval manuscript replicas in your classroom to instruct students in paleographic methods. If you are dedicated to critiquing postapocalyptic fantasy in your research, then show how you have students deconstruct episodes of *The Walking Dead*. If you study the role of death in Shakespearean drama, then show how you have your students stage one of the corpse scenes from *Hamlet*.

Remember to always stay on message.

8. You Don't Have a Conclusion

All professional documents should conclude with a broad gesture toward the wider import of your work. A line that dribbles off like "And I received positive feedback for that class" is painfully deflating to read. Finish strong. An example might be "In sum, all of my pedagogical strategies are dedicated to teaching the debates and controversies animating political life in ways that will remain with the student long after he or she leaves my classroom." Or "To conclude, whether in small classes or large, I am dedicated to bringing the insights of political science to students' lived experience, both at the local and global level."

I want to share with you a particularly awful teaching statement (with kind permission of the writer, discipline obscured). It isn't the worst teaching statement I've ever seen because nearly all first drafts of teaching statements are so uniformly awful that it is difficult to employ the superlative in this context. But this one is very bad indeed, and bad in a way that reflects the most common error of the genre, especially when written by women: hyper-emotionalism.

I have italicized all the words that invoke emotion and the kind of yearning and striving that is endemic to this genre, and I have bolded adjectives. The combination of emotionalism, striving, and adjectives makes this teaching statement a maelstrom of redundant feeling-talk in place of crisp and memorable substance.

> Teaching [my discipline] provides many opportunities to *stimulate* students' thinking about X and X. Students are more likely to learn when they are *comfortable* in the classroom, and when they are *engaged* with the material. To this end, I *strive to give* students *individualized attention* and to *foster* an understanding of the world around them through interactive learning.

The first paragraph is mostly pointless verbiage that states the obvious and provides little substantive content, none of it memorable.

When students know their teachers *care about* them, they are more **attentive** to and more **enthusiastic** about their studies. Each quarter, I *invest time and effort* into building *long-lasting relationships* with students. I *learn* their names, interests, and motivations for taking the course. I also design activities that *encourage* students to attend office hours, and I *invite* students to visit with me at cafés and restaurants during extended "office hours." In addition, I *make myself available* through email, instant messaging, and social networking sites. Like my colleagues, I have boundaries for office hours and availability online, but I *make sure* that students *never feel hesitant* to contact me. I *appreciate* that students have other *needs and concerns*, and I recognize that *personal problems* and learning disabilities can impede their studies. *It is also my experience* that many students do not ask for help. Therefore, I *take the initiative* to contact students who *seem uninterested or unresponsive*, and I *take note* when *I notice* a sudden change in a student's behavior. *Showing a little concern can go a long way.*

This paragraph is totally enmeshed in emotion-talk—all caring, striving, nurturing, and poor boundaries (despite the weird disavowal). It overuses "I" sentences, and is repetitive, taking nine sentences to make a single substantive point (I make myself available to students) that could be encapsulated in one. It sends a massive red flag to the committee that the candidate's priorities are skewed and she will not get her writing done for tenure. In sum, it presents the candidate as a perennial adjunct rather than tenure track material.

Students are also more **enthusiastic** about their studies when they are engaged with the material. In the classroom, I *make every effort* to create a **supportive** and **collegial** environment, in which students *feel* **comfortable** to *share* their ideas and to approach me for help. I begin each class with a **fun** and **engaging** activity related to course material. Sometimes, I *play* songs and ask students to interpret the lyrics. Other times, I *play* a short clip from a film or late-night comedy show. For example, in a class on X, I showed a clip on X from the film X. I also *invite* students to bring in songs, videos, and news articles for participation points. These activities allow students to participate in alternative ways, and they provide opportunities for students to see how X informs their everyday lives and experiences. During sections, I also incorporate **creative** but **purposeful** activities that *stimulate* students' interest in X. In addition to giving mini-lectures to clarify the readings, I use a combination of small- and large-group discussions, simulations, and *Jeopardy!*-like review games. For each class I teach, I also create a blog, where I post each week's agenda, discussion questions, and learning objectives. The blogs also provide an interactive forum for student-to-student and student-to-teacher communication, and they *allow me to present information* in multiple ways to *better accommodate* different learning styles.

This paragraph contains some substantive teaching methods but buries them in more feeling-talk. Also, she overuses lists and adjectives in describing the methods, and employs a term—"mini-lectures"—that is self-minimizing or juvenilizing. Finally, she has so little concrete substance about her teaching as tied to her discipline that little effort was required to disguise her discipline: as you can see, there are only a handful of Xs.

As an educator, I have a **unique** opportunity to help my students become better citizens who *care more* about the world around them. To make the most of this opportunity, I *examine* my own practices and *strive to* constantly *improve* upon them. To this end, I *seek* student feedback through the use of anonymous evaluations. These evaluations *help* students *feel more invested* in the course, and they *help me* know what and how to *change* in order to make my teaching more effective. If students come away from my class *caring even a little bit more* about X than they did at the start of the quarter, *all the better*.

This paragraph deploys the most hackneyed adjective of all—"unique"—and then catapults us back into feeling and striving land. While it is fine to refer to ways you improve your teaching, one sentence on this suffices. In this case, she over-narrates the point, then makes it again subordinate to the cause of emotions. Finally, her phrasing implies that all of her teaching needs intervention to be effective.

Through all of these errors of approach, this candidate renders herself, with the best of intentions, as someone with poor boundaries and questionable emotional distance from her students. Fortunately, she transformed the statement by the final draft. Unfortunately, I cannot share the revised document because it is now so detailed that her anonymity would be compromised. That's a good thing—it means that the revised statement has replaced generalizations with specificities, that it shows rather than tells.

TWENTY-SIX

....

Evidence of Teaching Effectiveness

Some job applications request a teaching portfolio or "evidence of teaching effectiveness." This goes beyond the basic teaching statement discussed in the previous chapter to encompass sample syllabi, proposed course descriptions, a list of courses, evaluations or a summary of evaluations, and the complete evaluations (both numerical and narrative) for one or two courses.

I will take each of these in turn.

The *sample syllabi* should reflect courses you have taught that are in some way similar to the courses you'll be asked to teach at the job for which you're applying. You do not need to write a new syllabus for one of the courses currently on their books (unless, of course, that is requested in the ad). Your purpose here is simply to give evidence that you know how to put together a class in a related area, with appropriate organization, subject coverage, assigned readings, and course assignments and exams. The syllabi you submit should be substantive and complete, with complete course descriptions at the top that demonstrate your pedagogical commitments in the classes. Don't excise the basic policy section; they want to know how you've dealt with issues of plagiarism and cheating. However, if your campus imposes pages of legal boilerplate, that does not need to be included.

Resist the temptation to create a "mega-class" to impress the search committee. I did this once, my first year on the job market, and a tenured friend said, gently, "Um, I'm not sure this class is actually teachable." Remember, they want evidence that your courses are viable for actual students. Keep the readings and assignments reasonable, and don't use the syllabus as a stealth bibliography of your dissertation topic.

Be particularly careful to match the quantity and difficulty level of the readings to both the level of course and the status and type of school to which you're applying. You may have been educated exclusively, in both undergraduate and graduate school, at Ivy Leagues or elite R1s, but those are not necessarily the types of schools to which you're applying. Adjust your expectations. An advanced undergrad class at an elite R1 can include a substantial reading load, while an advanced undergrad class at a regional teaching college, with an entirely different type of student body, should be dialed down. If you are unsure, Google syllabi for courses at the institution or other institutions of similar type and rank.

The *course descriptions/proposals* will be one-page sketches of new courses that you propose to develop. These documents are not complete syllabi with exhaustive policies and weekly assignments. This one-page, single-spaced document should include the following:

- Title of the course.
- Your name.
- Approximate level of the course.
- Envisioned enrollment of the course.
- A two-paragraph description of the course. Paragraph one will introduce an important theme or topic in the world that the course will address. By "in the world," I mean that it is an existing phenomenon that is worthy of study, and not some arcane and pedantic micro-argument about scholarly minutiae of interest to you, your advisor, and four other tenured professors in Norway. Please recall that syllabi are for *students*. The topic must speak to *students*. The second paragraph will describe the broad subtopic breakdown introduced by the course, and the readings or themes on which the course will be based. It will mention one or two innovative assignments. If there is room, a brief third

paragraph can show how the course fits into and advances existing initiatives and foci of the department.
- A "mini-syllabus": a single-spaced ten- or sixteen-line week-by-week list of the course topics.

The course will be read with an eye to its appeal to the students. Particularly if it's an undergraduate course, its appeal to undergraduates should be instantly apparent. The writing should sell. Don't be pedantic here. Consider starting with an intriguing question: "What do shows like *CSI* and *Bones* tell us about forensic science in America?" "Is the world running out of fresh water?" "What do Mark Twain and Danielle Steel have in common?" "One hundred and fifty years after the close of the Civil War, what is the status of race in America?"

The course should be innovative, and reflect new trends in your field(s). They already have old faculty doing old stuff. Your job is to do the new. It should capitalize on new technology and social media. These are transforming university pedagogy, and your job is to handle that for the other faculty who are too behind the times to figure it out.

It should be tailored to their department and campus. And its subject should relate to the job. If the job is for contemporary East Asia, don't submit your fabulous gender studies seminar, unless it is primarily East Asia based. If it is a gender studies job, don't submit your East Asia seminar unless it is primarily about gender.

It should not duplicate what is already there. They are hiring you to expand their coverage, not replicate it.

Your *list of courses taught* should include the names, the level, and the enrollment. Descriptions are unnecessary, although you can divide this list into undergraduate and graduate subheadings if you wish. If the position is an interdisciplinary or joint one, divide by department or area. Do not include course numbers; these are meaningless outside of the campus. Anth 1102 on one campus might be Anth 20 on another campus; the numbers just distract.

Lastly, you'll want a *brief summary of your evaluations*. I say "brief," because I do not believe it to be appropriate to send exhaustive archives of your numerical and narrative teaching evaluations from all of your classes (unless, of course, they are requested specifically).

These will most likely not be read, and may well exhaust the search committee by their sheer volume.

Rather, find a way to summarize your numerical evaluations in a table, and then give a sample of the written comments. Here are two examples, provided (and anonymized) by readers of the blog.

Teaching Evaluations for XXX University

	Overall	How much did this course contribute to your education? Consider factors as learning, exposure to new ideas, intellectual growth	How effectively did the instructor conduct class?	How would you evaluate the instructor's responses to your work?	To what extent was the instructor helpful to your learning outside of class?	Please rate your own level of effort in this course.
Introduction to XXX (Spring 2013)	6.24	6.4	6.6	5.8	6.6	5.8
Introduction to YYY (Fall 2012)	6.25	5.64	6.36	6.6	6.0	6.65
Intermediate XXX (Fall 2012)	5.81	5.2	6.0	6.0	6.25	5.6
Gen Ed Course XXX (Spring 2012)	6.28	6.25	6.25	6.0	6.6	6.3

Mean scores: 1 = poor, 7 = excellent

You might consider sending the *complete evaluation set, both numerical and narrative, from a single class.* That would allow for an objective view, rather than the edited view that arises from your picking and choosing narrative comments, for example. I would suggest sending a combination of summary of evaluations and one complete evaluation set (both numerical and narrative) for a single course.

No matter what you submit, in all of your teaching documents it is critical to be vigilant about the difference between your teaching *as a TA* and *as instructor of record.* In your selection of materials

Qualitative Written Evaluations
(scanned forms available upon request)

"I really enjoyed this course because I feel that it provided a lot of new information that I didn't know before. I also thought that Professor XXX really taught the class well with discussion questions and such. I liked the presentation style of the class with students presenting and also the professor."

"There was a lot of student involvement with small group discussion and bringing it into the larger group. Also, the presentations were interesting."

"She provided instant feedback on our reading responses and interview assignments, which I liked because I could see how I was doing throughout the semester. She also handed back our paper proposal rather quickly."

"My cultural perspective has been challenged many times and in effect has helped me form a more open mind. I could see our exchange students and their struggles and was able to form new friendships outside of the classroom."

"Professor XXX was very helpful and available for students who wished to speak with her regarding their research papers or presentations that they were giving to the class."

"Professor XXX was always willing to meet with me for a longer period of time regarding my work or just speak briefly about it. I really appreciated her willingness to help!"

to include, always prioritize the classes for which you were primary instructor. Only use TA materials if you don't have any instructor of record teaching experience. In general, if the narrative evaluations from TA discussion sections were excellent, include them, but not at the expense of equally excellent or even just solid alternatives from your solo-taught courses.

TWENTY-SEVEN

The Research Statement

The research statement is more variable in length than the cover letter and teaching statement. In the humanities and soft social sciences, two pages generally suffices. In general, I find that two pages allows for an elaboration of the research well beyond the summary in the cover letter, and gives the search committee substantial information to work with, while remaining attentive to the principle of search committee exhaustion. Some social science fields such as psychology tend to longer statements of three to four pages. In the sciences research statements are also longer (about four pages) often to make room for figures. Never simply assume that longer is better in an RS or in any job document. As always, I urge all job seekers to investigate the norms of their fields carefully, and follow the advice they receive on this matter from experts there.

Before moving on, let me clarify that the research statement I discuss in this chapter is the document requested as part of a basic job application. This is not the "research proposal" required by fellowship or postdoc applications. That genre of writing I discuss in part VIII.

Here are other rules:

- Use 11- or 12-point type and one-inch margins.
- Print on regular printer paper, not letterhead.

- Center your name and the words "Research Statement" at the top.
- Don't tailor overtly to a job ("My research will build on the strength of the department in X"). While you may subtly adjust your project descriptions to speak to the job, research statements do not typically refer to the job.
- Do not refer to any other job documents ("As you can see from my CV, I have published extensively . . .").
- Eschew grandiose claims ("This research is of critical importance to . . .").
- Don't go negative. Stay in the realm of what you did, not what others didn't.
- Minimize references to other scholars. The work is your own. If you coauthored a piece, do not use the name of the coauthor. Simply write, "I have a coauthored essay in the *Journal of X.*"
- Do not forget to articulate the core argument of your research: "In this dissertation, I argue that . . ." As a prompt device, you may use the line "In contrast to other scholars who have interpreted X as Y, in my dissertation I find that X is better understood as Z."
- Articulate a publishing trajectory, moving from past to present, from essays published to essays currently in preparation or in submission.
- Propose a second major project that is distinct and original compared to the first. Make sure you are not coming across as a one-trick pony.
- Use the active voice as much as possible, but beware a continual reliance on "I" statements.
- Do not position yourself as "extending" or "adding to" or "building off of" or "continuing" or "applying" other work, either your own or others. Everyone's work builds on the work of others; the point of job documents is to highlight the aspects of the work that are original and autonomous.

If unsure how to structure your research statement, use a six-paragraph model as follows:

PARA 1: A brief paragraph sketching the overarching theme and topic of your research, situating it disciplinarily.

PARA 2: A summary of the dissertation research. This may replicate to some extent the paragraph on the dissertation in the cover letter, but it must have more detail about the methods, the theoretical foundations, and, most of all, the core arguments. In the humanities and social sciences it is appropriate to include chapter summaries of the dissertation, approximately one or two sentences per chapter. In the sciences, the range of hypotheses, methods, and outcomes should be reflected.

PARA 3: A brief description of the contribution of the dissertation research to your field or fields.

PARA 4: A summary of publications associated with the dissertation research, including a plan for the book, if you are in a book field. Other ongoing research can be described here in more paragraphs in the event that you have other research.

PARA 5: A summary of the next research project, providing a topic, methods, a theoretical orientation, and a brief statement of contribution to your field(s). Mention publications, conference talks, or grants related to the new project.

PARA 6: A conclusion that briefly summarizes the wider impact of your research agenda(s) writ large—what do they tell us that is valuable and important, both for your discipline but also for a wider scholarly community, and, in some cases, for humanity in general.

When writing the research statement, keep the focus on the research itself, and not about your narrative of doing it. It is tempting to write a statement that goes something like this:

I work on transitions in the care of the elderly in Japan. I am particularly focused on the recent growth in government-run care facilities. I use ethnographic methods to address the nature of the care given in these facilities, and I explore how the care is received by the patients and their families. I believe such an approach is essential in a context of Japan's aging society. My dissertation explores one such facility in northern Japan.

Here the focus is on you instead of the research. Instead, write something like this:

The rapidly aging society is one of the primary challenges facing Japan in recent decades. Both the public and private sectors have hastened to respond to emerging needs of the elderly and their families. More than two hundred new government-run elderly care centers have been built in recent years. In my dissertation, I conduct an ethnographic study of one such facility in northern Japan, in order to explore the nature of the care provided there, as well as its reception by the elderly themselves and their family caregivers.

"I" statements are not verboten in most fields of the humanities and social sciences (sciences differ; check for your field). They just need to be minimized and carefully contextualized so that the research is always at the forefront, and your ego is secondary. It is a shame that this document is sometimes called a statement of research interests, because the one thing nobody really wants to know is what you're interested in. That is, if you view that as an opportunity to drone on and on about your private preoccupations. It's often quite a writing tic. "I am interested in. . . ," "I am particularly interested in . . . ," "Within this area a topic of particular fascination is . . . ," "Based on my interests in . . . ," "I have pursued these interests through . . ." and so on and so on, ad nauseam. If the word "interest" shows up once in a client's document, it nearly always shows up at least five more times.

Interest-talk is one of the biggest red flags of a job document, because it's self-involved. It suggests that you'll be a bad colleague, not a good one. The fact is, departments advertise because they need your labor. The nature of the labor will vary depending on the type of department and campus, and the job described. But they need you to teach specific classes that may have been named in the ad, and other classes that will round out their major in clear and deliberate ways. They need you to do research on topics that are consistent with the scholarly profile of the department as a whole and that strengthen the academic area specified in the job ad. They need you to publish articles and books that will a) meet their standards for tenure so that they don't have a hassle in six years, and b) bring fame and glory to the department. They need you to serve on committees and help the department run.

All of these things are entirely outcome based. You either do the publishing that they want to see, or you don't. You either teach the classes that they need and expect, or you don't. Good job document writing provides this evidence. Bad job documents drone on in a self-absorbed and self-regarding manner about your private fascinations, preoccupations, and obsessions—that is, your interests.

Here's an example of a bad statement:

> I have long been interested in the relationship between gender and transnational mobility in Japan. This led to my interest in Japanese women as transnational agents. My dissertation addressed this issue, and one fascinating conclusion of the research was that women's investment in transnational identities was not static but evolved over the life course. These interests led to an article I published in the *Journal of X,* which explored this subject further.

By the way, the word "fascinating" is another culprit. Here's the rewrite:

> My dissertation addresses the relationship between gender and mobility in Japan, specifically focusing on Japanese women as transnational agents. Based on fieldwork in Japan using X and Y methods, the dissertation concluded that women's investment in transnational identities was not static but evolved over the life course. I published part of this research in an article in the *Journal of X;* in this article I argue Q. I have another article on Y underway for submission this spring.

Finally, in your research statement and all academic writing, banish the words "attempt," "try," "endeavor," "hope," and the like. Too much academic writing depends on these and similar formulations:

- "In this research I hope to prove that . . ."
- "Through such an analysis I will try to show that . . ."

- "I believe that in making this argument I may be able to demonstrate that . . ."

A graduate school mentor once remarked, after glancing at the conference paper I had just shown him: "Do. Or do not. There is no try." The paper, a pretty standard effort, opened with the line "This paper will attempt to show that Japanese women are traveling abroad in increasing numbers in order to effect a quasi-feminist critique of unequal gender relations at home."

My mentor, channeling Yoda, was right—there is no try. If you did the research, and reached your conclusions, then stand by them. Why do scholars embark on their studies with so much doubt and so little confidence? Own your findings. Claim your ground. Take every sentence where you find these power-sucking words, and remove them. In their place, write:

- "In this research I prove that . . ."
- "Through such an analysis I show that . . ."
- "In making this argument I demonstrate that . . ."

And may the Force be with you.

TWENTY-EIGHT

What Is a Diversity Statement, Anyway?

The diversity statement is quickly emerging as the fifth required document of the typical job application. And because it's of such recent origin, nobody has a clear idea what it's supposed to do.

In general, the goal of a diversity statement is to demonstrate that you, as a candidate, have some awareness that historically underrepresented and economically disadvantaged groups have confronted obstacles in their access to higher education, and have been marginalized within and by the authorized knowledge commonly taught in university settings. The goal of the diversity statement is also to demonstrate that you bring this awareness into play in your research, teaching, and service, in concrete and thoughtful ways. As such, the diversity statement can take a variety of approaches.

It can address how you deal with a diverse range of students in the classroom, and incorporate a diversity of voices into your teaching materials and methods (rather than continually regurgitating the canon of dead white men, for example). But beyond that, the statement can show how your personal background and experiences have influenced your approach to your discipline, your research program, and your students. It can discuss how you support students, staff, and faculty in a variety of initiatives to improve equity of access to the resources of the university. It can consider how you address diversity in your own research topics. And it can consider how you prepare students for careers in a multicultural society. You don't have to choose just one of these angles; you can and should combine several.

Taking my own case as an example, from back in the day when I was an assistant professor, I might have constructed a diversity statement around a few central ideas. (Back then, this document was not required, so I never had the opportunity to actually compose one for myself.)

Doing my Ph.D. at the University of Hawai'i was, for me, a suburban haole girl from Pittsburgh, a trial by fire in American race politics. During my time in graduate school, the Hawaiian sovereignty movement gained a great deal of visibility, and I became acutely aware of the charged history of white presence on the islands. The anthropology department was deeply implicated in this politics, and by the time I finished my Ph.D., I had been well schooled in the mutual enmeshment of anthropology as a discipline with the history and epistemologies of colonialism. My teaching and research could not remain unaffected by this understanding.

Meanwhile, the classroom teaching experience I gained in Hawai'i taught me the challenges and opportunities of managing a multiethnic classroom. Speaking in broad generalizations, I had to learn how to keep the white students from dominating all classroom discussion. And I had to learn techniques to encourage the Asian and local students, who often come from cultural backgrounds that encourage a quiet deference to authority, to speak up. And I had to learn how to create space for Native Hawaiian students to express what were often critical perspectives on the taken-for-granted theories and methods of anthropology.

None of these things happened without conscious effort; I had to critically examine what I was teaching. Did the content of my courses thoughtlessly reproduce the standard white and Western model of legitimate knowledge? Or did it include a variety of voices from different subject positions of race, ethnicity, gender, and genre? Did my teaching methods squelch challenges to my authority, or did I create space for critiques and questions?

Later, after beginning my career as an assistant professor in the Northwest, when I had the opportunity to work with Native American graduate students from local tribes, I learned these lessons again, but in a new historical and political context. The presence, and the critiques, of Native American students changed the way I taught anthropology, trained students to work in the academy or on behalf of their own tribes, and conducted my own research. These changes caused me to question: What was the responsibility of anthropology—and the academy as a whole—to the wider community in which it's located?

I offer these thoughts not as an example but as a set of prompts. If I were to write my own diversity statement now, all of these questions would be replaced by declarative statements explaining exactly how my teaching, research, and mentoring reflected these provocations to work differently. If I wrote a diversity statement now, I would also weave my queer identity into it. How do I teach in non-heteronormative ways? How do I work to empower queer students to feel safe to speak in the classroom and conduct their lives outside of it? How do my scholarship and my professional life reflect a commitment to queer visibility, including working with queer professional associations in my disciplinary units? And having been a department head, I would include mentoring and supporting a range of junior faculty, and promoting—financially and administratively—initiatives on campus that engage diversity in a variety of forms.

Here is an example of an effective diversity statement:[1]

To demonstrate how I employ my cultural competency in the classroom, I will focus here on my work over the past two years with the University of X Biology Undergraduate Scholars Program (BUSP). Based on my experiences teaching college students, I expect the students in a biology classroom at XYZ Community College to be diverse in innumerable ways. My work with BUSP students exemplifies how I approach working with nontraditional students.

Growing up overseas, I know what it feels like to find oneself outside the dominant culture. In science the widespread image of a scientist is an older, white male who works in a lab. This pervasive image may be discouraging for students who do not "fit in" based on their own identities. The purpose of BUSP is to help students from historically underserved backgrounds, whose educational and economic circumstances limit their academic opportunities, to develop the skills necessary to succeed as life science majors. One of my goals as a biology instructor is to make sure that my students are exposed to the variety of ways that one may be a scientist. To accomplish this goal, I developed and taught a "Bio Boot Camp," designed to give BUSP students a head start on content and study skills necessary for the yearlong introductory biology course they take as sophomores.

I designed the Bio Boot Camp to be intense—we met daily for three weeks—and rigorous, but my priority was to help students enjoy the fundamentals of biology. The students who participated came from Anglo, Latino/a, African, Asian, and Afghani cultures, and the majority were female. My BUSP students met with several scientists from diverse backgrounds who did not fit the scientist stereotype. For example, we visited the University Botanical Conservatory and met with the conservatory director, Mr. X. As a former BUSP graduate, Mr. X exemplified a successful alternative career as a plant biologist. The field trip offered a memorable hands-on experience for students who had little previous practice with plants. On course evaluations many students indicated that this field trip was a highlight for them. Additionally, one student asked to volunteer with Mr. X at the conservatory.

I gave the Bio Boot Camp students a range of assignment choices to let them identify and explore their own interests. Some students chose to write children's books about photosynthesis and biodiversity. Others interviewed their parents, many of whom had immigrated to the United States, in order to learn more about the ecology of their ancestral homes. In class, the students explained and discussed their assignment choices, and they peer-reviewed rough drafts. The cross-cultural exposure was subtle, but by working together my students learned about one another and about different biological topics.

My awareness and appreciation of cross-cultural understanding grows continually. I work to maintain my fluency in Spanish because practicing a second language helps me appreciate the challenge faced by students who are simultaneously learning English and biology. As a mentor and a teacher I carefully listen to my students, and set aside my own perceptions of what biological concepts are "easy" or "hard" to understand because these assumptions are based on my own cultural and educational background, not that of my students.

This writer does not rest simply on a narration of the facts of her international background, but instead deftly weaves her understandings of the racial and gender norms of lab science into clear and specific classroom methods. This example, like all good writing for the job market, shows the candidate's engagement with diversity through concrete examples, rather than talking around it with generalizations, abstractions, and emotionalized good intentions. On the latter front, beware vague and saccharine sentiments like "I believe our differences make us stronger!" Due to overuse, these too function like white noise.

I suspect that some white, middle-class job seekers may fear or resent the diversity statement because it seems to privilege minority candidates. I hope that I've shown in this chapter that all job seekers can and should be able to show that they are prepared to teach people different from themselves, especially those people from historically underrepresented or economically disadvantaged groups. They can and should be able to demonstrate thoughtful strategies for putting this awareness into practice in teaching, research, and service.

At the same time, the diversity statement can be particularly fraught for candidates of color. They may be asked, point blank, "How are you diverse?" in ways that instantly tokenize them based on their identity. Philosopher Keisha Ray explains this in a thoughtful meditation on diversity and the job market. She writes, "How do you write a 1–3-page statement answering a question that you believe can be answered with a few words or a few phrases at the most, or even with just a picture of myself, given the acknowledged lack of diversity in philosophy?"[2] She concludes, "Answering questions about diversity forced me to confront the very likely possibility that I was used by philosophy and bioethics departments to satisfy HR requirements."

A reader once asked me how to answer the diversity question

"without offending anyone." I'm not really sure what that means. Different races and genders and sexualities, and so on, exist. We will all encounter people different from ourselves. Everybody has their own histories—their own places and families of origin, their inspirations, their trials by fire. You don't have to occupy a minority subject position to have a position on diversity. Early in my career, as a white, suburban, straight (at the time) young woman, I didn't offer much diversity to cultural anthropology (where white straight women are a dime a dozen, so to speak). But I had encountered questions of race and ethnicity in my training and life experiences, and the way I did my work changed because of it. Likewise, your experiences are your experiences. Your commitments are your commitments. Explaining how you work with different kinds of people, particularly those who struggle to enter and succeed in higher education, is not inherently offensive. It is an important and valuable exercise, and one that reveals a great deal about you as a candidate.

TWENTY-NINE

· ·

The Dissertation Abstract

All abstracts are difficult to write. It is hard to condense years of research into a small number of words. When it comes to the dissertation, this is amplified. Translating some ten years of work and hundreds of pages of dissertation into one or two pages of summary takes enormous effort.

At The Professor Is In I edit many dissertation abstracts for my clients from English, where this document is often a required element of job applications. I've learned that these abstracts commonly display two problems: 1) a grad student–ish obsession with literature review, betraying the writer's subordination to outside scholarly "authorities" and lack of conviction in his or her own intellectual project, argument, and/or contribution; 2) a fixation on the micro-topic of the research without a contextualization of the project within wider disciplinary concerns.

Fortunately, these problems can be easily fixed, because abstracts are among the most formulaic of all genres of academic writing. While the length may differ widely, the components of an abstract vary little. Here is a basic template for the dissertation version, approximately two pages in length, which will minimize the pitfalls mentioned above, and foreground both the original argument and its wider disciplinary contribution.

1. Big-picture problem or topic widely debated in your field (one or two sentences only)
2. Brief sketch of the literature on this topic (two or three sentences only)
3. A gap in the approaches to date, *without* criticism of other scholars (one sentence)
4. Your project, as it fills the gap (one or two sentences)
5. The specific material/texts/data that you examine in the dissertation (one or two sentences)
6. The theoretical orientation you employ (one sentence)
7. A summary of chapters (two or three sentences per chapter)
8. Your original conclusion/argument (one or two sentences)
9. Brief concluding paragraph pointing to the significance of the project (two or three sentences)

A good abstract will not merely sketch what the dissertation is about. It will also sketch why we should care. The fact that you decided to devote five or ten years of your life to the study of a topic does not in and of itself reassure us, the readers, that the topic is interesting or valuable. You actually have to do the work to prove that. So always cushion the chapter summaries, statement of theory and method, and core argument of your dissertation in a compelling setting of disciplinary or interdisciplinary import. That is why my template above devotes no fewer than three of its sections to disciplinary contextualization and contribution (numbers 1, 3, and 9).

Similarly, a good abstract will sketch the literature only as it supports and lays the groundwork for the writer's original research and argument. It will not subordinate the author's work to the work of others. That is why my template above devotes only one section to literature review (2).

A good abstract will focus on the research, not on the process of doing it, or a personal drama of discovery ("First I did . . . and then I did . . . and then I discovered . . . !"); it will limit the number of "I" sentences and eschew jargon.

It will also refrain from trite, cheap, and overused placeholder adjectives. What are those? Words like these:

- complex
- multivalent/multidirectional/multiplicious
- unique

Adjectives are not arguments.

The simple repetition of the words on this list, over and over in your documents, does not suggest that you have a coherent project, or make a compelling point, or advance an original argument. The adjectives on the list above are simply pointless. There is no Ph.D. research project that is not on a complex, multiplicious, or unique topic, and there is no analysis you can conduct at the Ph.D. level that is not complex, multiplicious, and unique.

Therefore, to use these words to describe your work is to say, precisely, nothing. They are white noise and devoid of meaning. Indeed, they make an implicit straw man move, because you are always implying that something "out there"—some topic, phenomenon, or analysis—is simple and unitary and entirely derivative. But that's patently untrue, so stop implying it. The implication cheapens your own work.

"Complex" is far and away the worst culprit—it is an epidemic. Here is a collection of (anonymized) cases that I gathered in less than one week at The Professor Is In.

- "This work surveys X composer's complex influence on the musical poetics of authors."
- "This book offers a more complex narrative of the relationship between sexuality, consumer behavior, and power."
- "Four case studies of X are used to illuminate this complex nation-building process."
- "A particularly effective means of demonstrating the complex cultural logics that form the commonsense assumptions underlying political power."
- "Many opportunities to discuss the complex interrelationship of structural and cultural forces that reproduces urban violence."

- "X's place was more complex and profound not only in the history of the nation, but also that of the region as a whole."
- "I challenge students to immerse themselves in the complex sociocultural contexts surrounding each text."
- "Chinese X actually has a long, complex history."
- "I examine the complex interplay of publishing, reading, and circulation that imbued regional fiction with meaning in early modern X."
- "My second article, X, analyzes the complex strategies employed by a highly acculturated ethnic population."

Transforming the adjective "complex" into the noun "complexity" does not help.

- "This role-playing exercise builds skills while also building a deeper understanding of the complexities of globalization."
- "Understanding this past complexity prepares us for the challenge of working to improve . . ."

And substituting some other tired adjective does not make it any better, either:

- "My research examines the intricate relationship between religion and politics in X."

If you want to see just how meaningless this adjective is, see how the above lines read without it:

- "This work surveys X composer's influence on the musical poetics of authors."
- "This book offers a narrative of the relationship between sexuality, consumer behavior, and power."
- "Four case studies of X are used to illuminate this nation-building process."
- "A particularly effective means of demonstrating the cultural logics that form the commonsense assumptions underlying political power."

- "Many opportunities to discuss the interrelationship of structural and cultural forces that reproduces urban violence."
- "X's place was more profound not only in the history of the nation, but also that of the region as a whole."
- "I challenge students to immerse themselves in the sociocultural contexts surrounding each text."
- "Chinese X actually has a long history."
- "I examine the interplay of publishing, reading, and circulation that imbued regional fiction with meaning in early modern X."
- "My second article, X, analyzes the strategies employed by a highly acculturated ethnic population."

As you can see, each sentence either works just as well or better without the adjective, or the loss of the adjective reveals the sentence to be absurdly simplistic to begin with ("Chinese X actually has a long history").

Thus we see "complex" revealed for what it is: a cheap and lazy substitute for actual engagement in ideas. In your abstracts and all of your writing, you must do better, and dig deeper. Find things to say about your dissertation that are meaningful and substantive, and not just placeholder adjectives that mimic substance while saying nothing at all.

PART V
....
TECHNIQUES OF THE ACADEMIC INTERVIEW

THIRTY

············

Academic Job Interview Basics

While most young scholars can, with effort, learn to discipline their job document writing to follow the rules I explain in this book, few can overcome their insecurities and anxieties for the academic job interview without a great deal of trial and error. It is my hope that this and the next few chapters can prevent some of the worst errors.

Remember that interviews are about image management.

One of the biggest challenges job candidates confront is mastering a professorial affect in your speech. Unfortunately most job candidates sound far more like undergraduates than like professors. You might think that graduate students would tend toward the excessively pompous, but generally you don't sound nearly pompous enough. The casual, approachable style that the undergraduates in your TA classroom love is harming you on the job market. You race through your words, mumble, and fill your talk with "um" and "ya know" and "right?" What most job candidates lack, that actual professors have in spades, comes down to one thing: self-importance.

It may seem counterintuitive that the same grad student who sounds so grandiose in a job document would sound querulous and wheedling in an interview, but there it is. Both are, after all, signs of the same fundamental anxiety.

Think about the professors you know. Now think about how they talk. They sound self-important. Professors don't race breathlessly through their words. Their slow, deliberate delivery is a core professorial conceit. Professors tend to savor their words like the priceless gems of brilliance they believe them to be. They relish them. They h-y-p-e-r-articulate them, the way Ross used to do on *Friends*. Like Ross, cherish your final consonants, because they are your allies. Contractions, however, banish. Practice saying this: "I. Am. quiTE convinceD that they. Are. correcT in their startinG PREmiseS, although [pause for skeptical affect] I migHT dispuTE soME of their con-clu-sioNS."

Don't forget to gesture widely, expansively. Opine. Assert. Dare I say it, explicate. And above all, remember to pause. Pause, and stroke your metaphorical beard. Nod sagely. Think deeply. Inhale. Then—and only then—respond to the question. This is the classic professorial move. Learn it.

Be particularly alert to uptalk: the upward ending lilt that transforms every declarative sentence into a question, especially if you are a woman. "My work is on Nigeria? And I conducted fieldwork in Abuja? And I looked at women active in the informal economy? Like? You know? Traders?"

You think nobody would do uptalk by the time they've finished a Ph.D.? You would be wrong, my friend. About half of my female interview clients have this habit, and a small proportion of the men. And 100 percent of those clients are unaware of how much they do it. Without checking through self-recording and mock interviews, it is hard to know. And changing it requires a change not just in speaking, but in thinking. It is necessary to examine the feelings of insecurity that motivate this habit. It takes mental effort to become comfortable with the authority that is communicated through a strong falling tone at the end of every sentence.

Similarly, attend to your body language—take up all the space to which you're entitled, and maintain a level gaze and steady eye contact. International candidates, take note that in the United States, a firm handshake and steady eye contact are cultural practices that are associated with a range of virtues such as maturity, reliability, and authority. Do not bring habits of deferential behavior appropriate for other cultural settings into your U.S. tenure track interviews. Women, attend to unconscious habits of twisting your hair, fiddling with jewelry, and smiling incessantly. Smiling at natural moments is fine; smiling constantly through every response is a gendered behavior of deference.

All candidates, record your mock interviews to identify odd body language such as staring at the ceiling, evasive eye movements, tilted head, bobbing and swaying, distracting hand gestures, and slumped, downcast shoulders. These are all daily sights at the live Skype Interview Interventions we do at The Professor Is In.

Authority is communicated, of course, in the substance of your responses as well. Insecure words such as "try," "attempt," "hope," "wish," and so on, which I introduced earlier in writing, are even more damning in speaking, where they tend to be incessantly repeated through unconscious habit.

The graduate student default to the negative is also a bugbear of the interview. Take a question like this: "Tell us about your plans to revise your dissertation into the book." Left to your own devices, you will likely respond:

> Well, the dissertation isn't really in a publishable state yet. My third chapter is still missing some major elements on the prewar period that I need to add. I will need to visit the University of Tokyo library to access some of that material. I haven't really submitted the manuscript to a press yet because I'm waiting to resolve issues like that before I do.

Here is a positive response:

> My former mentor has invited me to visit and use a collection of prewar materials at the University of Tokyo library this summer. I'll be incorporating that material into my third chapter, and in the meantime, I'll be drafting a proposal of the book to send to presses next fall.

Look forward to what you will do, not backward to what you have not done.

Anticipate ten to fifteen questions that you are likely to be asked, and write out one-to-two-minute outlines of responses to these, and practice until they are second nature. Don't memorize blocks of text per se, as you don't want to sound robotic; rather, use the outlines as conceptual landmarks that you consistently hit. I discuss some specific questions for which you should be prepared below. Remember that the interview is a dialogue and not a monologue. Always speak briefly to give the interviewer the opportunity to respond "How fascinating, tell us more," or alternatively, to move on to the next question if time is short.

In all responses remember that the goal is not to share all you know, but rather precisely what you know that meets the advertised needs of the position and/or the question specifically being asked. "Tell us about some classes you would develop for us," is not an invitation to spend twenty minutes explaining seven different classes you have in your head. It's an invitation to take five minutes to introduce two: possibly one at an intro level, and one at an advanced level, and both of them oriented precisely to the job at hand.

I once worked with a client, a Korean art historian, preparing for an interview in Asian art history at an institution located in a major West Coast city. I asked her to describe a course she would develop, and she responded with a course on the local Asian American art scene in that city. It was a fascinating course, but it was entirely wrong. The job was for an Asian art historian, not an Asian American art historian. Furthermore, there was already a well-known Asian American art historian on the faculty. A quick Google search revealed that he already offered a course on the local Asian American art scene. Had my client gone in with this course, she not only would have squandered her chance to share the expertise they were actually seeking (on Korean art) but she also might have alienated this colleague.

In another case, a Renaissance literature specialist applying for a Renaissance literature job offered as her first proposed course a class that included readings by Don DeLillo. It was a fascinating course, and she may well, after being hired, have gotten to teach such a course. But at the twenty-minute conference interview stage for which she was preparing, it was, again, entirely wrong. Because any course to be described in that short initial meeting needed to foreground the actual Renaissance.

The most important thing you can do to prepare for an interview is to review the candidate platform that you established for the market, which I discussed in chapter 8. Know your core stances and distinctive messages on all major elements of research and teaching, as oriented toward the particular campus, department, and job you're applying for. In order to achieve that orientation, of course, you must know the campus, department, and job inside and out. Make and study a departmental cheat sheet that lists the faculty and their areas of study and recent publications. Be familiar with the recent history of the department—the areas it is known for, and the new initiatives it is developing. Meditate on the ad and prepare customized responses that refer to the specializations mentioned in it.

For all interviews, sketch outlines of responses to basic questions, and practice them in front of a mirror and in front of friends, and at mock interviews in your department, over and over and over again, until they become second nature to you. Practice them while wearing your interview suit, since unfamiliar clothes can distract.

How do you anticipate interview questions? You can find lists online, but many of them are long and overwhelming. The hapless candidate looks at a list of thirty-five questions and feels, "I can't possibly prepare all that!" But, in fact, interview questions fall into distinct categories. If you can master the categories, you can prepare responses to a handful of basic types of questions that will carry you through some 90 percent of all interviewing situations.

As an exercise, let's look at this list of questions below:

- "How is your dissertation different from other work in your field?"
- "How does your dissertation intervene in the field of X?"
- "Who are the biggest scholarly influences on your work?"
- "What are your publication plans arising from the dissertation?"
- "Have you spoken with a publisher about your book? Where do you stand in negotiations?"
- "What is your research program for the next five years?"
- "What are your immediate and longer term publication plans?"

- "How would you teach a large intro class in your/our discipline? How would you teach our introductory course? Which text would you use? What kinds of assignments would you use?"
- "How would you teach our core theory seminar? Who would you have them read?"
- "How would you teach our methods course?"
- "Name two specialty courses you would teach, one undergraduate and one graduate."
- "What inspires your teaching?"
- "How do you see your work fitting into our department?"
- "What do you think the most important intellectual debate is in your/our field?"
- "Can you envision any collaborations with faculty currently in the department?"
- "How would you incorporate undergraduates into your research?"
- "We are hoping to build a strength in X. How would you participate in that effort?"
- "We don't have a lot of funding for the kind of equipment/travel that you require for your research. How would you work with this?"
- "Our campus is very student focused. You come from an R1. How do you see yourself fitting in?"
- "Our campus has high expectations for publication for tenure. How do you see yourself handling the expectations?"
- "Do you have plans to apply for any major grants? If so, which ones?"

These are all legitimate possible questions. But there are so many of them! How can you prepare? Looking more closely at them, you can see that the questions fall into seven basic categories:

- Your dissertation
- Your short and longer term publishing plans
- Your place in the field

- Courses you can teach—both general and specialized
- Your teaching philosophy
- Your interest in program building
- Your understanding of the financial and organizational context of the department

With the exception of the last one, these map neatly onto your candidate platform, and that platform will provide you with the foundation for your responses. The final category is what you master through your study of and tailoring for the particular campus, department, and job.

Occasionally you will confront a challenge, or even a hostile question: "What you've said is all very interesting, but isn't this really an outdated question in light of . . . ?" For any such situation, you want to master the art of what I call academic jujitsu. Take the force of the questioner, and instead of confronting it head on, courteously sidestep it and allow it to flow past you.

Here is an example:

Q: What you've said is all very interesting, but isn't this really an outdated question in light of . . . ?
A: Thank you for raising that question. Indeed at first glance it might seem that with the advent of X, the question of Y is less urgent, and that has even been argued by scholars such as P and Q. However, I would suggest that while X has raised important new questions, the issues of Y remain unresolved because they require a different kind of attention to [and so on back into the current of your project].

Here is another example:

Q: Doesn't your conclusion contradict what Nelson has proven with regard to X?
A: I'm glad you brought that up. Nelson does address a similar theme in his research. However, Nelson's question is really a different one from mine. While he focuses on X, I actually

begin from the perspective of Y. A perspective on Y helps us to keep the focus on Q, which is critical in light of recent changes [and so on back into the current of your project].

Et voilà, in each case, you are talking about your research, and not somebody else's—either the questioner's or some other scholar's. Interviewers don't need to hear about anyone else's research but yours. It is not their interview. It is your interview; keep the focus on your accomplishments.

And always finish strong. Don't end, feebly, with, "Um, did that answer your question?" Maintain firm, healthy boundaries: "Next question?"

Remember, they have short-listed you because of your expertise. Never grovel, apologize, or hedge. Speak out, audibly, with confidence and firmness and squared shoulders. Banish your graduate student behaviors, and comport yourself like a young, up-and-coming professional with things to say and points to make, hotly pursued by a whole posse of search committees, and securely confident in the impact you will make on your field.

THIRTY-ONE

·····················

The Key Questions in
an Academic Interview

Here I offer to you a quick and dirty list of what I often call the "facepalm fails" of the academic interview. These are the questions that are so obvious that you often forget to prepare for them. And then, encountering them, you fall flat on your face, in a particularly humiliating way (because they're so obvious), and get shunted out the door. The awful thing about the facepalm fails is that they are generally among the first questions that are asked in an interview. I incorporate all of these into the Skype Interview Interventions my team does with clients, and they trip clients up every single time.

"Tell us about your dissertation."

Too many job seekers do not know how to simply and clearly and concisely describe their dissertations in a way that makes us understand what it is about, how you did it, why we should care about it, and how it intervenes and advances your field, in three minutes or less. Five sentences should suffice:

1. "My dissertation, [title], examines [the topic]."
2. "Specifically, it analyzes [the specific phenomena studied]."

3. "I use X methods and Y theory to establish [the method and theory foundation]."
4. "I discovered/found that [observations and findings]."
5. "I conclude that [core argument]."
6. Bonus sentence on contribution: "While many scholars have argued that X should be understood as Y, my research reveals that X can be better understood as Z, showing the importance of P to the study of Q [statement of contribution to a field]."

"Tell us about your publishing plans for the next five years."

This is primarily a quantitative, not qualitative question. It is actually about your suitability for tenure. Yes, that's right. At the interview stage for your tenure track job offer, they are already evaluating your tenurability. Your questioner is seeking to discover whether you understand the nature of a publication arc for purposes of tenure. Your questioner does not want a ten-minute description of the journal article manuscript that you're still writing. She wants a quick and well-organized trajectory of publications from the past through the present and into the future, through your tenure case six years hence (and don't forget: your tenure file is gathered and sent to reviewers in year five).

"As you can see from my CV, I already have an article out based on the dissertation, in the *Journal of X*. I am currently finishing a revise and resubmit of another chapter from the dissertation for the *Journal of Y*. After that is complete I will turn my attention to a book proposal, and plan to have that completed and submitted to presses by the end of the fall semester. I am considering the University of X Press and the University of Y Press. I expect to have the book manuscript finished by spring 20XX. After that I'll be turning my attention to a major second project, which I can describe in more detail if you are interested."

"How would you teach our intro class?"

When you get a tenure track job, you aren't suddenly elevated into a magical sphere in which you spend all day stroking your beard and thinking profound thoughts about arcane subjects. You become a harassed and overworked junior faculty member. One of the duties that may well fall to you is to teach the intro class with hundreds of students. Get a plan for that, and whatever you do, do not start waxing nostalgic about your own halcyon days as an undergraduate in such a class.

Here is the basic rule of describing a course:

1. Title and optional short sketch of topic
2. Main takeaway point
3. Textbook(s) (if low undergrad) or readings (if high undergrad/grad) with brief explanation
4. Broad organization/roadmap of the course, with about three "landmarks"
5. Examples of innovative assignments
6. Conclusion

Let me describe each point in more detail.

Title: The title should be engaging and appeal to students. After the title, if it is a new course, and not one already on the books, one or two sentences will sketch the topic of the course in the context of the discipline. If the course is one on the books, then no explanation of it is necessary.

Example: "I would like to teach a course called Japan Imagined. It will explore representations of Japan in Western accounts from the seventeenth century to the present, focusing on shifts that accompany Japan's changing political and economic status vis-à-vis the West."

Takeaway point: One sentence will describe the point that you want students to take away from the course.

Example: "The point I want students to take away is that our image of 'Japan,' which students imagine as timeless, has actually shifted continually to reflect Western economic and political anxieties."

Textbook/readings: This is the part that almost everyone forgets. Briefly sketch the major readings in one or two sentences.

Example: "We'll read John Dower's *War Without Mercy* and Anne Allison's *Millennial Monsters,* among other texts, to get a sense of the scholarship on the politics of representation in a context in which Japan actively produces its own global self-representations. I'll also have students read primary documents such as Portuguese explorer accounts, Commodore Perry's journal, and WWII propaganda."

Broad organization/road map of the course with "landmarks": Quickly, in one or two sentences, sketch the organization of the course, from beginning to middle to end. This is not an exhaustive week-by-week, topic-by-topic description of the entire course, which will bore your listeners to tears.

Example: "We will start with Portuguese explorers and move through Commodore Perry and the American 'opening' of Japan, WWII and the occupation, and Japan's rise in the 1980s, ending with the ongoing recession and the transnational circulation of Japanese anime, manga, and video games."

Assignment: One sentence on a memorable assignment.

Example: "I have the students play video games such as Tekken and Pokémon, do an in-class demonstration of the Japanese cultural and linguistic elements in each game, and report on the ways these elements are discussed on the American Internet discussion boards devoted to the games."

Conclusion: One sentence that links the course to the wider course catalog, curriculum, or departmental agenda. This proves that you think like a colleague who understands that anything you teach must work within a larger curricular logic and scaffolding.

Example: "In this way students gain a foundation in contemporary Japanese history and Japan's image vis-à-vis the West that they can carry forward with them into more advanced courses in the major and their senior project."

In sum, in just a few scripted sentences you will summarize the course in a dynamic, memorable way, anticipating major questions and leaving no gaps:

"I would like to teach a course called Japan Imagined. It will explore representations of Japan in Western accounts from the seventeenth century to the present, focusing on the shifts that accompany Japan's changing political and economic status vis-à-vis the West. The point I want students to take away is that our image of 'Japan,' which students imagine as constant, has actually shifted continually to reflect economic and political anxieties. We'll read John Dower's *War Without Mercy* and Anne Allison's *Millennial Monsters,* among other texts, to get a sense of the scholarship on the politics of representation in a context in which Japan actively produces its own global self-representations, and I'll also have students read primary documents such as Portuguese explorer accounts, Commodore Perry's journal, and WWII propaganda. The course will start with Portuguese explorers and move through Commodore Perry and the American 'opening' of Japan, WWII and the occupation, and Japan's rise in the 1980s, and end with the ongoing recession and the transnational circulation of Japanese anime, manga, and video games. In the class, I have the students play video games such as Tekken and Pokémon, do an in-class demonstration of the Japanese cultural and linguistic elements in each game, and report on the ways these elements are discussed on the American Internet discussion boards devoted to the games. In this way students gain a foundation in contemporary Japanese history and Japan's image vis-à-vis the West that they can carry forward with them into more advanced courses in the major, and their senior projects."

"How would you teach our methods course and/or core theory seminar?"

You will have to serve the needs of all (or many) of the students in the program. Many of them will not be working on your area of specialization, but you will still have to show that you can add value for them through the work of several core seminars. One of these is the methods seminar. Have a plan.

The theory seminar is rough, so be prepared. If they're mean, they'll quiz you. The relevant theory will, of course, depend on your field. Taking the example of cultural anthropology as a case study, this could mean speaking knowledgeably about Marx, Weber, and Durkheim and then moving up through people such as Freud, Adorno, Levi-Strauss, and Foucault, while also giving honor to anthropologist standbys such as Malinowski, Evans-Pritchard, Radcliffe-Brown, Boas, Harris, and the other members of the canon. Sure, you can complicate things by bringing in critiques based on race and gender and sexuality, and so forth, but never think that you can entirely substitute the critical or marginalized voices you might personally prefer for traditional foundations.

"Name two courses you would develop for our department."

Have one undergrad and one graduate course always in your pocket. If the job is a SLAC, then have two undergrad, one lower level and one upper level. It goes without saying that these should be tailored according to the campus, department, and job at hand. Remember the Korean art historian and the Renaissance specialist from chapter 30. Use the template introduced previously to organize your responses.

"How would you mentor graduate students?"

This one's tough when you're just starting out. Don't default to the self-juvenilizing "As a graduate student I have been so fortunate to have had marvelous mentoring . . . " It doesn't matter that you're not even out of grad school yourself; you must be able to articulate a grad student mentorship philosophy from the standpoint of a faculty member, if you are being interviewed at an R1 institution.

Here is an example of one way to approach this question:

Graduate students at different levels will have different needs. First-year graduate students will be struggling to simply adapt to the demands of graduate school, and for those students, I would focus on helping them navigate the expectations of the program, its requirements, and basic academic reading and writing skills.

Mid-program students who are involved in establishing their dissertation projects will need assistance in formulating an original research project, and then gaining a command of the theoretical schools of thought and the various methodologies necessary to conduct it. Teaching skills in grant writing is also important at this stage.

With more advanced students I focus on academic writing skills, and work with them to plan ahead for conferences and presenting work in public.

As graduate students finish the program I would focus on the job market and other professionalization skills such as fellowships, postdocs, and networking. Overall I want to support students in both their scholarly growth as well as their professional development.

"Tell us about your second project."

Tenure track searches are expensive, draining, and time-consuming. When a search is done and a hire is made, outside of a tiny group of Ivy League schools that may not tenure their assistant professors, the understanding is that the person hired is suitable for tenure. Anyone who does not appear tenurable will not be offered the tenure track job to begin with. Nobody wants to go through the Sturm und Drang of a tenure track search for nothing.

The research profile, in order to be successful, has to show, as I explained above, what we usually call an "arc" of scholarly productivity, and sometimes call a scholarly trajectory, through tenure. This arc or trajectory articulates strong forward momentum from the dissertation through the refereed publications deriving from the dissertation, through a "major next project" that emerges organically and coherently from a set of consistent scholarly or thematic preoccupations, with funding, conference papers, and publications based on this second project anticipated or achieved. The arc demonstrates, more than anything else, that the candidate will not become deadwood after tenure, but will continue to produce high-profile scholarly work during the sabbatical year post tenure, and into the foreseeable future.

We have all heard about how at certain elite institutions two books are now required for tenure. That is still the exception (although be prepared for that if you are applying/interviewing at one of those schools). At my two R1 institutions, two books were not required, but a second book-length project clearly articulated and anticipated through funding, conference papers, and some preliminary publications absolutely was. You could not get tenure without the second project. The second project demonstrates that you are not a one-hit wonder or a flash in the pan, but the real deal, a scholar of the first rank, with a sustained program of research that continues out into the future.

This second/next project might, in reality, be something totally random that you conjure out of smoke and mirrors for the sake of the job market, and then only retrospectively narrate as part of a consistent and sustained scholarly project. That's fine. Conjure away. Whatever the project is, it demonstrates that you think like a tenure track—that is, tenurable—faculty member, and not like someone who is marking out their career semester by semester, or year by year.

"You come from an X kind of school. How would you adapt to a campus like ours?"

When, as is so often the case, you are coming from an elite Ph.D.-granting program and applying to a lower-ranking school that doubts your commitment, the best approach is to tell the simple truth. If you genuinely believe that you will be happy in a nonelite, regional, or teaching-heavy environment, then you should just say so.

The language might sound something like this:

"I have a commitment to the type of teaching that is done at Rural College, a commitment that has grown stronger the further that I have moved in my career. I look forward to hands-on work with students, and appreciate the campus's commitment to X. In addition, my family resides in the area/my research will thrive in the area/I have a personal connection to the area."

Note that no frantic claims were made of an "ideal fit," or the like. Rather, legitimate sentiments were expressed in a calm and factual manner. This is the best you can do to reassure a skittish search committee. I cannot promise that they will believe you. But you are certainly entitled to tell them the truth.

When you visit an urban school, have some thoughts prepared on working with urban/returning students. When you visit a rural comprehensive, speak to the appeal of the size and scope of the campus. When you visit a SLAC, be prepared to have a spiel on the liberal arts education and incorporating undergraduates in your research. When you visit a lower-ranking school, speak to the gratification of working with less-privileged students. Remember that most campuses feel insecure about something. They are always testing to make sure you really like what they are.

Note that in the example language above the presence of family in the area was mentioned last, not first. Be aware that this personal connection bears mentioning only if an institution is small, low-ranking, or located in a far-flung region . . . that is, an institution that you can imagine might have trouble attracting or retaining hires. However, if the institution is one of the top-ranked institutions in the world, hotly coveted, and the object of academic dreams, then mentioning the existence of family and friends in the area comes across as laughable. Nobody prioritizes Harvard because family lives nearby. If your family does live near Cambridge, sure, that's icing on the cake and a great thing. But don't mention it in the application because it makes you look, simply, clueless.

"Do you have any questions for us?"

Bad responses include:

- "No."
- "Uh, I guess not. I can't really think of any offhand."
- "I'd like to ask about your spousal hiring program."

- "What is your department's relationship with the dean?"
- "How is your department viewed on campus?"

These latter two are actually excellent things to try and intuit at the campus visit stage, indirectly and subtly. But they are not questions to be asked in an initial interview, because they make you look oddly judgmental and put your respondent on the spot.

The vast majority of the questions clients tell me they are planning to ask are inappropriate, and sometimes even potentially harmful to their candidacy. Why? Because they don't realize that the questions they ask are only putatively about gathering information; they are actually further communicating your suitability for the job.

Let me explain further. My partner Kellee Weinhold currently handles the bulk of the Skype Interview Interventions at The Professor Is In. Kellee and I were chatting the other day about her Interventions this past fall. She said to me, "What clients always need to understand is that the question is not the question! They always think the question is asking X, but it's actually asking Y; they just don't know it!"

We talked more. We came up with some examples of common questions, in which clients routinely misapprehend what is really being asked.

1. Tell us about your research.

You think they care about your research. You say way too much about tediously narrow interests.

No. As I've explained throughout this book, the search committee wants to learn about how your expertise fits into their departmental needs as expressed by the job ad, and connects with the work of the people doing the interview (which is why your methodology and contribution are actually the most important portion of your answer). Also that it is quickly getting funded and published in ways that bode well for tenure. At the same time, they are checking for how you express yourself, if you're engaging to talk to, and how self-absorbed you sound.

2. Tell us about your plans for the next five years.

You think they want to hear about your interests and motivations in the life of the mind in huge, grandiose, boring abstractions. This is the equivalent of someone asking you how to get from LA to New York City by car, and you start the answer: "The corn of Nebraska is beautiful in late summer!"

No. It's not about the corn. Instead, you'll need to explain how, leaving on X date, on Y road, you'll make it to Z city by sundown. Then, starting the next day, you'll reach Q by sundown. You will give the step-by-step route complete with mileage goals and destinations along the way. They don't need to know your feelings about the scenery.

Same for tenure. Tenure is a destination that must be reached in careful and well-planned stages. The search committee needs to know: 1) that you understand what tenure at their institution means and 2) that you have a plan, complete with dates and locations, to get there. All framed within their concerns, R1s and elite SLACs prioritizing research goals, along with teaching and a tiny bit of service, and middle-ranked SLACs and others prioritizing teaching goals, always informed by research and a greater degree of service.

3. Tell us how you would teach our big survey course.

You think they want to hear how you're going to make those undergrads finally grasp the point of transnationalism, once and for all. Or modernity. They must know modernity. Or intersectionality, goddammit! They MUST. BE. TAUGHT. INTERSECTIONALITY.

No. They do not want to hear that you are going to dogmatically hijack their big intro course and make it into an altar to your personal theoretical preoccupation. They want to know that 1) you get that you will be teaching big survey courses, 2) you get what the discipline expects students to learn in those courses and have a plan to assure students learn it.

Even though they are hiring an expert in the class dynamics of gender in Latin America, it does not mean you will hijack their Introduction to Anthropology class and teach it entirely through a Latin American Marxist gender theory lens. In other words, they want to know that you will not take their courses off the rails and leave them with ill-prepared students in their 200 level courses.

4. Tell us how you see yourself contributing to this department.

You think they want to know the courses you will propose, and how much you love students (and admire the faculty).

No. They need to see you making specific, substantive connections between your work and the work being done by current faculty in the department, at thematic and/or topical levels.

They also want to know how you will raise the profile of the department and/or its students (depending on the institution) both on and off campus. Working groups. Interdisciplinary collaborations. Professional affiliations. Programs. Initiatives. Field schools. And yes, courses. But really the courses you propose only go so far.

5. Tell us why you want to work here.

You think they want to know how great their department will be for you and all the great things you will do with all of their great resources.

No. That is self-absorbed. This is not the time for more "me, me, me" and how the job is going to serve you. They want to know that you understand the university, the department, the faculty, and have concrete ideas about how you can connect, build, and engage with its stated programs and priorities.

And finally:

6. Do you have any questions for us?

You think the purpose of these questions is to gather information.

No. These questions are more ways to elicit information about you. Your questions reveal what you prioritize; they always expose your values. You must manage them for what they disclose. You must show them that you are thinking about what they think you should be thinking about. Always with an eye to your tenure case.

If all your questions are about teaching, and it's an R1, you look like you don't belong.

Kellee told a story of her brother (who works for the U.S. Forest Service) and a recent search he chaired. He and his colleagues asked, "Do you have any questions for us?" He told Kellee that the candidates fell into two groups: those who asked something like, "How often am I paid and what are my benefits?" and those who asked something like, "I was looking at X project that you did last year, and it really intersects with my work; I am interested to know if you have plans to further develop X? I would like to be involved." Kellee's brother: "Who do you think made the short list?"

So, looked at in this light, it's important to think carefully about the questions you ask the search committee. Your questions should show an understanding of the departmental and campus profile and mission. Beware questions with a simple yes or no answer, that hinge on resources, or that imply judgment. Thus, "Is there a lot of collaboration in the department?" is bad, because it's a yes or no question, and if the truthful answer is no, your interviewers will feel embarrassed. "You seem to be lacking classes in X; are you looking to increase that coverage area?" is bad, because it is all judgment.

"I'd like to know more about sources for research support on campus" is a good way to phrase a question because it is open-ended. The department members can take their response in a range of different directions. A yes-or-no question, by contrast, shuts down conversation rather than opening it up. The pitfalls are, of course, situational, based on the status and rank of the institution. "Do you provide automatic junior sabbatical for assistant professors?" is quite fine when asked at an R1. When asked on the campus of a major research university or similarly elite college, that question demonstrates that the candidate understands the exigencies of earning tenure there, and is already prioritizing the research support that will ensure his or her success down the road. On such a campus, a lengthy series of questions about teaching, for example, or (god forbid) service, will tell exactly the opposite story: that you don't understand the requirements of an R1 tenure case, and may well be unprepared.

Finally, this question about automatic junior sabbaticals allows the responders to brag a little bit. They might say: "Well, all new faculty on campus get X automatically. In addition, the department provides Y, and then beyond that, you are eligible to apply for Z. All of our assistant professors have been successful so far."

But when asked at a regional teaching college, the question, "Do you provide automatic junior sabbatical for assistant professors?" might only elicit an "Uh, no," and bad feelings. Tenure at such a campus will be based substantially or entirely on teaching, and the institutional budget may provide for no research support at all. So asking about research support will communicate that you don't understand the exigencies of your eventual tenure case there, and also that you don't really get the campus and its culture. You are also causing the responder to potentially lose face. Far from being able to brag, the search-committee member is forced to state, baldly, "There is no substantial research support on this campus; any support must be found by you independently through grant-writing." The responder is not going to enjoy that experience, and it is not going to work in your favor as a candidate.

At a campus like this, you would do better if you asked: "I'd like to know more about sources for teaching support on campus." The search-committee members may be able to be eloquent on that question. And they will enjoy the warm and fuzzy feeling that you get their college and what they do.

Once again, the questions you ask are not really strictly about the information you gather. Rather, they are—in their substance as well as their form—another way that you demonstrate your preparedness for the job and your collegiality.

The following are just a few possible sample questions. Remember that many people are reading this book, so make efforts not to simply copy these, but adapt them to your circumstances.

Questions for Interviews at Research Universities

- "I'd like to know more about sources of travel support on campus."
- "Could you tell me about teaching-release possibilities on campus?"

- "I heard that there is a junior sabbatical for tenure-track faculty. Could you tell me more about that?"
- "What is the breakdown of undergraduate and graduate teaching?"
- "I'm interested to know how the graduate students are supported. Could you tell me more about that?"
- "What level of graduate-assistant support is available to support research?"

Questions for Interviews at Teaching-Oriented Colleges

- "I'd like to know more about the students; what do they tend to do after graduation?"
- "I'd like to know about some of the ways that students are involved in faculty research (and here are some of my ideas about that)."
- "I'm curious about opportunities to lead field school or study-abroad programs."
- "I'd like to know more about the [fill in the blank] Club. What are some of its activities and how are faculty involved?"
- "I'd like to hear about opportunities for collaborative (and/or interdisciplinary) teaching on campus."
- "I'd like to know more about the advising and mentoring programs in the college. How do faculty work with students outside the classroom?"

These are only general suggestions. All questions should be developed in response to the specifics of the campus, department, and job. However, these can guide your investigations. As you can see, they are open-ended, show a degree of entrepreneurial energy, and clearly communicate (at the subtextual, or metatextual, level) the orientation of the candidate toward distinct institutional values. If you follow these general models, you can concoct your own list of appropriate questions for all of your interviews and campus visits.

THIRTY-TWO

....

The Conference Interview
(Including Phone and Skype)

You have submitted your cover letter, your CV, and your recommendations. And lo! You've been long short-listed, and invited for a conference interview! Congratulations. Now what?

The elite departments from well-funded schools will conduct the interviews in conference hotel suites reserved for the purpose, or at one of the search committee members' own hotel rooms. Less endowed departments will be forced to use the dreaded conference careers center, with its rows of tiny cubicles and awkward lack of privacy. Many departments now offer a phone or Skype alternative.

The conference interview is most of all about speed and first impressions. This interview may be only thirty minutes in length. The interviewers are on a tight schedule, with a large number of candidates being hustled in and out of a small, cramped interview space. It is awkward and exhausting for everyone.

If it is a 30-minute interview, and 2.5 minutes are taken up in taking your seat and greetings and 2.5 minutes in closing and walking to the door, that leaves 25 minutes for talking. If the search committee members have five questions to ask, and take 1 minute to ask each question, that leaves you a sum total of 4 minutes of speaking time per answer. Brevity is key. Do. Not. Ramble. Prepare well for all of the questions I introduced in the previous chapters.

Once I went to a conference interview for an Ivy League anthropology department. I entered the expensive suite in the conference hotel, to be greeted by a phalanx of Famous Anthropologists, with one of them, the Most Famous of all, stretched full length on the sofa, hand dramatically resting over his eyes.

The interview commenced, with Most Famous Anthropologist sighing his questions from his supine position. We had barely begun when my eyes fell on a dirty, half-empty glass of water on the table in front of me. I innocently inquired, "Is this the water for *all* the candidates?" and got to enjoy the spectacle of the Least Famous Anthropologist scrambling to replace it. Even the Most Famous Anthropologist half-rose from his couch in consternation. I was given a clean glass of water. I was not invited to a campus visit. I tell this story to make the point: Conference interviews are bizarre. Your task is to project an aura of calm and good humor no matter the circumstances (and steer clear of deliberately provoking the committee, until you're sure you don't want the job).

Prepare for the interview by learning who is on the search committee. You can ask. Once you know the likely interviewers, spring into action. Research their work, and the profile of the department as a whole. Familiarize yourself with their course catalog, and review their website to see their recent accomplishments. Check on the classes that new assistant professors are most likely to be asked to teach, and prepare ideas on how to teach them.

Because you have read the work of your interviewers, you may be able to mention it in the interview. They will love you if you can respond, "I would certainly consider assigning *your* recent article in an upper level class on political economy, because I think it provides an excellent case study from Eastern Europe." You have to be sincere, of course; insincere flattery just alienates. But if you can be, that is pure interview gold.

Use your detective skills to inquire into the financial footing of the department, and whether the department is in the midst of raising enrollments for student tuition income or seeking greater grant revenue. This is, of course, quite difficult to intuit for an outsider like yourself. But use the Internet to investigate the institution's financial news, and seek information about any recent budget cuts both in official news sources as well as in the blogosphere. If a campus, or college within a campus, is in intensive downsizing mode, chances are you'll find clues to that somewhere on the Internet. If it is, be prepared to talk about how you will teach large classes, develop new popular ones that draw large enrollments, and seek external funding.

What if you haven't been invited to a conference interview per se, but just an "informal chat"? The chat is never ideal. It's my personal opinion that search committees should interview or not interview. They should not drift around chatting in an exclusive and inconsistent way that ends up privileging some candidates over others. And it's not necessarily the candidate who chats who is privileged.

Nevertheless, chats happen. What to do? You can't easily refuse the invitation. If you are definitely going to the conference, and the inviting search committee member knows it, then you can't refuse to meet them without looking ungracious. Make no mistake: This is an interview. You need to be prepared with your elevator speech, some classes to describe, your immediate publishing plans, your next research project and how it will be funded; and some familiarity with the department/program/faculty/job at hand.

It is true that this is very much a conversation, so you must not pontificate. Be sure to keep the conversational ball bouncing back and forth at a good clip. Indeed, there might be small talk before and after, so think ahead about topics to discuss, such as the terrific panel you just heard.

Remember the injunction against clinging. I would hazard to say that this is where the greatest risks lie for candidates dealing with the chat. In an interview setting you are ushered in and ushered out. But chats have no clear beginning or end, and you could find yourself succumbing to the desperate and undignified temptation to trail along with the faculty member to their next panel. Resist. Cut the cord. Leave!

In fact, leave expeditiously, with a line like, "Oh, pardon me, this has been delightful, but I have to go—I'm meeting my editor at Duke in a few minutes."

Finally, a word on phone and Skype interviews. It is of paramount importance in a phone and Skype interview, which are rarely more than twenty to thirty minutes long, and which do not have the benefit of real human interaction and nonverbal cue exchange, that you always limit your responses to no more than one or two minutes at a time.

The pause is your friend! Do not fear silence. Remember how hard it is to absorb complicated academic topics on the end of a phone, and give your interviewers the chance to absorb what you've said and formulate a response. End your sound byte on a strong note that signals unmistakably *I have now finished speaking.* Then count, silently, to five (one Mississippi, two Mississippi) and either allow the next question to come, or resume with something like, "In terms of *future* research, I will be moving on to a major second project on X . . ."

Here are some pointers for the phone interview:

- Dress for the interview, as odd as that probably seems. Wearing your interview suit with shoes and the whole nine yards puts you into the proper frame of mind for the experience.
- Set up your interview space at a spacious desk or table, with plenty of privacy, and on that desk set up your laptop or index cards with some short mental cues that you can quickly refer to when responding. These would include: "Dissertation themes: X, Y, and Z"; or "Intro course textbook: A with B supplement," or "Methods seminar: bridge quant and qual." Don't write out long responses; you must be prepared to speak naturally, so stick to minimal cues.
- Make a one-page cheat sheet of the department and set it next to you, with the names of the faculty (search committee at the top), their research foci, and the title of a recent publication.
- Have a tablet and pen next to you to take shorthand notes as questions are asked. You may be given a compound question, such as "Tell us about your dissertation, how you got interested in the topic, and what you see as its primary contribution." Make a note of each part of the question to be able to address each in your response.

For Skype interviews, most of these same techniques apply. Obviously you will dress for the interview, and do not neglect the parts of you out of sight of the camera. Attend to your setting. Find an appropriate location in your home or office, and have someone check your backdrop on screen. You may need their fresh eyes to point out the dead plant or the crumpled Little Debbie wrapper on the shelf behind you.

Check the size of your head on the screen, and adjust. Don't sit so far from the camera that you appear like a tiny pinhead, but don't sit so close that they are looking up your nose.

You may set up a few cue cards and the department cheat sheet around your Skype space, but beware the temptation to look off-camera while speaking. It is fine to have a pen and paper in front of you to jot a note or two if compound questions are asked. When speaking, it is OK to make "eye contact" with the person whose face is on your screen, even though technically to look like you're making eye contact, you'd need to stare into the tiny camera on your computer. It's my contention that staring into that camera is so unnatural and difficult that the effort to achieve eye contact in that way will backfire in the awkwardness of your responses. So give yourself permission to indulge in the far more natural tendency to look into the eyes of the face on the screen.

The larger question about the Skype interview is, of course: If you are offered the Skype option in place of the in-person interview at your national conference, should you take it? It's impossible to say with certainty whether Skype interviewees are disadvantaged compared to those who interview face-to-face. However, no candidate should impoverish herself on the mere hope of being short-listed for a job, and if you do not otherwise have plans to attend the conference, are not presenting at the conference (obviously, as I note in chapter 19, if you are on the market, you should be presenting at the conference), and cannot easily afford the trip without adding to your credit card debt, then I recommend taking the Skype option whenever it is offered.

THIRTY-THREE

The Campus Visit

Campus visits are the most stressful part of the job search, but with practice, they get better. It helps if you know what to expect, and understand what each element of the visit is meant to accomplish. One thing I will say about campus visits: They're weird and unpredictable, and you have no idea what the unspoken agendas are as you feel them swirling closely around your head.

The Deciding of the Date: You do not have to instantly accept the first date or dates they offer. They have a schedule, but you have a life. If you have a legitimate reason for needing other dates, you may say so. In all things be courteous and flexible but not obsequious. This correspondence establishes the tenor of your relationship with the department. If you have other campus visits, be sure to drop that into the conversation: "Oh, I'm sorry, that date is out; I'll actually be visiting another campus that day." But don't reveal the name of the other campus; the mystery adds to your allure.

Do not attempt to piggyback visits to any other places on the campus visit. It is tempting, if you live on one coast, and you're invited to the other coast, near your family, or some archive, to inquire about tacking on a visit. Do not do it, even at your own expense. It may, entirely unintentionally, give the appearance of being selfish or instrumentalizing. I learned this the hard way from personal experience. There are two exceptions to this rule, however. The first is if a major conference coincides with the dates and region of your visit, you can inquire about scheduling around that. And if you have several campus visits in quick succession, you can inquire about flying directly from one to another.

The Email Correspondence with the Department Head: If the head contacts you to extend a welcome, or ask if you have any special needs, behave with dignity, professional reserve, and self-respect. If you have any food allergies, special needs, or so forth, mention them right away. I was once invited by the department head to a home breakfast (weird in itself) where my host served, with a flourish, a gourmet nut-filled granola. I had to decline, having an anaphylactic allergy to tree nuts. He was offended. I was mortified. He had nothing else to serve. I left hungry.

Don't let this happen to you.

The Thirty-Minute Visits with Department Faculty: Ideally you will have received a schedule ahead of time. It will likely contain back-to-back meetings with some ten to fifteen faculty members. When you get your schedule, make a cheat sheet on the people you'll be meeting, and do your best to commit it to memory, while you also carry it in your briefcase during the visit. As I explained earlier, the cheat sheet will have their area and specialization, and a recent publication, award, or achievement.

The point here: These are not a series of oral exams! Be pleasant. Conversational. Be ready for them to ask you a hard question or two about your work. Don't be afraid to repeat what you've said to others; remember your platform and stay on message. At the same time, you can embellish based on their individual interests. One of them might be preoccupied with a recent curriculum revision. Talk, then, about how you see a course of yours fitting in with that. Another one perhaps shares your area of geographical interest. Chat about your latest trip in-country. They are people, too; express interest in what they are working on, and find a way to relate your interests to that.

They already know you're smart from your work. Now they need to know you're fun and engaging to be around.

The Visit to the Library/Center for the Humanities/International Studies Center: These visits are about the department trying to please and impress you with the various resources available. These are great opportunities to ask how the department is involved in the center's activities, which gives you insight into how the department is viewed on campus. The people you meet in these contexts most likely have little impact on the search outcome.

The Job Talk: The job talk is the subject of the whole next chapter. For now, simply note that this is the highlight of the visit. The most important single aspect of the job talk is that whatever time frame they have given you, abide by it. Exceeding your allotted time is fiercely resented. Many people will have to leave for class or to pick up their kids from child care, and so forth. To ensure that every audience member gets to hear some part of the Q and A—a crucial element of your performance—you must stay on schedule.

Pitch your job talk high; don't dumb things down. But at the same time, make it engaging to a nonspecialized audience. Remember to describe your topic before you launch into analyzing it. We are not inside your brain, we have not spent a decade on the topic, and we are hearing about this thing for the first time. You must spend about one-fifth of the talk introducing the who, what, when, where, and how, and getting us intrigued. Then move into your analysis. Make sure to balance your data, texts, or materials and your theory-talk; don't overweight toward excess theory-talk, a temptation in some literature fields. Adjust this balance to the predilections of the department. Use plenty of visuals. And conclude strong.

The Q and A after the Job Talk: This is the downfall of many, many job candidates. Practice by scheduling a mock job talk and Q and A in your department (or with The Professor Is In!), before you ever go to a campus visit. You are not born knowing how to manage academic questions, especially when they are random, odd, or hostile. Schedule all the practice you can.

Be aware of department culture: Do they wish to have your introducer mediate questions, or have you do it yourself? Follow the custom.

Never forget that senior people should be called on first. Call on the most senior/emeriti first, because nothing is going to stop them from talking . . . so get it out of the way right away.

Do not call on a grad student first. Of course, you won't know with total certainty who is a grad student, but usually you can tell. There are two reasons: First, grad student questions can sometimes be off point, didactic, or self-aggrandizing. These questions waste valuable time for both you and the search committee. Second, the culture of some departments dictates that grad students are supposed to keep their mouths shut and listen. Faculty in a department often have a well-established Q and A choreography, with senior faculty launching immediately into a sharp challenge, with other middling faculty following up with softballs and soothing. Mistakenly calling on grad students prematurely runs the risk of irritating the faculty, who have pressing questions that they feel entitled to ask first. Of course, because you are never sure who is a graduate student and who is not, politely respond to all questioners possible over the course of the Q and A period.

Respond positively to all questions, for example: "That's an excellent question" or "You raise an important point; I'm glad you brought that up." Then, regardless of what the question actually is, turn the answer to something in which you have strength. That does not mean to simply repeat, over and over, your thesis. Be lively and dynamic and engaged with different ideas and challenges. But, when necessary, use the methods of academic jujitsu that I introduced in chapter 30.

The After-Talk Reception: This is the primary opportunity for many members of the faculty to get a chance to interact with you. It is not the time to kick back and chug multiple glasses of wine. Stay alert. Nurse a single drink and eat something neat and nonsmelly (cheese cubes are good; smoked salmon is bad). Mingle, and don't allow yourself to be commandeered by any one person. Remember that you need to speak most to the tenured members of the department, while certainly not neglecting the untenured. Don't get stuck with the graduate students. Be aware of who has votes and influence.

The Search Committee Interview: This is the real deal, an actual interview, so don't make the mistake of considering it a mere formality. Your answers will be closely examined, deconstructed, discussed, and evaluated. Do not assume that because you've interviewed before, and they have your written materials, you do not need to make a strong verbal presentation. Do not hesitate to refer to your written materials, with new emphasis. Example:

Q: What upper level course would you develop for us?
A: Well, you may recall the course syllabus that I submitted with my application, for a course on X. [Someone pulls it out of the file, hands it around, people study it.] Well, as you can see, I focus on P and Q in that course. As George and I were just discussing over lunch, I think it will have a lot of appeal for students, while also introducing them to some core current debates in our field . . .

The Meeting with the Dean/Provost: In the meeting with upper administrators, you will typically be given a basic rundown of tenure expectations, the salary range, the benefits offered by the university, leave policies, and so forth. Some deans play a role in searches and some don't. This interview may seem pro forma, but it isn't. I explain further in chapter 36; for now, note that you'll want to emphasize your success in bringing in money with grants, enthusiasm for teaching large courses, commitment to mobilizing social media in your courses, and willingness to teach in multiple disciplines in a downsizing environment. It is always safe to assume that deans and other administrators are thinking about saving money (even while their salaries may be squandering it).

The Real Estate Tour: Some campuses that are in beautiful, inexpensive locations like to use real estate as a means of courting candidates. It's weird and awkward to drive around in someone's car looking at neighborhoods, but like with the campus tour, be enthusiastic and gracious, without forgetting that you're still on stage. Note the condition of the car. I was once driven around by an associate professor in her aged, worn-out Toyota Corolla. It turned out to be an excellent indicator of faculty salaries.

Meals with Faculty: Between nerves and fielding questions, you likely will not be able to eat much at meals. Carry meal replacement bars with you and use them during brief breaks in your schedule to keep your blood sugar level.

Do not order wine at dinner unless it is clear that "everyone" is ordering wine. Then follow suit, if you drink alcohol. If you don't, politely decline, without going into explanations. Drink only one glass. Similarly, don't order dessert unless others initiate it. People may be exhausted and anxious to get home.

When ordering your meal, don't order the filet mignon; remember that everyone is on a budget. Be sure and order the neatest item on the menu. Being a dreadfully messy eater, I found it best to avoid pasta or soup or anything that drips. I was also cautious of flaky rolls and croissants that scatter crumbs all down my front, and yogurt that must be lapped up in an infantile way. A piece of meat or fish that can be quickly cut into manageable pieces will minimize any potentially distracting struggle with your food.

The Lunch with the Grad Students: In some departments graduate student voices are listened to very carefully indeed. In others, they're ignored. In all of my departments the grad students had one vote on searches, and the grad student representative on the committee was conscientious in surveying grad student opinions. These were shared with the faculty in a report, and were discussed seriously. Assume that the grad students play a major role in your fate, and show a high level of interest in and commitment to them. We hope this is sincere. But be aware that grad students are unpredictable. They can be your most enthusiastic supporters, but their insecure status can make them potentially reactive. You must make special efforts to show that you are excited about their work and want to know more about it. Share ideas and suggestions for readings with them, and in all things, construct yourself as their ally.

The Campus Tour: This is likely led by a grad student, so keep in mind the notes above. While on the campus tour, be curious, but don't gush. Also, try not to say anything that appears to unfavorably compare the campus with your home campus: "Wow, it's so small!" "Wow, how does anybody find their way around here?" "Wow, don't your legs get tired?" "Wow, is this all there is?" Be prepared with good questions: How is the campus over summer? Are the students politically active? Are there many international students?

The campus tour is the reason you must be sure to wear comfortable and weather-appropriate shoes.

The Meeting with the Department Head: The meeting with the head covers the nuts and bolts of teaching expectations, junior leave, the third-year review, and tenure. Come prepared to listen and take notes, and have intelligent questions to ask, such as "What is the typical teaching load?" and "How often do faculty get to teach graduate seminars?" and "How does the department engage with the Center for X?" No prima donna act here; for example, upon hearing the teaching load: "What? When will I get my *research* done?" The head needs to know that you are going to be a full-fledged faculty member and colleague, ready to take on your share of the tedious work of running a department. With absolutely no undignified pandering, simply demonstrate your preparedness to be a colleague, and do what it takes to get tenure (so you can keep being a colleague).

And a final note: *Be nice to the secretaries.* They can make or break your quality of life if you get the job . . . and they remember. Treat them with courtesy and respect. Be sure to thank them for the efforts they made to set up the visit. Take the time to talk with them when you have a few free moments. They do the lion's share of work in most departments and rarely are acknowledged for it. Make sure that you do.

THIRTY-FOUR

The Job Talk

The job talk is the jewel in the crown of the campus visit. You cannot bomb the job talk and still get the job. Yet candidate after candidate strides to the podium and promptly sinks their chances. Why are misunderstandings of this relatively simple task so rife? I don't know, but after years of sitting through and reading excruciating talks, I've assembled a checklist that, if you follow it scrupulously, will keep your talk out of the danger zone.

1. Make Sure the Talk Speaks to the Job Being Advertised. Candidates can be so obsessed with their own narrow projects, on the one hand, or so amped up about trying to be all things to all people, on the other, that they often miss the mark in pitching the talk to exactly the position being filled. If it's a nineteenth-century British literature job, then should your talk be about postcolonial literature? No. Should it be about Fielding? No. Should it be about twentieth-century film adaptations of Dickens? No. It should be about some aspect of actual literature written in the actual nineteenth century. Do interesting things, but don't forget that they have curricular needs that must be filled.

2. Have a Clear One-Paragraph Intro that lays out the topic and sketches the basic plan of the talk. "Thank you for having me. Today I'll be speaking about X. In the talk, I'll be exploring X from the perspective of Y and will be relating it to Z. I will show that X derives from/ causes/represents/signifies Q, and ultimately argue that X can be understood as P." Seriously, this is not that hard, yet nearly everyone forgets.

3. Resist the Temptation to Open with a Vignette. Yes, I know that you think your little vignette is perfect for illustrating everything that is amazing and interesting and colorful and compelling about your topic. But guess what? You've been working on this project for ten years, and know the place and time and context and dramatis personae like the back of your hand. We're hearing it for the first time, and know nothing. That great story about Vicente and the fish-monger? The one that instantly revealed to you the whole truth of the local economy? The one that inspired your whole dissertation? Guess what? We don't know who Vicente is. We don't know why fish are important. We don't know why they were even talking. We can't follow your story, because we don't know the place, or the people, or their motivations. Remove the vignette.

4. Take about Two Paragraphs to Explain Your Topic Clearly for first-time listeners. Think "undergrad lecture" for this introductory section. Basic. Simple. Clear. No theory, no disputes, no rhetoric. Just the facts: who, what, when, where, how.

5. Get to the Point. And Stay on Point. Don't spend seven pages in prefatory remarks and caveats. You should be into the main topic of your talk by the end of the second page. Make sure that the evidence mobilized and arguments advanced actually relate directly to the topic, without digressions. Make sure the point you prove is the point you meant to prove.

6. Advance a Clear and Logical Argument through the rest of the body of the talk, using your "stuff" (ethnography, literary texts, historical material, and so forth) to advance theoretical and conceptual arguments. Do not go overboard with either your material or your theory. The stuff and stories must ground the theory and concepts, while the theory and concepts must illuminate the stuff and stories.

7. Eschew Excessive Citation of Other Works and Sources. You don't need to pay obeisance to fifteen other scholars or bodies of work. No lit reviews here! Briefly and efficiently cite just one or two scholars as a kind of "pivot" to your talk—the moment when you move from describing a phenomenon to analyzing it conceptually. Point briefly to their innovations or interventions, and then quickly move to your own original and distinctive argument.

8. Advance an Original and Distinctive Argument. It should look like this: "From an examination of X and Y, we can conclude that X may be understood as Z." Don't be vague and "shed light on" or "contribute to the literature on" or " add to the excellent work on." This is not dependent, or derivative, or additive. It is your own original argument.

9. Use Decent Visuals that Illustrate the Points of the Talk while obeying a few basic rules of design—limited text on each slide, plenty of blank space, images that make sense to first-time viewers (undergrad lecture standards apply here, too), graphics and text large enough for the audience to see from where they are sitting, a manageable amount of content, and no weird and bewildering diagrams or flowcharts filled with tiny, illegible captions. This last thing is the bugbear of anxious social scientists.

Academic audiences are generally ambivalent about PowerPoint. They appreciate visuals as much as anyone, but they also resent the "dumbing down" that often happens in a PowerPoint-centric presentation. Be sure that the text stands alone as academic written text, and is not subordinate to slides. In other words, don't stand in front of the screen and say "And next, in this slide, we see that . . ."

Also, leave visuals that you do use on the screen for long enough that the audience can thoroughly assimilate them. One of the most common errors that nervous speakers commit is snapping through visuals too quickly. Your audience is seeing them for the first time. They need abundant time—several minutes most likely—to thoroughly study each one.

10. Insert Pauses for Interaction with the Audience. Know your talk well enough that you don't have to read it. Yes, it is often still the norm to work from a paper. But that doesn't mean you need to keep your eyes glued to it. While this may seem to contradict rule 11 and possibly rule 5, it does not. You can remain strictly professorial and formal, and still make abundant eye contact, gesture broadly, and in some cases move about the stage or podium area. To draw your audience in and monitor their reactions to what you are saying, you must watch them. Also, anticipating nerves, print the talk out in large double-space text so that it's easy to read, and don't be afraid to put stage directions into the text ("Insert quip here"; "Offer 'spontaneous' remark about X here," and so on).

11. Be Thoroughly Formal and Professional. This is not a chat. This is a formal presentation of research. It is meant to showcase your expertise and authority, not demonstrate that you are nice. Do not write the job talk in spoken form. For example: "So then I'm going to ask the question, 'What would happen if we look at X instead of Y?' And when I do that, a very interesting thing comes up, which I'm sure that you can anticipate, which is that focusing on X puts the whole topic of Z in a new perspective."

Instead, you will write: "Focusing on X instead of Y reveals a different perspective on Z, and that is the perspective that I will focus on today."

In addition, use formal words exclusively. This is not the place for slang and casual language:

"The novel is so interesting!"

"This outcome is super-cool!"

"Isn't this result amazing?"

"This guy was, like, the rock star of informants!"

Minimize your use of "us" and "we," as in "We can see here that the image . . ." and "What we all know about intersectionality is . . ." I'm not saying you have to jettison them entirely, but they are vastly overused, chatty, and come across as presumptuous ("What do you mean 'we,' job candidate?").

Use humor sparingly. Search committees and audiences always

appreciate knowing that you have a sense of humor, but the job talk is not usually the place to demonstrate it. A witticism, if it arises naturally from your materials, or some mishap in your presentation, is certainly appropriate. But beyond that, let your sense of humor emerge in your conversations throughout the day; in the job talk, give your research the serious delivery that it deserves.

12. Be Aware of Your Body Language. Keep your gaze level, head held high, stance firm, feet strongly planted (no winding or twisting your feet below the podium), shoulders squared, and your hands calmly on the podium or gesturing. I once worked with a stellar R1 client who had a brilliant project, fabulous teaching skills, and a terrific intellectual pedigree. And then we did a run-through of her job talk on Skype, and she crumbled before my eyes. Her typical self-assurance was nowhere to be seen. She ducked her head, bobbed, and swayed. Her eyes darted from side to side. Her hands twisted into knots and fluttered like little fish. "No, start over, try it again!": Three times we went through it. When we hung up I was still concerned. On her visit, she did fine and got the job. But she told me afterward, without that Skype practice she never would have realized just how much she let her nerves show through her nonverbal habits.

13. Banish the Following Phrases: "is worthy of study," "deserves study," and "merits study." The fact that you are studying it proves that it is worthy of study. Saying these words makes you sound like a junior grad student trying to convince a skeptical advisor of the value of a dissertation topic. And while we're here, remember to jettison the words "try," "seek," "hope," "attempt," and "endeavor."

14. Have a Strong and Inspiring Finish. Do not dribble away with "So, yeah, uh, I guess that's it. . . . Um, does anybody have any questions?" leaving the audience to squirm in their seats and wonder when to clap. Finish strong. Assertively. With a clear falling tone in the final words, then a pause, and then a confident gaze with half smile taking in the whole audience, and a strong and gracious "Thank you." Then another pause for applause, and then, "I'd be happy to take questions" (or acknowledge your moderator rising out of his or her seat to moderate questions for you).

Academics often forget that academic speaking is a form of performance. And as with all performances, the buildup to the conclusion, and the conclusion itself, are in some ways the most important elements. The finish sits in the air, vibrating, and stays with the listeners for some time. It's true that in an academic talk, questioners often jump in aggressively; nevertheless, a strong finish, more than almost anything else, demonstrates the speaker's confidence and élan.

15. Be Prepared for the Q and A. In my years on search committees, it was the Q and A that most often destroyed candidates. Given enough time and help, most people could pull together a decent talk, but the Q and A separated the wheat from the chaff. Remember that by the time you give the job talk, you've already proven that your work, on paper, is good. What the job talk proves is that you're intellectually vibrant and dynamic and that you can defend your work against challenges, while remaining open to intriguing new scholarly possibilities and conversations. Be friendly, good humored, and affable, and not cringing, obsequious, or pandering.

As I mentioned earlier, master the art of academic jujitsu; when directly challenged, acknowledge the value of the questioner's point, but then turn the focus away from their agenda and back to your own. In other words, never, ever respond "Oh, wow, I really wish I'd had time to talk about that and it's a total oversight that I didn't include it. I'm really sorry about that." Instead respond, "You raise a valuable point and it's certainly one that I considered. However, my findings showed that the primary issue here is, in fact, X, and so it was to that that I turned my greatest attention."

Of course there are occasional variations in the genre of the job talk: Some places will ask you to include in your job talk a teaching demo, a quick survey of future work, plans for classes, and so on. Of course you must do what is asked. But if you're being asked to give what is still the default job talk—the research paper followed by Q and A—then the checklist above will guide you.

THIRTY-FIVE

....

The Teaching Demo

Teaching demos are standard at teaching-focused institutions, and may turn up at R1-type campus visits on occasion. Sometimes the teaching demo replaces the job talk, and sometimes it is required in addition to the job talk.

The teaching demo can be organized in several ways: around a visit to an existing classroom borrowed from a colleague's regularly scheduled class, around a "class" conducted with students assembled for the purpose, or as simply a demonstration of a hypothetical class presented before a group of faculty.

Just as the job talk is the single most important part of a campus visit to a research institution, the teaching demo is the most important element of a visit to a teaching-oriented college.

The scary thing about teaching demos, of course, is that unlike job talks, which follow a pretty predictable format of talk plus Q and A, they incorporate an unknown element: the students. How will the students react? Will they do the assigned readings? Will they talk? Or will you be marooned in a desolate space of deafening silence and dashed career hopes?

Advance research is the key to success in the teaching demo. The most important thing to determine is the general academic level of the student body. As soon as you've been told the topic and level of class, use the Internet to research similar classes on campus (preferably in that department) to discover standards of reading

expectations and typical types of assignments. This is critical because you may be coming from an institution where the expectations differ. Do not assume that the students at the teaching demo
will behave the same as the undergraduate students in your department at your Ph.D.-granting institution. If you or your advisor have
colleagues who teach at this type of institution and department, solicit their advice.

It is wise to steer clear of either an all-lecture or all-discussion
format. Unless given specific instructions, prepare a good but short
lecture, with highly regimented discussion or classroom activities
to follow. With a completely unknown group of students, planning a full-hour lecture could be the kiss of death, while planning
a loose and spontaneous class discussion carries too many risks.
And, indeed, the agenda of a teaching demo is a bit different from
the agenda of an actual class. While in your own classroom you may
loathe lecturing and be a firm practitioner of student-led learning,
in a teaching demo, they want to see some demonstration of classroom authority. A certain amount of lecture, in this context, is not
out of place, even if it's not your preferred pedagogical method.
However, it would be a mistake to lecture exclusively. So come prepared to use your Socratic methods, quick-and-dirty exercises (such
as fast free-writes), and superior discussion leadership skills.

Sometimes you'll be asked to suggest the reading. Keep any assigned reading short, and prepare some backup close-reading pas-
sages that students can do on the spot.

The department may assign you a topic, or they may ask you to
choose one. In either case, do not use the teaching demo as an
opportunity to beat the dead horse of your research for the ump-
teenth time. That is what the job talk is for. Faculty must spend a
great deal of time teaching outside their core research areas, and
the teaching demo proves your willingness and ability to do so. Of
course, you can introduce some of your work if it arises organically
from the topic or discussion, but remember—the teaching demo is
not about you per se; it is about the students. So look up from your
notes, keep a close watch on them, be alert for signs of boredom
and disaffection, encourage all participation, even the most tentative, and don't be afraid to dig into genuine debate.

Particularly if you've had prior experience only as a TA, remember that your goal is to draw the students out and interact with them like a professor. You'll have all the normal challenges of teaching: silent students, someone monopolizing the conversation, ill-conceived remarks, and the like. Don't be excessively nice; you must exhibit firm leadership. While a relaxed, casual, and approachable discussion style might work wonders in your TA discussion section, be sure to channel your inner professor in this exercise. You want an aura of command.

Last, don't forget one of the perennial rules of good teaching: the wrap-up, in which you tie up the class with a "what we learned/practiced/discussed today" summary that brings the class period to a firm closure. As I wrote earlier, a strong ending is key to a strong performance, so don't dribble off with an awkward laugh and a "Well, I hope that answered your question, ha ha, so, um . . . yeah." Conclude your thoughts with plenty of time to spare (avoid the frantic, undignified trying-to-be-heard-over-packing-up-noise syndrome), thank the class for their attention, and bid them a cordial farewell.

....

THIRTY-SIX

How to Talk to the Dean

Many, if not most, campus visits still include a visit with the dean, and this is often the least understood element of the entire experience. What in the world do deans talk about?

I have never been a dean, but I certainly spent time talking to them as a job candidate, and later as a faculty member and department head. In those capacities I observed that deans tend to fall into three general patterns in their interactions with job candidates: the explanatory, the budgetary, and the intellectual. These are not necessarily mutually exclusive categories.

When a dean is taking the explanatory route, she will use her thirty minutes with the candidate to explain the position, policies, and campus. She will typically focus on the compensation package, not just salary range but also the benefits and retirement plans, the general policies about third-year review and tenure, and the raises associated with promotion. In cases like this, the meeting with the dean is easy for the candidate, who mainly just listens.

When the dean is preoccupied with budgetary concerns, she will ask questions that relate, directly or indirectly, to money. This can include inquiring about a candidate's past success with major grants; plans for future grants; budgetary requirements for labs and research and plans for fulfilling them; willingness to teach large classes; commitment to interdisciplinarity and cross-listing of classes (that is, filling multiple teaching needs with a single line);

and feelings about being the sole representative of a field in the department or on campus.

This last subject is particularly treacherous for candidates. In the course of the conversation you might inquire, very reasonably, "Are there plans to build the program in X and hire other X specialists in departments such as Y in the next few years?" The dean responds, "Of course we'd always like to build in every worthy direction, but in the current financial situation, hard choices have to be made, and there's a good possibility you will be the only X specialist for the foreseeable future." And then she looks at you expectantly.

Here is how you probably will want to respond: "What? Well, I hope that there will be hires at *least* in the Y department because I can't be expected to carry the weight of an entire program on my own." And that would lose you the job (at least from the dean's perspective).

The correct answer is, instead: "I see plenty of opportunity for growth with even a single faculty member. With strategic collaborations with Y and Z scholars in departments such as A and B, and leveraging the resources already on campus in the form of C, I can imagine creating opportunities for students in the areas of Y and Z even without the addition of another dedicated line."

That is the language of the neoliberal campus, and it is how you deal with a dean who is taking the budgetary line.

When a dean prefers the intellectual approach, she will take the opportunity to quiz you on the state of your field and its most important directions of future growth. Common questions in this vein include:

"What do you think are the most important current debates in your field?"

"How do you think your field will change the most in the next ten years and why?"

"What is the single biggest challenge facing your field right now?"

"What is the most important text published in the last five years in your field, and why?"

This tactic kills two deanly birds with one stone. On the one hand, she evaluates your intellectual breadth and confidence. On the other hand, she gets a candid perspective on the emergent trends in your field, against which she can judge and evaluate what the current members of the department are talking about and doing. If three candidates come through the dean's door all telling her that the most important new trend in the field is X, and nobody in the department is currently doing X, the dean has a useful insight into the department and its limitations.

Sadly, most job candidates are ill prepared to deal with the intellectual dean's line of questioning.

Many years ago a senior anthropologist colleague of mine told me a story about his meeting with the graduate students during a campus visit to an Ivy League anthropology department. "What are you reading right now?" he had asked them eagerly. "What is the book that everyone is reading and talking about?"

The graduate students paused, looked at one another, and thought for a while. "*The Nuer,*" they finally responded. "Yeah, everybody is reading *The Nuer.*"

The Nuer: A Description of the Modes of Livelihood and Political Institutions of a Nilotic People is a foundational text of British social anthropology written by E. E. Evans-Pritchard and originally published in 1940. A core element of a History of Anthropology seminar reading list, *The Nuer* is a book that "everyone" reads only if "everyone" is conceived of as first- and second-year anthropology graduate students in a very old-fashioned department indeed.

What my friend was asking, but what the graduate students entirely failed to grasp, was not what is everyone reading *in their classes,* but "What is the thing that everyone is reading that is exciting, new, and controversial, and that has the department riled up, thinking, and talking?" That is, what is the book that is changing our field?

Although it's a different set of circumstances entirely, this story encapsulates the problem of green job candidates confronting an intellectual dean. The green job candidate is likely still absorbed by their recent history of taking classes, sitting for comprehensive exams, and enduring the dissertation defense. This narrow set of experiences is designed to test whether the student has read enough, knows enough, is legitimate enough, to be "passed" as a credible practitioner in the field.

The dean, however, has no such agenda. The dean, who is most likely not in your discipline, is prepared to accept that you are, of course, perfectly credible as a practitioner of your field. What the dean is testing is whether you are, or are poised to be, a *leader* in your field, someone who isn't preoccupied with reproducing the old (*The Nuer*), but who is busy creating the new.

The best job candidates will be prepared to answer the kinds of intellectual dean questions I listed above with confidence and vision. Don't neglect to prepare for these questions, even if a dean interview is not on your schedule. These questions have a pesky habit of popping up from the search chair, the department head, the graduate students . . . all sorts of people. As you aim for a position as an important scholar in your field, you must leave behind your graduate student frame of reference, and learn to think and speak like an intellectual leader.

THIRTY-SEVEN

·······················

They Said What?
Handling Outrageous Questions

I could write a book on the outrageous questions my readers and clients have shared with me from their interviews and campus visits. Federal employment laws dictate that questions cannot be asked that appear to discriminate on the basis of sex, race, nationality, religion, or age; however, these laws are not widely or completely understood among the professoriate. While some of the faculty will have heard vaguely that they shouldn't ask certain types of questions, and many colleagues you meet will make great efforts to stay within the bounds of the law, every department seems to have at least one faculty member who simply doesn't get it, or doesn't care, and who routinely asks questions that are illegal or at best outrageously inappropriate.

Common examples include the following, many of which were shared by readers of The Professor Is In blog:

- "Are you married?"
- "What will your husband do if you take this job?"
- "Do you have children? How will you manage your research with a family? Do you plan to get pregnant?"
- "Will you be unhappy here away from your own people?"
- "Are you really black?"

- "Aren't you going to want to retire soon?"
- "Are you a lesbian?"
- "Why do you think you, as a woman of color, can relate to our students?" [Awkward pause.] "I'm not saying our students are rednecks but . . ."
- "Our dean wants us to get more black students in classes. You're a white woman. How will you help us achieve that goal? Be specific. We're in trouble here."
- "Just how Jewish are you?"
- "So, I notice your blended Irish-Jewish last name. I've often wondered how Catholic-Jewish weddings work out in the long run; I have to admit that my research hasn't led me to believe in the longevity of interfaith marriages."
- "I see from your materials that you've never been to Greece. I'm highly skeptical of hiring a colleague in classics who hasn't been there. Can you explain why you haven't made that happen in your scholarly training? A more serious candidate would have prioritized differently."

Why are these questions asked? In a few cases, particularly with questions about family and children, they may arise from an ill-conceived effort to establish a friendly human connection. In other cases, of course, the message is clear: You don't belong here.

So how do you respond?

It rarely behooves the candidate to confront the questioner, even if what you want to say is, "Illegal! I'm not answering!" While there is no good way to deal with a bad question, you can minimize engagement with the question, and refocus attention to the job itself. Never accept the identified problem of your identity; instead focus entirely on your skills and qualifications for the job at hand.

Q: Are you married?
A: Yes [or no]. Going back to what we were talking about at the meeting/over coffee/in the interview, I want to tell you more about that workshop I'm organizing on . . .

Q: What will your husband do if you take this job?

A: My husband and I have always supported each other's careers, and that will continue. Going back to what we were talking about at the meeting/over coffee/in the interview, I want to tell you more about that workshop I'm organizing on . . .

Q: How will you manage your research with your children?

A: I am very well organized and always stick to both weekly and monthly plans of work; I lay out my research and writing goals and organize my time to meet them. Going back to what we were talking about at the meeting/over coffee/in the interview, I want to tell you more about that workshop I'm organizing on . . .

Q: Will you be unhappy here away from your own people?

A: I am excited to be anywhere I can focus on my research/teach in my discipline. Going back to what we were talking about at the meeting/over coffee/in the interview, I want to tell you more about that workshop I'm organizing on . . .

Q: Are you really black?

A: Yes. Now, going back to what we were talking about at the meeting/over coffee/in the interview, I want to tell you more about that workshop I'm organizing on . . .

Q: Aren't you going to want to retire soon?

A: I am just starting out on all of the publishing I plan to do associated with my dissertation, including my first book manuscript, and I have an exciting second major project planned after that. I'd like to tell you about those. . . .

Q: Are you a lesbian?

A: Since I focus on X topic area, I haven't found that my sexual identity has much bearing on the outcomes, or on my work in the lab. Going back to what we were talking about at the meeting/over coffee/in the interview, I want to tell you more about that workshop I'm organizing on . . .

Q: Why do you think you, as a woman of color, can relate to our students? [Awkward pause.] I'm not saying our students are rednecks but . . .
A: In all of my classes I value a diversity of viewpoints, and I use specific pedagogical techniques to make sure all students feel heard. For example, I . . .

Q: Our dean wants us to get more black students in classes. You're a white woman. How will you help us achieve that goal? Be specific. We're in trouble here.
A: I have been committed to recruiting diverse students into the field of X, and working with them closely to succeed in the program. Studies have shown that one of the primary obstacles to students of color entering the X field is Y; I overcome that by focusing on Z. . . . [Note that the candidate does need a substantive answer here—just one that does not engage in any way with her own racial subject position.]

Q: Just how Jewish are you?
A: My religious practice has never really played much role in my academic identity or lab research. Going back to what we were talking about at the meeting/over coffee/in the interview, I want to tell you more about that workshop I'm organizing on . . .

Q: So, I notice your blended Irish-Jewish last name. I've often wondered how Catholic-Jewish weddings work out in the long run; I have to admit that my research hasn't led me to believe in the longevity of interfaith marriages.
A: I do have an interesting family. Going back to what we were talking about at the meeting/over coffee/in the interview, I want to tell you more about that workshop I'm organizing on . . .

Q: I see from your materials that you've never been to Greece. I'm highly skeptical of hiring a colleague in classics who hasn't been there. Can you explain why you haven't made that happen in your scholarly training? A more serious candidate would have prioritized differently. [This candidate came from a resource-poor program that did not provide research support for this kind of travel.]

A: My research is focused on X and Y, and I had abundant resources through P and Q to be able to complete my dissertation, two published articles, and a book manuscript based on the work. I will certainly look forward to traveling to Greece for my next project, which is on . . .

Remember that you do not have to pick up what the problematic questioner is putting down. You have control over your responses. Also remember that you are not obliged to volunteer information out of a codependent concern for your questioner's comfort.

SC member: Are you married?

You: Yes. [Silence. Resist the overwhelming codependent urge to elaborate.]

SC member: [Silence. Waiting.]

You: [Smile pleasantly but noncommittally.]

SC member: Um, so, what does he do?

You: He's an academic. [Silence. Resist the overwhelming codependent urge to elaborate.]

SC member: Ah. What will he do if you're offered this job?

You: We both have independent careers; right now I'm focusing on mine. [Resist the overwhelming codependent urge to elaborate.]

SC member: Yes, but would he come with you if you got the job?

You: We are both pursuing our own job searches; right now my focus is on my job search, and I'd like to answer any questions you might have about my candidacy for this job. One thing I was excited to speak to you about was the workshop I recently organized on . . .

Taking this tack requires almost superhuman self-control, because of our seemingly hard-wired tendency to fill in silences and overexplain, especially in any context in which we feel anxious or insecure. Nevertheless, remember: You are in control of your own information. You are required to share nothing that you don't want to.

The trouble with illegal questions, of course, is that sometimes they aren't questions at all. They are just comments that circuitously work to effect a policing of boundaries between those who do and do not belong. Sometimes faculty will turn on a candidate simply for bearing a resemblance to a problematic outsider. On my own very first campus visit, for example, which occurred just after I had been living in Japan for two years, an old-school, on-the-verge-of-retirement British-trained social anthropologist suddenly burst out at me, in the middle of a hallway conversation, "Would you stop bowing and apologizing like a goddamned Oriental?"

Or faculty will objectify or tokenize the candidate's identity. An interviewer at a Catholic institution told a Jewish candidate wondering about a statement of faith requirement, "We have lots of Jews on the faculty! Here, have a list! That should make you feel better, right?" Sometimes the message is couched evasively by imputing the discriminatory attitude to another colleague who is not present. As an African American job seeker told me, "One interviewer said to me, 'I think they should hire African Americans but it's so difficult—I know Professor X. He is my neighbor. Our children play together. He's my friend. He will not agree to any candidate who is not Jewish.'" Sometimes a group of faculty will attempt to retroactively distance themselves from the problematic faculty member and his behavior, which is nevertheless tolerated in the moment. As the candidate asked the question about interfaith marriages above explained, "The department had apparently taken bets as to whether he would say something about it, and apologized profusely when I returned."

It goes without saying that no such ham-handed distancing effort is any less inappropriate (or shows any more class) than an openly discriminatory question. They are all other-ing to the candidate, and put the candidate in an impossible position. How is one to respond to any of them? "Oh, no, sir, I'm definitely not Oriental"? "That's great! Jews love being on lists!"? "Well then, I'm sorry I'm black and not Jewish"? "Ha ha, that certainly was funny when he insulted my parentage. Hope you at least made some money off of it!"?

Before moving on, I want to pause to point out that a lot of what search candidates call "illegal" questions may not technically be illegal. But they are absolutely inappropriate, and may well be ambiguous enough that they could lead to lawsuits alleging discrimination, and often do in hiring contexts that are more litigious than the academy. Not every grossly inappropriate and discomfiting question necessarily falls into the illegality. I am no lawyer and no expert, so beyond this I direct you to investigate further with human resources at your institution. In the meantime, master the art of redirection, as with toddlers.

THIRTY-EIGHT

Waiting, Wondering, Wiki

The job search is so entirely out of your control that it is easy to obsess about the tiny places where you exercise some agency. At no moment in the whole process is the lack of control more crushingly apparent than in the gaping void after the campus visit is over. The only step available to you after returning home is sending a thank-you note. Consequently the etiquette of the thank-you note receives an inordinate level of candidate concern, and I am asked about it at least once a week.

It is appropriate to write an email thank-you to the department head, to the search committee chair, and to the department secretary who helped arrange the visit, and then to any other faculty member with whom you feel you formed a special connection. Just a couple of lines are fine:

> I'm writing to thank you again for hosting me on my campus visit. I thoroughly enjoyed the opportunity to get to know the search committee and the department. I remain very interested in the position. I will look forward to hearing from you.
>
> SINCERELY,
>
> SIGNATURE

You do not need to thank every single person you met, although you can if you wish.

It is appropriate, if you wish, to send a thank-you card to the department, addressed either to the department head or to the departmental secretary, but it is not required. Emails are the norm.

Now, moving on to other anxieties of the follow-up: the protocols for awaiting a decision, dealing with the dreaded jobs wiki, and whether you can ask for feedback when you don't get the job.

Without question one of the most demoralizing aspects of the job search is the silence that typically follows after each stage of the application process. You submit an application and . . . nothing. You get a conference interview and . . . nothing. You come home from your campus visit and . . . nothing. It's a sad fact of our uncivil times that some of the former courtesies of professional life have fallen away, leaving nothing but an empty void. Countless searches conclude without the department even informing unsuccessful candidates that they are no longer under consideration.

What should you do? Well, I'm sorry to say, my advice is to just wait it out, and don't ask. The fact is, calling the department to ask about the status of the search is a painful and humiliating and ultimately pointless exercise. If they want you, they will call. For most job seekers, the call will not come. Sorry.

If your conference is imminent and you need to make plans based on a possible conference interview, OK, go ahead, if you must, and write an email to the department secretary to inquire. (Do spare a moment to consider the secretary who is fielding inquiries from a pool of several hundred applicants.) Otherwise, don't bother. There is no mystery here. There is no confusion or delay or problem with the search or Gmail or your university server. What there is, is the fact that you probably have not been short-listed. It's painful and shocking and devastating, and no amount of reading all the dire warnings will prepare you for the dismay and panic you feel the first time it happens to you.

I remember the first year I was on the market in 1995, an already brutal time in anthropology. I got not a single callback from the first set of applications I sent out; I thought my local post office was experiencing some sort of malfunction. Surely, there had to be some mistake.

There was no mistake. I was confronting competition from

graduates of the top programs of the land, and I was sending out painfully bad application materials. But the memory of that deafening silence, my bewilderment, my growing humiliation, my slowly dawning understanding . . . all these things are as fresh in my mind today as they were that fall. What I learned then is true today: If they want you, they will call you.

In an inhuman system that doles out humiliation by the bucket load, it is important to do what you can to retain your dignity.

This brings us to the dreaded jobs wiki. Every job seeker knows the depredations wrought upon the job-seeking population by the jobs wiki—the discipline-specific, open-source listing of current openings that is updated by readers when they get invitations at each new stage.

When you go on the jobs wiki, the news is never good, because you don't go there to find out that you got an interview invitation. No, the jobs wiki tells you only what you didn't get, but somebody else did: a request for materials, an invitation to a conference interview, a campus visit. As outspoken higher education critic and provocateur Rebecca Schuman wrote in her witty post on the subject,

> The wiki is like that social-skills-impaired friend you had in high school, the one who points out your giant, throbbing zit or inquires about your recent breakup as if you had never thought to be sad about it before. Just because it nominally and often tells the truth doesn't mean you should hang out with it.[1]

In the gaping communication void that now characterizes the academic job market, the wiki stands in as the public commons of shared information for a confused and desperate populace. Here's an example from the 2013–14 anthropology list. In parentheses are the dates of the updates, and the "x7" and the like represent the number of readers who can confirm that they, too, passed each follow-up stage of the search:

> *This position [Y] was just posted, and they seem to want a specialist in Z. Does anybody know the story here?*
>   *Email acknowledgment of application. (11/14) x7*

Any news?

Zilch. The silence on this one makes me wonder whether the funding dried up.

I don't know. . . . What with all the holidays/finals/conferences, the two months doesn't seem unreasonable.

A few other search committees I'm waiting on have been similarly silent, but it's frustrating—I can commiserate. (1/15)

They have narrowed it down to 12 people. They request two publications and three reference letters. (1/22) x4

Any news on campus visits? (2/18)

Department is still waiting for approval of finalists. (2/19)

Received official invitation to visit campus during the second half of March. (2/28)

ON-CAMPUS INTERVIEWS SCHEDULED. (2/28)

And there you have it—your dreams crushed, in the space of a few lines.

But is the jobs wiki all bad? Well, it is when you obsess over it, and everybody does, at least for part of their time on the market. It's an addiction, and it'll get you.

"[Here's] a harsh truth," Rebecca Schuman elaborated. "Once you start chasing the wiki dragon, it can consume your entire life. Not only will it wiki-waste your time, but you will be sorely tempted to believe everything you read on it, even things that are made up. (And fabrication happens, especially later in the cycle.) You may also feel absolutely, wrenchingly terrible about yourself even if you do get an interview or two, because you will look at all the 'success' on that list and wonder why you didn't get 20."[2]

But if you can manage your addiction, the jobs wiki can help you. Because so few departments provide information to job seekers on a timely basis, the wiki allows you to accurately track whether or not you should plan to attend a conference on the hope of an interview. If you know you have no interview, you can skip the trouble and expense of the conference with complete peace of mind. As one job seeker told me, "I didn't get any conference interviews last year and after the initial disappointment, I found a sense of relief in knowing that I could focus on enjoying my winter break."

The wiki only goes so far, however. When you have made it all the way through the campus visit, and have met the department members face-to-face, then the quest for feedback takes on an entirely different and much more personal dimension.

If you are rejected after the campus visit, can you ask why? Yes, you can, although you probably won't get a response. Departments are constrained from providing substantive feedback from unsuccessful candidates, either because of real or imagined HR rules, or because of embarrassment. They would just as soon you quietly disappear.

But even vague feedback can be enormously helpful. When asking, stick to general, nondesperate sorts of questions. That is, avoid something like "Why didn't I get the job? I matched your ad perfectly and had a great time on my visit!" Instead, frame it more like "I would like to ask if you can provide any feedback on my materials or visit that would provide insight as I move forward in my job search."

When I was a search committee chair and department head, I used to long for certain candidates to contact me afterward so I could alert them to their major errors. I could not have gone into great detail, but I could have shared some observations: "Your job talk was not well organized, and you seemed unprepared for many of the questions." "You did not relate your research very clearly to the stated foci of the job ad." "You didn't seem to have given much thought to new classes in the area we're trying to develop." "It was difficult to determine your publication trajectory."

Nothing mean or aggressive or gratuitous was necessary. Just basic feedback.

I personally think it is an ethical obligation for department heads or search committee chairs to provide this kind of feedback to an unsuccessful candidate seeking information. If a phone call is more comfortable than an email trail, do it that way.

To candidates, this feedback is invaluable. Use it as you plan your next applications. And stay focused, as best you can, not on your own grief and regret about the Job That Got Away, but on the things you can do moving forward, both on the academic job market and beyond.

PART VI

· · · · · · · · · · · · · · · ·

NAVIGATING THE JOB MARKET MINEFIELD

THIRTY-NINE

Good Job Candidates Gone Bad

With careful study, candidates can often identify the content and organization errors of their job documents, but they often remain unaware of problems of emotional tone and affect that color their writing and speaking during the job search. I've written about hyper-emotionalism and excessive humility elsewhere in the book. Here I identify five more errors of approach.

1. Narcissism

Narcissism, in the context of the job market, is obsession with your own process. Yes, we know that graduate school is an epic journey of discovery, and that you're excited about this journey. However, your drama of discovery is not interesting to search committees. Later, when you're colleagues and have plenty of time over lunch, the story may be worth sharing. But in the harried contexts of job documents and interviews, you need to stay on point. Which is not an exhaustive blow-by-blow account of all the utterly fascinating, unique, and original things you did in your Ph.D. program, but simply the facts of your research, publication, and teaching.

Here's sample narcissistic language: "I have always been fasci-nated by X, and that led me to pursue an inquiry into Y for my dissertation. First I approached it from the angle of Z, but then I realized that a methodology that emphasized A would yield more insight. I had the privilege of taking a class with Professor B, and inspired by that I came to the conclusion that C . . ."

Here is the replacement: "My dissertation focused on X, using the Y method. I argue Z."

Bottom line: They want to know what you researched, concluded, and published, and when. And what you'll do next.

2. Grandiosity

Grad students tend to veer between two extremes: I know nothing and I know everything. The latter position is an overcompensatory response to fear of the former. As you gain experience you find a middle ground of calm confidence. However, at the point of applying for your first tenure track job, these two extremes predominate.

Most of this book has attacked the former—that is, the grad student default to "I'm not worthy." However, here I highlight the pitfall of the latter: "I am a genius, I tell you, a *genius*." This position is, of course, communicated not directly, but indirectly through what I've come to call grad student grandiosity. Grandiosity can be seen in purple prose, pretentious verbs and adjectives, pedantic or tendentious claims for the originality of your work, bragging, and judging.

Grandiosity is most often found in excessive claims for the work's import:

"My work transforms understandings of civil society."

"My book will serve a milestone function in the academic panorama, and all major academic libraries will be interested in this work."

"My work represents a case study of balance between the academic mission of uncovering understudied phenomena and the intellectual duty to spur global debates on the current world."

"This is an essential topic in our own time."

"I call this framework X/X, much like Michel Foucault's knowledge/power paradigm."

"As Western academia's first comprehensive work concerning . . ."

"My dissertation, then, not only offers a novel interpretation of a central figure, texts, and topics in the history of Western thought; it enlarges disciplines and discourses of crucial interest to academic and wider public audiences."

Self-important, overblown, "fancy" words are another clue:

"The abiding concerns of my research pertain to the relationship of . . ."

"The dissertation draws together nascent theories of . . ."

"Because skills acquired in the classroom can perdure for a lifetime."

"My emphasis on rhetorically situated teaching reticulates well with service-learning courses."

Pretentious modifiers are always a sure sign of grandiosity:

"The relationship between X and Y has been a troubled and, at times, tragic one in both the distant and recent past. Untangling its intricacies requires a perspective hearkening back to a point at which the traditions were indistinct."

As is the impulse to judge and condemn other scholars' failings, usually using the overblown modifiers and fancy words mentioned above:

"The ill-considered tendency, here, to rationalize the X as merely illustrative of narrative exploits or symbols of elite status limits the interpretative potential of these objects. This narrowed perspective undermines the dense materiality of the X themselves, from which a broad field of valuable insight is lost."

"Postures that correctly see in the Q century 'the first century of X' (for example, Y and Z) risk presenting those traditions as spoken into being by X, thus relying on X for the very definition of their objects of inquiry."

"The very act of making the term X plural is enough to bring the ire of several scholars in the field."

"To date, even the most thoughtful proponents of a model of continued interfusion between X and Y in the Middle Ages (for example, A and B) leave unanswered questions of . . ."

There is pedantic lecturing:

"The twenty-first century can be characterized by change and transaction. In this environment it is important that undergraduate education teaches students how to learn. It is more important that students know how and where to find information than to know all of the answers. Be able to challenge core assumptions rather than share the standard one. Recognize a variety of viewpoints rather than molding experience to a single viewpoint."

"Besides classroom and lab group responsibilities, community science outreach is an increasingly important and relevant aspect of science education. Whether it be through demonstrations and conversations in high schools, malls, and community organizations or media and public lecture discussions, scientists, and especially X, should reach out and describe what we are doing to the general public and how the field of X improves and affects lives in a positive way."

And there is pretentious posturing about teaching:

"These methods play to my strengths as a pedagogue."

"Both my dissertation and classroom work evince a strong interest in . . ."

"My classes are also praxis spaces, which require my teaching to be iterative."

"A meaningful problem within which the student is invested and the resolution of which will stimulate the student's creative and analytical abilities, this is . . ."

"One of my primary teaching goals is to 'de-fetishize' both the triumphal globalization of the modern and the obstinate parochialism of the past, and show why both are true but partially . . ."

It also arises in the tailoring sections, when a candidate presumes to judge the department and its faculty:

"I find X's work on Y particularly admirable, as it is consistent with my own approach."

"I find the department's commitment to X impressive and worthy of praise."

"I find the program's position on X correct and would support . . ."

Sometimes candidates claim a broader view than they are really entitled to:

[ABD candidate]: "Over the course of my academic career, I have always . . ."

And sometimes candidates combine the grandiose and the over-humble:

"My thesis hopes to be part of this crucial conversation . . ."

It is easy to see why job candidates fall prey to grandiosity. Their position could not be more insecure; it's natural to overcompensate. However, effective documents will eschew grandiose claims, and will present the record calmly, without excessive rhetorical flourishes, and with a focus on just the facts. Yes, your work is valuable, but let us come to that conclusion ourselves, OK?

Bottom line: Your dissertation is important, but it is not literally earth shattering, and you are not single-handedly rescuing your field from extinction. Tone it down.

3. Self-Juvenilization

Grad students remain in an extended juvenile status long after their peers outside of academia have moved on to fully adult lives. The outcome is that job seekers may experience themselves as more juvenile than they are, and fall back on self-juvenilizing habits in their efforts to appeal to search committees.

The most common form this takes is the exhaustive narration of graduate school minutiae such as courses taken, comprehensive exam fields, encounters with professors, and adventures of research. This is another form of sounding like a grad student.

Some examples are obvious. "While a grad student in the English Ph.D. program, I . . ." is a sure giveaway. Delete any language that depicts you as a student—either grad student, or, God forbid, undergraduate (read below for more on that). However, most cases are more subtle and involve constant references to grad school process/status. Language such as the following:

> "*After my defense* I will develop a book proposal . . ."

> "I am writing an article *based on chapter two of my dissertation* . . ."

> "I am giving two conference papers *derived from this dissertation research* . . ."

> "*After receiving feedback from my dissertation committee*, I will incorporate revisions into the book manuscript."

> "*As a graduate student teaching assistant*, I taught a course on . . ."

> "*I have six terms of experience as a TA* in the X course, and in that course I focus on . . ."

> "*I not only autonomously taught these three courses, but I was also responsible for creating the syllabi and lesson content.*"

The final three examples are rampant in teaching paragraphs. The final example is a case of overexplaining your record in a way that inadvertently makes you look less experienced, rather than more. If you simply explain how you taught the class, you look like a faculty member. If you laboriously articulate that you were "responsible for creating the syllabi" and so forth, you look like a grad student.

In a similar vein, nobody but you actually cares what chapter your article derives from. They care that you wrote an article, and that that article is published in a high-ranking journal. To anxiously look backward to the chapter it once was is to rehearse your grad student anxieties in public.

Because you have already devoted one or two complete paragraphs to describing the dissertation, its topic, methods, theories, conclusions, and contribution in the cover letter and research statement, there is no reason to keep referring back to it as the context for other professional accomplishments.

The second way candidates juvenilize themselves is in the evocation of childhood identity. "As a child growing up in Bangalore," someone might say, or "When I was a young girl my father always told me . . ." or "Having gone to an all-girls school, I am familiar . . ." I hope it is clear by now that one must never speak of oneself as a child.

Candidates will also wax lyrical about their glory days as undergraduates at small liberal arts colleges when applying for jobs at SLACs. This I call the scourge of liberal arts mush. Here are examples, adapted from actual client letters:

> "I attended a liberal arts college and loved it. During college, I grew enormously intellectually and culturally."

> "I recently visited X College to attend a symposium, and was inspired by the sense of enthusiasm and innovation exuded by faculty and students. The small size of the student body was also inspiring. I attended Y University (which had two thousand undergraduates) and recall with gratitude the close and productive relationships I enjoyed with faculty. Some of them changed my life and set me on my current path. I would leap at the opportunity to develop similar relationships with undergraduates and faculty."

> "Becoming a member of the X College community and fulfilling my passion for liberal arts education would be both an honor and a privilege."

Stop. Just stop, with the love, the honor, the privilege, and the inspiration.

Biologist and blogger Terry McGlynn, in a 2013 column in *Inside Higher Ed*, observed that "many people who apply to liberal arts colleges mention that they were liberal arts college students, suggesting that this experience gives them a better preparation for the job of a liberal arts college professor." He goes on to remark, dryly: "This argument is both pedestrian and non-compelling."[1]

I consider it embarrassing and sycophantic. And profoundly ill conceived. Your fond memories of happy days as a carefree undergrad cavorting about the finely groomed lawns of Wellesley have absolutely no bearing on your suitability for a competitive position as a tenure track assistant professor who must teach at an advanced level, maintain an intensive record of research productivity, and fulfill administrative needs. Of course you must show an understanding of the liberal arts institutional mission, with some specific ideas of how you'll contribute to it. This is different from teary-eyed nostalgia.

Bottom line: Your job documents focus on your academic profile and potential, not on some imagined appeal of your youth.

4. Arrogance

This problem arises most visibly in interviews, in the candidate who talks endlessly about himself to the exclusion of all else. A professor chairing a search once wrote to me to share such an experience with a candidate who far exceeded his allotted time for the research presentation. "He saw me gently signaling," she wrote, but "decided his material was so interesting that he felt it better to take an additional 20 minutes."

This same candidate neglected to ask a single female faculty member in the department about her work. "He met with 10 female faculty, and somehow forgot to say the magic words: 'Tell me about your research,'" the search committee chair noted.

Demonstrate interest in your interviewers. It's true that you are the one being interviewed. But at the stage of the campus visit, they actually already thoroughly know your research. What they are evaluating is your collegiality. Make the human connection, and remember basic principles of sociality: express interest in others, don't talk exclusively about yourself.

Be particularly careful that you're not falling into unfortunate and offensive gender stereotypes. In the words of my search committee chair: "Asking female faculty about the shopping opportunities in the town, but not about their research, isn't the best move."

Bottom line: Remember that a professor is a colleague. Even when she's a woman.

5. Victimhood

The market is awful and it's easy to feel like a victim. However, beware the temptation to take on a victim identity—the identity of the unsuccessful job seeker whose failure proves that it's all a crapshoot, and a con game and nothing that the candidate does has any impact on the corrupt and nepotistic outcomes of tenure track hiring.

Of course, it goes without saying that the job market in the broadest sense is terribly, patently unfair, in that several generations of Ph.D.'s are now victims of an exploitative system that trains them for jobs that no longer exist, and denies that fact. But that doesn't mean that every single outcome is uniformly unfair, or mysterious, or inexplicable, or that every single application outcome is nothing more than a "crapshoot," in the common idiom of post-academic critique. In fact, there is a correlation between the record, the quality of job documents, and the outcome. It is not a perfect correlation, and it is not a correlation that overcomes the basic fact of evaporating tenure track jobs and the wholesale adjunctification of the academy. But it is a correlation nonetheless.

I find it tremendously frustrating that so many unsuccessful job seekers look at their record, and look at their unsuccessful outcome, and complain about the unfairness of it all—without taking a moment to look at their body of writing and speaking that mediates the two—the application documents themselves and their interview skills. One is not born with these things. One acquires them through dedicated effort, sustained practice, deep self-critique, and a willingness to grow and change.

Some of the most vocal public proponents of the crapshoot position, who use their failure to find a tenure track job as proof of the outrageous corruption of the entire academic enterprise, turn out to have job documents that are appallingly bad. I know, because I have had the chance to work with some of them. In some cases, what they were sending out was virtually unshortlistable. After revising it, they have at times encountered different outcomes.

Those most at risk of making a career of victimhood are usually the people most deeply invested in the belief that teaching "should" count for more than research on the job market, and that years of adjunct experience "should" be highly valued, if the ideal of the academy is to be achieved. Many things about the academy should indeed be different. They are right: teaching should be more valued. However, what we know is true is that the university "ideal" is a thing marketed on university websites for the purpose of attracting tuition-paying students, and teaching plays a small and ever decreasing role in that commodity. Application materials must, again, speak to the real circumstances and priorities of search committees in a rapidly downsizing industry, and not the dreams and wishes of candidates.

Changing your individual practices will not guarantee you a job when tenure track jobs barely exist. But changing your individual practices will allow you to control what can be controlled about the job search, and, more important, allow you to maintain a sense of agency about your own fate, whether that lies within the academy or outside of it.

Bottom line: Don't be a victim. Change what you need to, when you need to. Up to and including leaving behind the dream of the academic career.

FORTY

···········

Fear of the Inside Candidate

Most people on the job market fiercely resent the inside candidate, assuming that he has endless advantages over external applicants.

I am here to say that in my experience, this is not true. Indeed, I have often seen the inside candidate get passed over for the job and then suffer the humiliation of watching the tenure track hire proceed in front of him.

The reason that inside candidates tend to do poorly is that they misunderstand the difference between an adjunct and a tenure track search. Adjunct hiring is often decided based on personal relationships, but tenure track hiring? Almost never. Tenure track hiring is cutthroat, and is dominated by an ethos of aspiration. This means that the unknown, who promises seemingly limitless possibility, will almost always prevail over the known, a mere mortal.

Unfortunately, inside candidates often rely on relationship-talk, assuming that their proven dedication to department teaching and service, their "niceness," and their self-sacrifice will win friends and influence people. What niceness, teaching, and service do, for an adjunct, is ensure that you are a perpetual adjunct.

Here are examples of this kind of writing (adapted from actual letters):

"It has been an enormous pleasure and privilege to teach at your department and I would be honored to continue on in a permanent capacity."

"I have been deeply impressed by your commitment to student mentoring and have striven to improve my own mentoring skills during my past year here."

"As you know, my course on Whitman was very popular! I, of course, benefited from the Whitman resources that we are fortunate to have at our library."

"I was honored to be given the duty of directing our Undergraduate Major Association and in that capacity I organized pizza and movie nights, which our students told me were the highlight of the semester."

The word that comes to mind here is "smarmy." Smarmy does not get tenure track jobs.

It is not coincidental that all of these clients were women. I won't say men never do this, but if there was ever a pitfall that women are particularly prone to, this is it.

The only way that the known can compete with the unknown is to present themselves as if they are similarly unknown, or at least, only incompletely known. That is, by submitting materials that make little reference to relationships in the department, and articulating a scholarly profile mostly or completely independent of the department. Of course you should not take this to a bizarre extreme; you DO know them. But don't lean on these relationships, don't build your case around them, don't depend on them to prove your legitimacy or appeal.

The tenure track candidate sells herself on her profile as a scholar. Even at a teaching-oriented school, the tenure track hire is a scholarly hire. And scholarship is not warm and fuzzy. Scholarship is rigorous. It is, by its very nature, not easily accessible to people outside the scholarly circle. The proper ethos of a scholar applying for a tenure track job means remembering that they want you for what they don't see but respect nevertheless, which is your expertise and authority in the field and your productivity.

If you instead pander to them, cater to them, overtly appeal to them, and try to play off of preexisting personal relationships and your ethos of "giving" to the department, you are defining yourself as, fundamentally, not tenure track material. This may be disillusioning. But it is true. I can hear many of you arguing with me. I know your arguments. I've heard them all before. Trust me, they're wrong. Your selfless sacrifices on behalf of the department will not buy you a tenure track offer.

Before I leave the subject of the inside candidate, I will pause to note that you, my reader, might perhaps wonder how to ask if there is an inside candidate for the job to which you're applying.

You do not ask if there is an inside candidate.

I don't care if you strongly suspect that there is, and have good reason to believe the whole search is a completely pointless charade because they obviously already have somebody chosen. It doesn't matter. You must not ask if there is an inside candidate.

Why? Because it's Just. Not. Done. And they will never tell you the truth in any case.

FORTY-ONE

Wrangling Recalcitrant References

The struggle to keep a supply of effective and updated reference letters arriving by deadline is one of the major stresses of the entire job search enterprise.

Even when your relationship is warm and supportive, it feels awful to have to go back to the well over and over, year after year, asking for letter after letter. It is worse when the relationship is neglectful or antagonistic. There are advisors who simply refuse to respond to requests for letters, spoiling their advisees' chances for jobs and fellowships. The advisee has little recourse. In 2014 I had two clients lose their positions on a conference interview short list because a referee failed to submit a letter in time. While in previous eras search committees may have taken the extra step of allowing the candidate to find and submit a replacement letter, in the frantic, bullying atmosphere of searches today, this seems to be an increasingly abandoned courtesy.

At the same time, with the intensification of searches, advisors now have to write a larger number of letters for each advisee. As a job seeker, there are ways that you can reduce this burden and ease the process. A frantic email request at midnight, one day before the due date, with no email address or mailing address or description of the job, is not going to yield optimal results.

A considerate way to request reference letters is to create an Excel spreadsheet with columns for each job/grant specifying:

- the deadline
- the contact email/website
- the snail mail address (still essential for the heading of the letter, even when it is sent electronically)
- the contact person's name
- the description of the job or grant
- notes with ideas for tailoring

This spreadsheet should be created at least a month in advance of the deadlines. Given this spreadsheet, referees need only cut and paste addresses into the letter file, and quickly add a few points of tailoring for the job at hand. With the bulk of requests sent well ahead of time, the occasional last-minute request can be accommodated without resentment.

If you are a job seeker and your references are providing letters on time, by all means continue to request them. Do not fall into codependent tendencies to "protect" them from "too much" work by preemptively turning to a reference letter dossier service (dossier services store generic letters provided by referees and send them out to search committees for a fee). It is not your job to caretake your referees and adjust your needs to their assumed convenience.

Of course, even with efforts such as these, some job seekers cannot reliably extract letters from their referees. In such cases, you may consider turning to dossier services such as Interfolio. If your advisor has proven that she cannot be counted on to provide letters on time for your job and postdoc and grant deadlines, then you will want to consider a dossier service. Similarly, if your advisor has told you point-blank that he refuses to write personalized letters for students in general/you in particular then, again, you may have to use a dossier service. If your advisor is ailing, elderly and infirm, or dead, then, too, a dossier letter is an excellent thing to have.

However, outside these conditions, it is my position that job candidates should hope for and expect personalized letters for every job and postdoc to which they apply and should look long and hard at advisors who balk at that responsibility. A faculty member certainly is not obliged to write for every student who asks. But a faculty member is obliged to write for those students whom she genuinely supports. Please recall that with the marvelous invention of computers, professors no longer have to inscribe each word of every letter laboriously by hand. A few edits to name and address, with a few fresh words speaking to the job or grant, and voilà, a personalized letter can be supplied with but a few minutes' work. Ph.D.-level training is slow, painstaking, and highly individualized. It is not a mass-market process, and it never can be. Its extreme personalization, based on a relationship built over years between a graduate student and his/her advisor, means that every Ph.D. student finishes with the personal imprimatur of that advisor. These relationships at the heart of the graduate enterprise are reflected in the lengthy, detailed, and personal letters of reference that the advisor and committee members write for the student.

Even when an advisor has many advisees, all applying to multiple jobs, tailored templates minimize the time and effort involved. Advisors can streamline their letter writing by maintaining a set of four or five letter templates for each applicant, tailored for particular types of jobs. In my case, I maintained letter draft files for my advisees pre-drafted for research-oriented anthropology jobs, teaching-oriented anthropology jobs, research-oriented Asian studies jobs, teaching-oriented Asian studies jobs, and also postdocs. Because so much tailoring was already done within each of these templates, very little remained to be done for individual applications. It is, of course, the advisee's responsibility to feed the writer updated information about publications, conferences, grants, and awards in new versions of the spreadsheet, so that the templates can be kept current.

I would argue that if a letter writer is proving unreliable or obdurate, then the solution is not always to give up and settle for a dossier letter, but to consider finding a different letter writer. While the advisor's letter is difficult to replace for the first couple of years after the Ph.D., you are not tied to other committee members. In all things, be aware of field conventions. English leads the way in dossier letters, while my own field of Anthropology remains invested in the personalized letter.

Not only does Interfolio institutionalize advisor abandonment of the letter-writing responsibility; it is also the perfect sign of the neoliberal regime in that it transfers the costs of applying for jobs from the institution onto the candidate, who increasingly has no choice but to pay for each letter generated, adding to the obligatory and non-optional costs of the job search.

In 2014, the Modern Language Association signed an agreement with Interfolio to formalize its use for most job applications in MLA fields. This agreement makes Interfolio's services free or low cost to candidates for some positions. On the other hand, of course, it tacitly authorizes the generic letter. Interfolio marketed this new plan to job seekers by touting alleged "ease of application," "transparency in the hiring process," and, best of all, "allowing scholars time to be scholars." Interfolio elaborates: "Whether you're a candidate for a position or a member of a Search Committee, the necessary work takes time away from your primary roles as a scholar. So, whether you're using our dossier service, [or] our confidential letter writing service, we want you to be able to work as quickly and efficiently in these tasks so you can return to your primary professional role."

Because apparently the one thing scholars don't do is go to much trouble to help other scholars get jobs to continue being scholars. Interfolio's tagline is "Free the faculty." Who on the job market is more in need of protection and accommodation, after all, than the tenured faculty reference letter writers?

The increasing reliance on Interfolio is part of the transfer of costs and responsibilities of the job search from institutions onto individual job seekers who can ill afford them. When advisors, departments, and jobs impose the use of Interfolio on job candidates, it is also part of the neoliberal transformation of the academy. However, when professional organizations dictate the use of Interfolio for applications, then resistance may well be futile. The personalized letter may go extinct.

FORTY-TWO

Managing Your Online Presence

The days of asking "Should I have a website?" are past. You have an online presence. The question is—are you managing it? This is no time to passively wonder when you'll ever get around to creating a website. Rather, mobilize all the abundant resources of the Internet to proactively pursue your academic and career goals. I'm no techie, and my website (which I built in 2010 and in 2015 still maintain myself) is not particularly sophisticated or elegant, but I do know that a legible and well-curated online presence is central to a professional profile at this point in time. As Kelli Marshall writes in an excellent compendium of advice on this matter, "In a nutshell, if you do not have a clear online presence, you are allowing Google, Yahoo, and Bing to create your identity for you."[1]

During your job search, you'll very likely be Googled by somebody on a search committee. Faculty do not usually do this to try to expose unsavory information about you, but rather to get a broader sense of your profile. As one R1 tenured professor told me, "I'm not looking for social 'dirt' on candidates, but want to see what their professional/academic online presence is. If nothing comes up, for me that is a bad sign. I would rather see them engaged online in some fashion—blog, Twitter, grad student conference, panel listing at the national conference program, publications, academia.edu, anything really—than nothing at all."

The things search committees are looking for will, of course, reflect the field, the position, and the committee member's own preoccupations. For example, rare is the position in English these days that does not include a digital humanities subspecialty, and search committee members there will seek evidence of your involvement with digital humanities initiatives. If the faculty member is someone who is invested in public, open-access scholarship, they'll certainly be curious to see if you are active in those circles. Similarly, they may look for teaching materials such as syllabi and course evaluations, or even wander into RateMyProfessors.com, although never fear—no faculty member is ever likely to take those findings at face value. On the research front, search committees might want to access your publications and conference talks.

Search committees may well find nothing from an online search that wasn't already apparent in the application materials. And that's fine. Your online profile doesn't have to provide more data points, but it does give a richer impression of you as a candidate. A survey of your Internet footprint will reveal things about your social style—are you reserved? Sarcastic? Opinionated? Supportive? This speaks to your potential collegiality. It also reveals the academic circles in which you participate. This speaks to your academic community.

The important thing is that you manage your online impression in a proactive way. Marshall writes, "The best advice: Search your own name, particularly if you're going on the job market and perhaps also if you're going up for tenure. See what committees will see when they engage with you digitally." Creating your own website that brings together the disparate elements of your profile allows you to be in charge of your message. Remember your platform? Your website can foreground each of its elements. The goal here is a carefully curated image that is consistent.

Your website does not need to be complicated. Standards of Web design in academia remain low, and nobody will judge you for a rudimentary approach. If it's functional, it's fine. It is no longer necessary to know HTML, and using drag-and-drop site-builders like Weebly, Squarespace, and Wix, you can build one in a day.

The landing page of the website will feature your photograph. Your picture does not have to be a posed portrait, but it should be serious. No shots of you at the beach, or running a marathon, or playing with your baby. All of these things are fine to do, but they are not fine to foreground in your professional self-presentation. Another option is an action shot from your research site, lab, or classroom. No matter what type of photographs you choose, attend to your clothing. No halter tops or bathing suits or cocktail dresses or bare chests or beer logo T-shirts (and yes, I've seen all of these). For consistency, the photograph you use should also be used across other platforms, such as Google+ and Twitter.

Besides the photograph, the landing page will feature a short, non-jargony summary of your profile in research and teaching, and current projects. Additional pages will feature your CV, teaching info (syllabi, course descriptions), publications, recent or upcoming talks, and so forth. You can embed videos of your presentations or teaching, add links to academic articles as well as public writing, and include student projects. Keep the content professional, and for the most part eschew family, hobbies, and pets.

It is not essential that you blog. If you do blog, give thought that the content is consistent with your platform, and does not contradict or distract from it. Beware highly polemical content, which can alienate readers, and unserious content ("I was watching *The Bachelorette* last night and . . ."—unless, of course, your research is on reality TV!).

Think also about quantity. You want the blog to act in support of your academic profile, and never to overwhelm it. If you post every day, but have no record of refereed journal articles, search committees are absolutely going to draw the conclusion that your priorities are not where they should be for tenure. Make no mistake about that.

If the thought of putting together a simple website overwhelms you, you can, of course, consider a basic academia.edu page. Minimalistic and not really customizable, academia.edu still offers the flexibility to post most of the elements of your record, including papers, talks, CV, syllabi, and student work. The same goes for a Google+ profile. Both academia.edu and Google+ have high rankings in Google search algorithms, so they're likely to be the first things seen.

No matter what platform you use, keep it up to date. You'd never send an outdated CV for a job, so don't let your online profile reflect an outdated record.

Turning now to the question of social media: Many graduate students avoid sites such as Facebook and Twitter out of fear that a social media presence will somehow harm them. This is unfortunate. Social media allows for connection, and connection allows for networking (a far more comfortable networking than stalking a stranger at a conference, sweaty business card in hand). Networking creates relationships, and relationships lead to publishing opportunities, conference invitations, and, ultimately, jobs.

By engaging your scholarly circles on Facebook and Twitter, you expand your reputation exponentially. You make online friends, some of whom translate into face-to-face friends and collaborators. When you apply for a job, you may have a foot in the door, and it helps. Twitter may not get you a job directly, but it brings you to the attention of the people who may one day be hiring.

But use caution. In a notorious case from summer 2014, Steven Salaita, a professor of American Indian studies, saw his tenured position at the University of Illinois at Urbana-Champaign rescinded (after he had already given up his previous tenured position and moved across the country) as a result of incendiary anti-Israel tweets he made over the summer. The Salaita case raises a host of serious issues related to free speech and academic freedom, and reflects a chilled environment of surveillance of faculty social media activity. However, for job seekers the primary lesson to be drawn here is not to reject Twitter. It is to use Twitter constructively and conservatively. The Salaita case notwithstanding, search committee members don't typically dig deep into your timeline to unearth compromising material. So don't be paranoid; just be smart. Use social media, but keep the content engaged but "appropriate" according to today's conservative standards of public discourse. I personally deplore the implications for political discourse and critique that this "conservative standard" implies. But either way, I reiterate, for the purposes of your job search, the benefits of social media still outweigh its risks, as long as you are willing to acknowledge that you are operating in an increasingly surveilled environment.

Besides Twitter and Facebook there are other sites to consider, including LinkedIn, Instagram, and so on—the list grows and changes constantly. Not all of these are necessary—indeed, don't spread yourself too thin. Any social media presence should support your academic productivity, not compete with it. While it's possible to feel overwhelmed by the demands of the Internet, the ease with which it facilitates connections, networking, and the exchange of ideas makes it indispensable to your career, as long as you manage it with care and caution.

....

FORTY-THREE

Evaluating Campus Climate

If you're seeking your first job, you'll likely accept an offer almost anywhere, because in this market, beggars can't be choosers. But if you have a choice to turn down a possible offer, and, frankly, even if you don't, it is wise to examine campus climate as thoroughly as possible. In the former case, so you can make an educated decision about taking the job, and in the latter case, so you can accurately anticipate what you'll find there once you arrive.

I learned the hard way that heartbreak can arise from failing to properly grasp the campus climate for a position under consideration. I failed to heed the warnings when I went to my campus visit for a tenured position at the large Midwestern R1 that I eventually fled in despair. If I had paid more attention, I might have seen signs of the issues that eventually defeated me, and saved myself years of anguish. Of course, it's hard to say. The fleeting impressions of two days on campus will not necessarily justify turning down a job that looks perfect on paper.

Still, there are things you can do to gather your impressions. Be a good detective, and know what you're getting into.

The first thing to do is visit the student union. During some break in your schedule, if you have one, get a cup of coffee and plant yourself right in the middle of wherever is most crowded. Eavesdrop on conversations and take in the vibe. Are the students lively, excited, engaged? Do you hear talk about books and ideas? Or only who got wasted last Friday night and who's going to get wasted this Friday night?

At one campus visit to an elite West Coast institution, I was flabbergasted at the sheer intellectual force emanating from the students around me in the union. I grasped as never before, in that moment, the gulf between the place at which I had trained, and the place at which I hoped to be employed. By contrast, at Midwestern U, I might have noticed that the student union had little intellectual energy. Because you've been so thoroughly shaped by your own Ph.D. institution, you may not know exactly what questions to ask on a campus visit to pinpoint these differences (and indeed any questions that loaded would be a poor choice). But the student union can communicate volumes about levels of student preparation and support, the rigor of intellectual life, and campus morale.

While in the student union, study the flyers and posters. Is the campus lively and full of interesting events? Do you see four different campus Republican groups, but no Green Party? Or the reverse? If the queer community is important to you, do you see signs for queer events and groups? These posters, as well as any online calendars of events, will show you how easily you'll find like-minded souls among the faculty and student body.

Pick up the student newspaper and browse the editorials. Are they far to the right? To the left? Read the articles. Are they substantive? Do they engage with campus life in a meaningful way? Or are they shallow and painfully full of basic grammatical errors and logical flaws? This was another clue I missed in my Midwestern U visit. These things tell you more about the caliber of the student body than anything a faculty member will say.

Observe mealtimes during the visit. At lunches and dinners, do the faculty chat easily with one another? Do they show a familiarity with one another's families? If wine is served at dinner, do people kick back over a bottle or two and dig in for a long, lively evening, as was the case at my visit for my first job? Or do people stick to a single glass, and wrap up dinner as quickly as possible, as was the case at my second?

Conversely, is anyone drinking too much? I was once at an East Coast campus visit where I was driven to and from dinner by a senior faculty member who was obviously drunk, and who, I came to learn, was a well-known alcoholic. His behavior and the efforts of other faculty members to manage it had shaped the department in a host of unfortunate ways. That job I removed from consideration.

Pay particular attention to the grad students, as they are the canaries in the coal mine. You cannot just come out and ask them "Are you happy?" "Are the faculty jerks?" or "Is this department as crazy as it seems?" They will never reveal department secrets to you. But you can ask "Do you feel your needs are met in the department?" or "Do you have a voice in governance?" Simple questions like these will unleash a torrent of candid remarks. By reading between the lines, you will be able to tell whether the department has a supportive and democratic ethos or a cold and hierarchical one, and whether problems in the department are solved or left to fester.

If you are concerned about issues of gender, race, sexual orientation, disability, and so on, make your best efforts to inquire (indirectly if necessary) with others who share your identity about their satisfaction in the department. Don't fail to study campus data for information on demographics, promotion rates, and so on.

Pay attention to the audience for your job talk. Is it widely attended by both faculty and grad students, who listen carefully and engage deeply? Or, do you find yourself speaking to a half-empty room? At the campus visit with the alcoholic faculty member, the department secretary constituted one-fifth of the assembled audience for my job talk. Fortunately I had a choice.

In the end, you'll never know with absolute certainty what you're getting into. But by using your human senses and studying the clues I describe here, you can piece together a portrait of the campus as a place to work and live.

FORTY-FOUR

When You Feel Like You Don't Belong

I think it's safe to say that almost everyone feels like they "don't be-long" in the academy at one point or another in their graduate training and job search. It's such a closed, insular, and elitist sys-tem, and so profoundly based on status jockeying around grada-tions of knowledge and ignorance (Do you know more than me, or do I know more than you?) that people come out of graduate school hazing mostly having absorbed the firm idea that they don't know anything, and that this fact must be concealed at all costs.

There are gradations, of course, and those gradations will likely track along lines of privilege.

Academia was a system created by elite white men and for elite white men, and elite white men continue to dominate its ranks, particularly at the level of full professor and administrator. While I know and have worked with white men who struggle mightily with feeling intellectually unworthy, these types of struggles are magni-fied when the scholar deviates from the norm. Women, students of color, first-generation students, queer and older students . . . all of those coming from marginalized positions fight a mighty battle to claim a space at the academic table, and to find a voice in academic debates. They also often find themselves cut out of the academic prestige circles or relationships through which cultural capital, un-taught knowledge, and opportunities flow. The elite (and white) old boys' network is a real thing.

One common response to this state of affairs is Imposter Syndrome, which refers to the constant nagging doubt that, regardless of your achievements, you are about to be exposed as a fraud. Women are far more prone to Imposter Syndrome than men, due to countless forms of policing of female behavior around speech, dress, and assertiveness throughout their lives. For many women, the default to "I must be wrong" is almost automatic, and rarely consciously recognized. When this is imposed on top of the incessant judgments and critique of grad school training, it can become debilitating.

Imposter Syndrome strikes hardest when someone feels isolated and, by virtue of their identity, somehow deviant from established systems of academic authority. It's likely to be felt keenly, in some form or another, by anyone outside the norm for any reason—race, gender, sexuality, class, body size, physical limitations, family educational status, and so forth. It's likely to be reinforced by microaggressions that those who deviate from the norm experience in an ongoing way throughout their academic career.

If you feel uncertain about where you belong in the academy based on elements of your identity, there are several steps you can take.

First off, in establishing your platform, be conscious about the degree to which you link your identity and your scholarly profile. The choice is completely personal, but should always be intentional. Do you wish to make your own identity a foundation for your research, framing your identity as well as your research both as interventions in your field? In other words, as a lesbian of color, for example, is your agenda to speak up on behalf of lesbians of color in the academy overtly, and prioritize lesbian of color viewpoints in your research and the content of your courses? That is fine, but know that the more you do, the greater price you will likely pay. While some jobs will welcome, even invite, such embodied interventions in the epistemological and methodological practices of the field, more jobs remain "generalist" and will be wary of candidates who appear "polemical" or, as it's commonly and evasively phrased, "too narrow." Search committees are happiest when they can acquire a "diversity" candidate who does not in any way disrupt established disciplinary systems of knowledge and practice. For most jobs out-side of ethnic studies or women and gender studies, if they can hire a lesbian of color who does what appears to be "neutral" and "ob-jective" research unconnected to topics of race, gender, or sexual-ity, that is a "win" (from the hiring institution's perspective). Do not proceed in ignorance of that fact.

Second, be sure that your identity is clear in your job documents, if you count as a diversity candidate. In the United States, racial minority candidates typically qualify, while queer, first-generation, and other candidates do not (although queer candidates count for diversity purposes in Canada). Sometimes this is field dependent. While in the humanities women are by no means a specially re-cruited group, in the STEM fields they certainly are. When commu-nicating your diversity identity, it is best to link it to the substance of your record in some way, rather than simply announcing "By the way, I am black" (for example). In my work with clients, I find that they tend to either not mention their identity at all because they don't know how, or else devote an entire paragraph of the job let-ter to a long, involved story about the painful trials and tribulations they had to overcome to get the Ph.D. and how passionate they are about mentoring students in similar circumstances. Both of these are mistakes. The first, obviously, because diversity hiring is a door that you want to make sure is open to you, if you qualify. The sec-ond, because even when speaking of your identity, you still have to remember the basic rules of job documents: Show, don't tell; es-chew adjectives and emotion; focus on professional outcomes not personal process; remain factual and evidence based. This is par-ticularly so when a person of color is engaging with a white search committee that does not want to be uncomfortably reminded of the existence of racism.

One good approach is to open the teaching paragraph of your job letter with a phrase like: "As a Native American/African Amer-ican/Latina/queer/disabled scholar, I am sensitive to issues of di-versity in the classroom/I prioritize a diversity of perspectives in my classroom/I make a point to include a range of diverse voices in my classroom. In all of my courses I assign readings by X and Y, and incorporate projects that include P and Q." You can then add a line such as, "Because of my background I am familiar with challenges faced by students of color/queer students/students with disabilities, and am committed to mentoring them for success in the university setting."

Why does this work? Because it makes your identity an asset in your work for the department. You are showing in concrete and evidence-based ways how your identity informs and enriches your pedagogy, and by extension the pedagogical offerings of the department as a whole. This is just one example, of course. You can make similar pitches related to service, although be very wary of that, as excessive service is the single greatest threat to minority candidates' well being and tenurability.

You can, of course, write similarly with regard to your research, but the advantages here, in terms of the job search, are not as clear. Departments are going to be less moved by invoking diversity in research than teaching, because departments are less interested in understanding race than they are tokenistically demonstrating to higher administration, accrediting agencies, state legislatures, and the community at large that they offer the concrete, and commodified, value of "diversity" (i.e., brown faces) directly to their student-consumers.

In any case, the larger point here is this: A flat statement of identity, or a story of struggle based on identity, is valuable in many contexts but not in job documents, because these do not do the work that your job documents need to do. To be effective, your identity must be shown to inform your contributions to the department, and that is most easily achieved by demonstrating how it is mobilized in specific contexts of classroom teaching and student mentoring.

Third, carefully consider your articulation of profile in your job documents. Marginalized candidates may want to use the classroom as a site of critical intervention on politicized topics. Departments, however, may need assurances that you can also teach generic bread-and-butter topics in the discipline. So along with that innovative interrogation of homophobia in popular media, be sure to also give an example of teaching general theories of communication. Along with the class on Japanese American internment, include the class on historiographical methods. Remember that no new hire gets to teach exclusively in their niche. Everybody in traditional disciplinary departments has to show the ability to teach the discipline at large. Yes, this is the imposition of traditional (white/male) disciplinarity as the unmarked norm, situating the study of race, gender, sexuality, etc., as marginal "special interests."[1] Nevertheless, this stance informs most hiring decisions.

Fourth, do your homework. Before you apply, after you apply, and particularly before you go to an interview or campus visit, investigate: How is the campus for people like you? Mobilize both the Internet and your personal network. However, don't contact the search committee ahead of time to ask anxious preemptive questions such as "I'm worried about the environment for women in your department." Few departments will respond well to that during the search process itself. After an offer is made, there is more opportunity.

Fifth, when you are invited for an interview, you are entitled to seek any necessary accommodations, and should do so courteously but firmly and nonapologetically. Be specific about what you require in accommodations for disabilities. Don't expect them to read your mind. In a minor but illustrative example, I have an anaphylactic allergy to tree nuts (but not peanuts). When I visit a campus, I can't simply tell them, "I can't have tree nuts at meals," because people without the allergy have no idea where tree nuts hide or even what tree nuts really are. Left to their own devices they will cancel the harmless peanut (not a tree nut)-filled Thai restaurant, and take me to the Middle Eastern restaurant that has pistachios and almonds in half the dishes. It's on me to explain, "I can eat X but not Y. Z restaurants are safest." Always be a clear advocate for yourself and your needs.

Sixth, while on campus, investigate its climate thoroughly, using the techniques I discussed in chapter 43. Be a detective, and remain alert to every clue. See if you can quietly feel out the environment by talking with those who share your identifications.

Seventh, you may indeed encounter jerks on your campus visit. They may ask you inappropriate questions, as I discussed in chapter 37. It is often said that "you are interviewing them as much as they are interviewing you." This is a very weak truism indeed in a desperate job market where you'll take just about any job offered regardless of conditions. Nevertheless, you want to know what you're getting into, and who is a likely ally and who isn't. You can draw valuable conclusions from a close, critical observation of your potential colleagues. Any inappropriate questions you encounter, as well as other colleagues' reactions to these questions, will reveal useful insights into the political and emotional landscape of the department. An African-American historian I know reflected on one dinner during a campus visit: "While I sat discussing my research with the department chair, two faculty members directly across from me—both white men—began a loud and slightly uncomfortable argument about whether or not lives improved for African Americans after the abolition of slavery." He continued, "I remember thinking, *'Don't say anything. Be quiet. Focus on the other person, don't forget about showing that you fit!'* " He went on, "The amount of effort to remain poised with a department chair while two potential white colleagues debated black lives as an abstract concept was considerable, to say the least." Even without reacting in the moment, however, he knew that this department would not be a comfortable one.

What to do in a situation like this? Whatever you do, don't lose your cool. The campus visit is no time to blow your top, get angry, get snarky, or lecture faculty on racism or employment law. At the same time, be protective of yourself, even in a desperate market. I strongly believe that nobody should take a job at which they feel explicitly attacked or disrespected. Take the high road in the moment, and file all impressions carefully to evaluate and discuss with trusted comrades later.

Eighth, and this is a hard one, try not to go into the market in a defensive stance. It's easy to dread all the judgments that might be awaiting you, but remember that graduate school inculcates a level of paranoia that is not always completely rational. Don't forget that while you hold fast to your political and ethical convictions, like all candidates you still have to demonstrate your work's significance, originality, and import according to broad disciplinary standards and norms. As much as possible, relate your work to themes compelling to the discipline at large. A candidate who is unsuccessful might assume, "I was rejected because I was X," when the reason for the rejection is that the job documents did nothing to communicate the broad contribution of the project to those search committee members who might not share or immediately understand the client's identity and agenda. In a broader sense, as I write above, this is of course still the imposition of traditional disciplinarity as the unmarked norm. But if you can demonstrate how you operate within the unmarked norm, you will be able to enter the institution and effect the change you want.

A case in point from work with a client. This client was a queer sociologist, and in her cover letter she described her research on an American queer cultural practice in terms that could be summarized something like this: "This queer cultural practice by queer people expresses queer identity and represents queer empowerment (for queer people). My Queer Studies course shows how this is the case." She asked me why I thought she wasn't getting any traction for Sociology jobs, and if it was because of homophobia.

I told her that indeed homophobia is always a possibility and there certainly may be faculty members who are thinking (consciously or not), "Ew, queer person! Yuck!" But this is, I told her, far from the only (or even main) problem with her candidacy. I said, "Your project reads like queer cheerleading. It does not read like sociological analysis. You don't engage with sociological theory at all, and you don't demonstrate any investment in teaching Sociology outside of a narrow scope of queer topics, or being able to engage with graduate students working on any thematics except queer ones." Going back to her job documents, we reframed the approach, so that it read something like this: "This queer cultural practice is an example of [sociological concept]. It can best be understood through the lens of [sociological theory]. I examined it through [sociological methods]. I argue that it represents [sociological analysis]. It is a useful example of [sociological phenomenon] when teaching courses such as [mainstream Sociology course]." With this adjustment, she instantly represented herself as competitive for a much wider range of potential positions. Homophobia is real, but so are broad departmental teaching needs.

I'm not saying discrimination doesn't happen. It happens in all kinds of ways. Not just in overt hostility and policing, but also in an overt or covert impression of tokenism, as discussed by philosopher Keisha Ray, who tried to make sense of a suspiciously large number of initial interview invitations she received (59). "When you are different and you are aware that departments are increasingly being required to at least show they have made an attempt to hire diverse faculty, you start to question why you are really conducting an interview."[2] She wondered if she was there just "so faculty can show their dean or HR department that at least they interviewed someone diverse?" The African American historian quoted earlier concurs. "There's a sense of insecurity that followed me on the market: Was I being evaluated as a diversity hire above my scholarship? Did other people think I was?"

What can you do? Subject all elements of your research, teaching, application materials, and interview performance to a rigorous and unflinching scrutiny, to check if you really made the best case for yourself that you can in the broadest and most inclusive way you can. And approach the process with a balance of caution and curiosity. As the historian, who ultimately found a satisfying tenure track position at an institution that is "mostly white but conscientious and friendly," concludes: "I've found that a polite half-smile (even if it has to be pasted on at times), quiet question asking, and doing due diligence in reading up on your potential institution will help you navigate the process considerably."

Ninth, if you are offered the job, and have a choice about taking it, mobilize your network to study the larger environment of both campus and the locale. Will you be safe? Will you be comfortable? Will you find a critical mass of people like you? If you decide to take it, be proactive. Use your network to find connections to help you in your transition. Seek advice on everything from where to look for housing to which gym to join to where to get your hair done. Things like this are important to your comfort and well-being; don't minimize them. If offered the position, remember that discrimination is more intense at the stage of tenure than it is at hiring. Any minority new hire (an African American in almost any department, a woman in STEM fields, and so on) will likely have to meet a considerably higher bar for tenure than their white male counterparts while being subjected to impossible service demands. Confront this truth immediately, and start right away laying the groundwork for what will likely be an inequitably demanding tenure case.

Tenth, when negotiating your contract, be vigilant. Women are generally offered less than men. Minority candidates may find themselves saddled with an unreasonable service expectation. While running a new certificate program in African American studies may sound exciting and inspiring, it's also death to your tenure case in English if it's not accompanied by significant reductions in your teaching and research load. Beware the lowball offer and the excessive service expectation both. Work with a trusted mentor who is in your field and familiar with the type and rank of department you are dealing with. Ask them to help you ensure that your offer includes fair and reasonable service expectations and compensation, and make sure that all negotiated elements are spelled out in writing.

A note on salaries: I explain in my chapters on negotiating that one should never under any circumstances trust the national salary average tables published in the *Chronicle of Higher Education* and such places, not because they are untrustworthy, but because salaries are so variable at the assistant professor level, and so contingent on completely local department, college, and campus economies, that national averages almost always lead you astray in your particular negotiation. In other words, averages are helpful as aggregate data; they are treacherous for a particular negotiation. Don't instantly assume that discrimination is at play when salaries don't match what you expect. Work with your mentor to investigate.

Finally: If you don't get the job, try to hold onto a space of calm. It may have been because of who you are. And it may not. It's difficult to say. There are so many variables in any search that nobody can anticipate them all. Keep working to make your record irrefutable, be realistic about the systemic obstacles to finding permanent work in the academy, and lay the groundwork for moving on to post-academic options.

Do women, people of color, and others in marginalized positions have to do twice as much to get half the credit? Why yes, yes they do. A 2014 study, for example, established that women in sociology are 51 percent less likely to get tenure than men, even when equivalent in research productivity. In computer science, they are 55 percent less likely. The researcher's conclusion: "Women must be more productive than men if they want to earn tenure at a research university."[3] Is any of this fair? No. But if you want the goal of an academic career to work out for you, construct a record and a set of application materials that make you hard to reject, and be vigilant, if and when you get an offer, that you set yourself up to avoid excessive service and teaching, and meet the highest possible bar for tenure, to which you will likely be held.

FORTY-FIVE

What If You're Pregnant?

All of the regular challenges of the job market are magnified when you are pregnant or dealing with a newborn baby. And then there are additional problems particular to your status: When should you disclose the pregnancy, and should you seek accommodations? What if you're put on bed rest during the height of the interview season? And what about bias? Academia is all about the mind, and doesn't easily accommodate the demands of the body. A visibly pregnant woman may not look like a "real" scholar in the eyes of some faculty members, and may indeed make some interviewers openly uncomfortable. Yet the number of pregnant job candidates is steadily increasing as more and more women go into the academy, and departments are under pressure to accommodate their needs. Compared to years ago, a pregnant job candidate has a good chance of being able to juggle her pregnancy and the job search with some hope of success.

If you are or will shortly be visibly pregnant and have received an invitation to an interview, it is probably wise to inform the person at the department with whom you've been corresponding that you are pregnant. "By the way," you might write, "I just wanted to mention that I'm six months pregnant. This will not impact my visit in any way; I mention just so nobody is too startled when I arrive."

I suggest this because, while your state of pregnancy may not impact your interview performance, springing a pregnant belly on an unsuspecting search committee or dinner group might not produce ideal results. Given the questionable social skills of so many academics, wildly awkward or inappropriate comments are not hard to imagine. If possible, forestall that possibility with a little advance warning.

If you are invited to an interview or campus visit, and then find yourself put on bed rest, request the accommodation of a Skype alternative. More than one of my readers has shared a story of conducting a full day of faculty interviews and job talk from her hospital bed, and still getting the job.

Once you have the baby, you're confronted with a different set of challenges. If you're breast-feeding, you will have to pump. If you are pumping, ask for the accommodation of a quiet, private, hygienic space. We hope that this will be a comfortable, private office, but readers tell me it may well be a bathroom or even a broom closet. Wherever it is, make sure your schedule includes an adequate number and length of breaks to pump, as well as a refrigerator for storing the breast milk. You will have to spell out these requirements in detail; don't expect them to know.

When your newborn doesn't take a bottle, you will either need to speed-wean her, or bring her along. The latter is no mean feat, but it has been done. Readers who accomplished it brought a family member to the visit, at their own expense, to care for the baby and take her to the department for regular nursing breaks.

It probably helps if you can make the arrangement for these accommodations with a female secretary or faculty member who is familiar with the requirements of pumping or nursing. But don't assume a man will not assist in this, although chances are younger men will have more cultural knowledge of nursing and pumping than older ones. This type of accommodation request is becoming more common, and departments are gaining experience in dealing with it.

As you anticipate your baby's arrival, be clear on one thing: your life will change drastically and your productivity will, for a period, evaporate. If you are currently pregnant with your first child, you probably have plans for finishing this article or that chapter, or going to this or that conference, one or two or three months after the birth. I am here to tell you, that is probably not going to happen. You will not be writing or giving public talks for a number of months.

When you do get back to work some months later, you will discover that your work will have to be done in fifteen- or thirty- or, at best, sixty-minute chunks, and nothing will ever feel finished. This is not your imagination. Nothing will ever really be finished, the way it was before you had a baby. Life with a baby is a life of juggling competing nonnegotiable imperatives, and your academic tasks now have to be scheduled amid a surprisingly inflexible routine of day care, naps, playtime, mealtimes, and bedtimes. Add to that the hormonal fog that will envelop you for some part of the baby's first year, and you'll find that your pace of writing and your focus have both dropped.

Don't worry—you'll get it all back. And you'll be happier for it. What you need to make that happen is, above all, reliable child care. Line up child care, and then line up backup child care for when your first line of child care falls through.

Speaking of hormones, your moods might swing wildly during pregnancy and after the birth (mine certainly did, not that anyone could tell the difference). That's normal. But if you find yourself chronically depressed, angry, or withdrawn after your baby is born, unable to bond with your baby, or feeling suicidal, get help. That is postpartum depression and it is serious, but it can be treated.

In the meantime, if you're planning a pregnancy while on the job market, my advice is finish every last piece of writing you can before that baby arrives. Write like a maniac every waking instant up until you actually go into labor. If you're working on an article, finish it and submit it to the journal. If you are doing the dissertation, finish a complete draft if you can. And if you think you'll be needing a job talk, well, write one preemptively, even if you haven't yet gotten any invitations, or maybe even submitted any applications. These are the last precious months you will have before your life is turned upside down by a really cranky, adorable stranger who cries constantly and sleeps little and needs you all the time. You don't want deadlines hanging over your head while you get to know this little being, so get as many of them out of the way as you can before she arrives.

FORTY-SIX

·················

What Not to Wear

One of the saddest sights in the hotel conference hall is the ineptly dressed interview candidate—the one in the ill-fitting suit with too-short sleeves and too-long pants, rushing through the halls clutching a tattered old backpack. That person smells of desperation. Don't let it be you.

Yes, we all know that many actual faculty members dress like slobs. Nevertheless, interviews require interview wear. Make yourself look like you are already employed and earning a regular income. Is this classist? Yes. Academia is classist, and knowing how to dress is one of the codes of belonging you must master. Clothing marks you as an insider, and micro-practices will differ based on your particular discipline, field, and subfield, as well as the institutional norms appropriate for the rank, type, and geographical location of the school at which you're interviewing. All have their own sartorial sign systems that should not be ignored.

When I was a first-year assistant professor at West Coast U, we ran a search for a senior cultural anthropologist. One candidate came for his campus visit from an Ivy League school. As he launched into his job talk, I noticed that ever so naturally, without breaking stride, he quietly removed his suit jacket, and ever so insouciantly, rolled up his sleeves. He may even have loosened his tie. Why? Because he'd scanned the room there in the Northwest, and realized that his dark blue East Coast Ivy League suit was entirely out of place in that shaggy, casual environment. He needed to look a bit more like an "insider," and within a few minutes, he did. He got the job.

As a junior candidate you will, of course, need to err on the side of formality, and think twice before removing your jacket. But the story does illuminate the ways that attentive and experienced candidates attend closely to their sartorial surroundings.

In this chapter I'll focus first on recommendations for women who present as women. I'll spare a few words for men, and then finish with some advice on professional wear for gender nonconforming women.

For women who present as women, a new, stylish, well-cut, fitted gray, brown, or black suit, or skirt and jacket, or dress and jacket combo, should be acquired fresh for the interview season. This must fit you at your current weight. It must also fit you properly through the shoulders and across the bust, and hit you at the proper spot on your hips and wrists. If you are uncertain, find someone with fashion knowledge and taste to evaluate these matters of fit. An objective opinion is usually valuable in matters of weight and fit.

Have your hair cut and styled in an actual current style, not dragging or sproinging about in the stringy or unkempt clump so commonly seen in our graduate lounges. Also, no barrettes. You are not nine. Ponytails are tricky; they can look childish or stylish, depending on how they're done. Get some expert advice on yours, if you have one. Meanwhile, remember that it is not actually illegal for an academic to have a trendy haircut. You will be astounded at what a good haircut does for your confidence.

Makeup is optional, of course. If you use it, lean away from Wet N Wild and more toward L'Oréal and Revlon. No need to go into the overpriced department store brands at this stage in your career. I like Revlon ColorStay because I put it on in the morning and don't have to think about it again for a few hours. ColorStay Ultimate Liquid Lipstick comes in a variety of campus-appropriate neutral shades and is durable. Keep in mind that a good lip stain also makes a really long-lasting blush.

This is just me, but even if you don't wear makeup, take care of your skin. I learned about skin care from my many years in Japan, where they take it seriously indeed.

Wear conservative jewelry to job talks. Conspicuous jewelry is fine for large conferences, but not at job interview situations where it might distract. Beware of jangling bracelets, which, I once found out to my chagrin, can make quite a racket on a podium.

Take out your tops and look at them. Are they stained? Get them cleaned or pass them on. Are they ripped? Fix them or pass them on. Your interviewers notice. Also, iron your shirts. I know there's no time. But iron your shirts.

Your blouse must button completely over "the girls." There must be no gapping of any kind. Wearing a camisole underneath a gapping blouse is not an acceptable solution. Your breasts must be, as Clinton Kelly of *What Not to Wear* used to say, locked and loaded, and covered in their entirety by your clothing. Cleavage and bra straps are unacceptable in any academic setting. Leave the spaghetti straps to the undergraduates. Choose tops that don't have to be tugged at to preserve modesty.

Readers have asked what to do when you're busty and blouses just don't work. I am not unfamiliar with this problem. I typically either sew up the placket of blouses to turn them into de-facto pullovers, or else I use Commando Matchsticks, a double-sided fashion tape made for closing up offending gaps.

On a related note, the fitted jacket is the job candidate's best friend. The best fitted jackets look both hip and professional and can be combined with any skirts or pants in your wardrobe. However, all jackets have to be tried on at the store. The best and most expensive jacket will not do its magic if it doesn't fit your body, so don't try to buy jackets online. Jacket shopping can be grueling, like shopping for swimsuits. Put in the time. It's worth it for the effect: Remember that a good jacket covers a multitude of sins.

Pants or skirt? The perennial question. It doesn't matter unless it does in your field or location. The important thing is to be comfortable. Just leave behind any trailing earth mother skirts you wore in graduate school (or is that just the Northwest?). You are a young professional; you have to look like one. Old-timers bemoan the homogenization of the assistant professoriate, in their sea of dull gray suits. Nevertheless, own a gray suit (or again, the dress-jacket combo). Just make it really, really stylish, and wear it with killer shoes.

If you are a person who wears heels regularly, wear a heel between one and three inches. If you don't and won't, that's fine. But I don't recommend ballet flats or Mary Janes, or anything that bears a resemblance to little girl shoes. If you do wear heels, make sure they aren't too high or too skinny. Above three inches, and you're tottering. Avoid stilettos and kitten heels—they stick in sidewalk cracks and grates, and trip you up. A wide stacked heel provides the stability that keeps you from falling over as you walk around campus or approach the podium. Be sure your shoes are comfortable, and do not wear brand-new shoes unless they have been tested for comfort. At the same time, the shoes should be fresh and not worn down in the heel or sole.

For campus visits, there are some additional considerations. At the typical campus visit you are picked up at the airport and taken to dinner. You will need to be appropriately dressed on the plane, in dress pants and a blouse or sweater, with a cardigan or jacket. A matching suit is unnecessary at this stage. Don't wear linen or silk or any fabric that wrinkles. You might want to take a quick trip to the restroom before arrival, to brush your hair, check your makeup and jewelry (make sure no earrings fell out), and maybe brush your teeth.

Pack your clothes for the visit in a small carry-on and do not check. Checking bags leads to awkward delays that nobody wants to deal with when they are likely anxious to get you to dinner. Carry your interview materials in a shoulder bag briefcase, and let the carry-on and the briefcase be all that you carry with you on the trip.

The next day is likely your big day on campus, going from eight a.m. to at least eight p.m., with the job talk. This is the day you wear your interview ensemble. Make sure your underwear is comfortable, fits, and stays put. If you're going to wear a Spanx-type of undergarment, test it ahead of time so you know it won't ride up and need tugging at. This goes for all your clothes. I was once at a campus visit and halfway through the day realized my skirt had worked its way around so that the zipper, kick pleat, and rear bulge was in the front. It didn't help my already shaky confidence.

Your clothes should be freshly washed or dry-cleaned and pressed. You may, if you know that you're a bit of a slob, pack an extra top/shell in your briefcase against the terrible possibility of spilling pizza sauce down your front at lunch with the graduate students.

Pack all of your regular toiletries, hair products, and the like. Do not depend on whatever random products you find in small travel sizes at the drugstore, or the hotel they put you up at. They will not perform the same, and you don't want to end up with weird, flyaway hair or moisturizer that you find out, too late, you're allergic to, when you're in the high-stakes environment of a campus visit. Go to the trouble of getting travel bottles and filling them with your products.

If you are heading into unfamiliar cold weather for your campus visit, get a quality, stylish cold-weather dress coat. Coats of this type can often be found secondhand; don't make a significant outlay for what might be only one northern campus visit. Conservative East Coast campuses still expect the classic woolen dress coat, but in the Midwest of the Polar Vortex, make sure you prioritize warmth. A chic scarf and leather gloves make everyone look good, but hats can leave you looking disheveled, so find a style that pulls on and off with minimal hair disruption.

Attend to your footwear if you're heading into snow and ice. When I lived in the Midwest, I always had luck with La Canadienne boots; they are insulated and made for cold northern climes, but still look chic. They have rubber soles that grip the ice, but you would never know by looking at them. I got endless compliments on mine, and still do, because I still wear them in balmy Oregon, just because they're really cute. They are not cheap, however. Look for last-season models at Sierra Trading Post. Or check out a cheaper alternative such as Sorel.

How to afford all this on a grad student or adjunct salary? Secondhand boutiques. Any college town worth its salt will have at least one and probably a handful of high-quality secondhand women's clothing stores. Shop at these, and you can cover most of your clothing needs. True, you're buying the undergraduates' cast-offs, and have to hate your life to some extent. But, whatever. I didn't buy new clothes until after I was tenured.

For men, what you wear will vary depending on your discipline. In the formal disciplines (political science, economics) you'll need to buy a new suit for the interview season, which fits you at your current weight, buttons across your middle, and which you have tailored so that the sleeves and pants hit you at the proper spots. This suit does not have to be a high-end suit that costs a fortune. A good department store suit from Macy's that has been tailored by their in-house tailor to fit you is completely acceptable. Just avoid the shiny $99 suit from Men's Wearhouse if you can.

In addition, you need a good quality department store shirt, which you have ironed to remove the package folds. You also need a basic tie of recent vintage, a new leather belt, decent quality leather dress shoes, and socks that match either the shoes or the suit.

Men, your hair should be recently cut. Facial hair continues to be acceptable in academia; just make sure you're well-groomed.

If you're in one of the less formal disciplines (anthropology, sociology) you don't need to show up in a suit, but you will want a good quality jacket and dress pants or khakis. If you are in theater or art history, you may be able to get by in black jeans and a hip shirt and tie. Check with mentors in your field.

One rule that applies to both men and women: Never carry a backpack.

Both men and women should invest in the best quality leather or microfiber briefcase that they can manage. Last season's models are often on deep discount at OfficeMax and other chain stores. T.J. Maxx and Ross are also excellent sources.

Now, all of my advice so far has been gender normative; what if you are not? Well, as a femme dyke who has lived with my butch partner for more than ten years, I've given thought to this question. A butch reader once wrote to ask for advice:

> I recently tried to girl-up my wardrobe, and it was pretty much a disaster (ranging from Oh Hell No, to my shoulders don't fit in any of these tops, to WTF, women's shoes [even the flats!] are dangerous). Not all

was lost, but given that presenting as a "conventional" woman is pretty much out of the picture, any advice?

I have advice. My partner is an old-school butch dyke. She's over fifty, and hasn't worn an article of women's clothing in many decades. For years she had her hair cut at the barber, although now she gets a really good men's haircut from a high-end hair salon. She had to work with them a bit to make them understand she wasn't asking for a "pixie," but now they're totally on the same page.

The "lesbian," "androgynous," "post-butch," "boi," and "FTM" moments passed her by unheeded. She is a butch dyke: That's the category. She wears men's clothes exclusively but does not consciously attempt to "pass" as male. She is, nevertheless, mistaken for a man with some regularity, especially when she's wearing a suit, or sitting down at a restaurant, or in Japan, where there just isn't any other cultural means to interpret her. But people almost always realize their mistake pretty quickly, and then some awkward moments ensue before the flow of conversation resumes.

A former journalist, she has not interviewed for a job in many, many years—whether it was as the publisher at a small newspaper, a tenure track position at an R1, or a major start-up—in which she did not arrive for the interview in a men's suit, with men's dress shoes, and a men's haircut. She has gotten most of the jobs she's interviewed for and has succeeded, and been promoted, in the institutions in which she has worked, despite the fact that in these institutions she is generally the only butch dyke, or conspicuously gay person, on the payroll.

Why?

In an ideal world we wouldn't have to ask why, because we'd know that she was being judged on her qualifications, skills, and character. But we know the world is not ideal, and people are judged on their appearance all the time. So why would a sartorial profile so obviously marginal, so obviously outside the mainstream, have no observable impact on her level of professional success?

Well, I'm not omniscient, so I can't say for sure, but I have a theory. And it's a theory my partner shares from her own subjective experience of her life. The theory is that she is more focused on what she's doing than who she is supposed to represent, and so people respond with similar ease to what she's bringing to the table, instead of getting hung up on what she signifies.

I know that's not terribly precise, but it's the closest I can come to articulating how it works. She doesn't hold up the dress style or the haircut or the masculine affect as any kind of barrier to other people, or to her own personality, which is very large. When you interact with my partner, you are instantly *in* an interaction—you're engaging with her, responding, thinking, reacting, talking, listening, joking, exchanging ideas. The substance of the communication prevails. She's quite charismatic, and people generally just want to keep talking. And know more. And get her onto their team.

Now, what does this mean if you, as a butch dyke, are wondering how to dress on the job market? Well, in a way, it is a message that applies to everyone on the market, butch or not. The message is this: You need to be comfortable with who you are. If you're butch, go butch. If you're androgynous, go androgynous. If you're femme, go femme.

Now, that would seem to contradict my perennial message that you need to wear potentially unfamiliar, formal clothes to interviews, clothes that might not be all that comfortable. But I'm speaking of a deeper level of comfort. My partner would not go to an interview in jeans and a collared shirt, even though that might be her most comfortable choice for daily wear. She wears interview-appropriate clothes, clothes that might chafe a bit, but that are both appropriate to the context and consistent with her larger identity.

I had a colleague years back who was a lesbian. Not a femme dyke; a lesbian. Which was fine. But she seemed to have this idea that she had to "pass" as extra feminine to be legible in the academy. Day after day she'd show up in pencil skirts and little heels, and day after day she'd walk stiffly and awkwardly around the department, the strain evident on her face. Now, granted, she had a job and got tenure and promoted and so on, so this is not some morality tale of how she crashed and burned because she wasn't true to herself. But it is a tale of a colleague who was excruciatingly uncomfortable in her own skin. I had another colleague, a butch dyke, who showed up for her campus interview in a three-piece suit and wingtips. She got the job, and proceeded to come to work in three-piece suits and wingtips for her first couple of years on campus. Over time she acquiesced to the laid-back vibe on that campus, and ratcheted down the formality level, but she never stopped dressing butch. She's done fine. Sure, she stands out. That comes with the territory. You're never going to be a butch dyke, or gender-variant in most ways, and not stand out. But standing out is different from being "a problem" and "rejected," and "unemployed."

I get that not every campus around the country is going to be equally open to candidates showing up dressed in gender-bending ways. The South is more conservative than the West and Midwest, and small schools, and certainly church-related schools, will be far harder nuts to crack in this regard than R1s and Ivy Leagues. It's a risk to show up for an interview, or any high-stakes encounter (such as meeting my mother) dressed like a guy. But what's the alternative? Are you going to fake it? Do you think you can? I'll bet you can't. And the strain is going to show and undermine your performance in a host of overt and covert ways.

Ultimately, my advice is this: If you're a butch dyke, go to that campus interview dressed as a butch dyke—not in your jeans and leather jacket, and not in wrinkled chinos and a short-sleeved poly blend shirt, but in a really nice suit and dress shirt, and quality shoes, and socks that match your trousers, and a fresh haircut—because you don't want to get offered a job under false pretenses. They need to know who you are. And you need to know who you are. And then, when you get the job, your productivity, teaching, contributions, and collegiality will prove your value to your colleagues and the institution. As I said in chapter 44, you'll probably have to work harder for tenure and be held to a higher bar. But once there, you can work on aging gracefully as a butch professor, and setting an example for the baby butches finding their way.

FORTY-SEVEN

Covering the Costs

Talk of wardrobe inevitably raises the question of finances. While the expense of a job search wardrobe can be minimized, as I noted, by relying on the quality secondhand clothing boutiques readily found in cities and most college towns, other expenses of the job search are not so easily handled. And since the majority of graduate students are carrying significant debt from their undergraduate and graduate schooling, the costs of the job search are a major impediment. How to manage them? In this chapter I turn first to some recommendations for hacking the conference circuit, and then end with some observations about how to choose among different work options while remaining on the job market over several years.

I have argued that conferences are critical to a competitive academic record, and we've seen that conferences are also a prime location for networking, as well as for the conference interview stage of the search. But conferences are also one of the greatest expenses of the academic job search, and one of the causes of Ph.D. debt.[1] Unless you are independently wealthy or have some abundant source of conference funding, you need to be selective.

It is not necessary to go to more than one national conference in your field per year, or if you are in an interdisciplinary area of study and can afford it, two. As I mentioned earlier, I attended both the American Anthropological Association conference and the

Association for Asian Studies conference annually. I rarely attended any other conference, and then, only with full funding. Don't add to your debt to attend any conference at which you are not on the program or don't have a specific job interview invitation. Attending conferences without presenting or interviewing is not a good use of your money, when money is tight.

If your interviewing school is offering the option of a Skype interview, consider taking it. More and more departments are turning to the virtual interview in recognition of the insupportable financial burden of conference interviews on unemployed job seekers. While you never know how a Skype interview is weighed against an in-person one, you can be sure that a one in (approximately) twenty chance at nothing more than a campus visit short list is not worth going into debt for.

If you do have a paper or interview (or, we hope, both) on the schedule, then the task becomes getting there and back on the cheap. Here are my hacks for cutting costs on the conference circuit:

- If the conference is within driving distance, carpool with friends to get there.
- If it requires a flight, see if friends or family will donate frequent-flier miles toward a ticket. Or see if your friends and family will contribute to a ticket fund.
- Be sure to check StudentUniverse.com and similar sites for budget tickets. Also check LivingSocial and such sites for deals; if your conference is at a major hub, you may get lucky.
- Use departmental or disciplinary Listservs to arrange shared transport from the airport to the hotel; also check out subway and bus schedules, and free hotel shuttles.
- Never stay at the overpriced conference hotels, unless you are with a group large enough to reduce the per-person cost substantially.
- Instead, use Groupon, LivingSocial, Airbnb, and similar sites to find cut-rate deals.
- Have a friend or relative contribute hotel chain loyalty points.

- Better yet, see if you can line up a couch to crash on; conference Listservs or craigslist may provide options if your network of friends and family does not.
- Stay at a hotel or motel with a kitchenette so you can cook simple meals.
- Beware of hidden costs, such as Wi-Fi. Motels will offer free Wi-Fi more consistently than hotels.
- Never use the hotel printers if you can avoid it, either for printing your paper or your boarding passes. These charge extortionate rates.
- Food costs are a challenge—plan ahead. While you may want to budget for one major dinner with your panel or some important colleagues, economize elsewhere. Pack food you can cook in your kitchenette (don't expect to buy ingredients at downtown markets). And exploit Groupon and the like for deals on food in the area.
- Maximize free breakfasts offered by your hotel or motel— try to find one with a substantial hot breakfast with protein sources such as sausage or, at bare minimum, a hard-boiled egg. A carb-only breakfast of waffles with syrup is going to leave you crashed and weaving by midday.
- If you want to meet someone to chat, consider doing it at the free wine and cheese events hosted by the major presses. You can score wine and a plate of food, and stand in a quiet corner to talk.
- Check if coffee is provided at the book exhibit during the day.
- If you're planning a panel meal, consider making it a lunch or breakfast instead of a dinner. In all cases, research to find cheaper restaurant options—they exist, they're just hard to find.
- Visit the book exhibit, but don't succumb to its lures, unless the book is one that you absolutely require for your work. The conference rate usually includes a 20 percent discount on the price.
- If you are getting reimbursed, save all receipts religiously. Create a system if you don't already have one—for example,

a dedicated pocketbook into which you transfer all receipts at the end of each day. Submit these quickly. Smart travelers do the paperwork on the plane on the way home, before anything has a chance to get lost.

It goes without saying, of course, that you will apply for all available conference funding from your home department and graduate college and any other available source semester after semester, year after year. I once had a client who told me that she stopped applying for funding after a certain point because she'd "already gotten so much," and felt she should "leave some for others." That is codependent self-sabotage. Your job is to take care of you; apply for all conference funding available.

Managing conferences is just one small element of the financial calculations of the job search, of course. In this day, when most candidates stay on the market for multiple years, the most urgent calculation becomes how to weigh various work options against the imperative to keep researching and writing to maintain a competitive record. When confronted with the option of adjuncting, living off of savings, or taking a nonacademic job, for example, how does one choose?

As I remarked in an earlier chapter, this type of calculation will depend on a host of factors that are distinctive to you and your individual case: How much debt do you currently have? How close are you to finishing and defending? How much have you published to date? How much teaching experience have you already gained? For the purposes of discussion, I will lay out some scenarios.

If you are a typical ABD who has not had the chance to get a lot of experience teaching, then you'll want to prioritize gaining that through adjuncting for a year or so. On the other hand, if you are an ABD who's been in the adjunct trenches for years (and has not been able to finish and defend your dissertation, or get any publishing done, because of it), then avoid more adjuncting. Take this chance either to live on savings, seek the support of family if that is available, or get a nonacademic job, while you focus on finishing the dissertation and publishing peer-reviewed articles.

If you have unmanageable debt, then prioritize financial stability, and any kind of job that will allow you to pay it down and perhaps even build some savings.

Remember that you can simultaneously try out a variety of things. In other words, send out an application for that statistician job at the Department of Labor you've been eyeing. Why not? You don't have to stop adjuncting while you do it. And you can keep sending out tenure track applications for economics jobs, too. There's no harm in trying a new option on for size and seeing how it feels. It is not disloyal to keep a variety of irons in the fire.

Do search committees have a bias against candidates with "gaps" in their record, either from adjuncting or from working outside of the academy? In general they do not, as long as the adjuncting or nonacademic work is done for a limited time, and hasn't interfered in a candidate's program of publishing, conferences, and grants. What is a "limited time"? I wrote in chapter 10 that three years is a reasonable length of time to search for your first job, on the condition that the outcome of these years is not crushing new debt or exhaustion. Those with family or other resources to support them financially can adjunct indefinitely if it serves them to do so. Others cannot and should not. When choosing among several options, make sure to go for the one that advances your personal cause. Do not become so in thrall to the cult of academia that you cannot see there are always other options to choose.

PART VII

· · · · · · · · · · · · · · · · · · · ·

NEGOTIATING
AN OFFER

····················

FORTY-EIGHT

Don't Be Afraid to Negotiate

On the American academic job market, negotiating the tenure track job offer is by and large expected. Unfortunately, most new Ph.D.'s have no idea how to do it. Desperation plays a large role, as many green candidates (and their advisors) believe they must "say yes before the department changes its mind." In addition, new Ph.D.'s fresh from graduate school or adjuncting may be so accustomed to being underpaid and undervalued that they have no idea of their actual worth. There is the emerging anxiety about rescinded offers. And last, the Work of the Mind mythology insists that attaching a price tag to your academic labor is déclassé.

I'm here to tell you that negotiating is normal, it is expected, and you should do it. This is your opportunity to gain the resources you need to be successful in your new position. These resources also increase significantly over time. Imagine this scenario: You are thirty years old, and you are offered an initial salary of $75,000, at an institution that provides a 5 percent retirement contribution and a 5 percent institutional match. With a 7 percent annual return on your investment, at age sixty-five, and 1 percent annual raises, you will have accrued the following:

Without negotiating:	$3,124,521 lifetime earnings	$1,238,522 retirement balance
Negotiating a 5 percent increase	$3,280,747 lifetime earnings	$1,300,448 retirement balance
Negotiating a 10 percent increase	$3,436,973 lifetime earnings	$1,362,374 retirement balance

With the 10 percent initial increase, you accrue an extra $312,452 in earnings, and $123,852 in retirement, for a total of $436,304.[1] And because future salary offers at later jobs are usually pegged to your previous salary, this impact could intensify over time. Michelle Marks and Crystal Harold, in a 2009 *Journal of Organizational Behavior* article, suggest an even larger impact, demonstrating that an initial salary of $55,000 rather than $50,000 would earn an additional $600,000+ over the course of a forty-year career.[2]

Thus, do not discount the impact of any increase, however small, in your initial compensation package. Don't allow reluctance, anxiety, or diffidence to stop you. If you are a woman, this is particularly urgent. Women are likely to assume that they can't or must not ask for "too much." As Sara Laschever, coauthor of *Women Don't Ask*, puts it: "[Women] over-identify with the other side. Women have this tendency to protect and take care of people. But you need to allow the other side to negotiate their side of the discussion. Women also tend to ask for too little. They should talk to people to get a sense of what men ask for and shoot for that. If you aim too low, not many places are going to say, 'No, you didn't ask for enough; take more.' You need to think about what your market value is."[3]

I have found these observations borne out in my negotiating work with women Ph.D.'s again and again. A well-conducted negotiation is not about asking for too much; it's about asking for what you are worth. What follows are my recommendations for conducting an effective and collegial negotiation.

Do not, under any circumstances, accept the offer the same day they make it. When they call or email, answer pleasantly and politely, "Oh, thank you. That is good news. I'm so pleased." And then say, "I'd like to know more about the offer. When can I expect a written offer by email?" If the department head tries to push you for a commitment, simply repeat, "I am very happy for the offer, but I will need to see the offer elements in writing before I can make a final commitment. I very much look forward to discussing this further after seeing the details. I hope we can begin soon."

Now, there are several things you need to know. Once an offer has been made to you, the institution in the vast majority of cases will not rescind the offer, or offer the job to anyone else, for a certain amount of time. While that amount of time may vary by institution, you typically have at least one week to contemplate your response, and possibly as much as two or three. During that time you are in the driver's seat. While unscrupulous or panicky or pushy department heads may try to hustle you, do not allow yourself to be hustled. You are now the one in charge.

It is true that rescinded offers happen more often now, for budgetary reasons, administrative foul-ups, or sheer institutional malfeasance. Check out the Academic Jobs Wiki's forum "Universities to Fear" for more stories of this nature, and read this book's chapter 50 carefully. For now, rest assured that only an infinitesimally small number of offers are rescinded, and by understanding the principles I explain here, you will reduce that likelihood even further. The most important thing you can do is confer with a trusted mentor as you evaluate the offer and craft your responses. There are too many unknown variables in a first tenure track job that you cannot possibly comprehend. You need help knowing how far to push and when to stop.

Before launching into any negotiation, expect to receive a complete offer by email that encompasses salary, teaching load, teaching releases, conference funding, start-up funds, moving expenses, and so on. Once you receive these, decide what you're going to come back with in negotiation.

The basic elements of a typical early career tenure track offer will include some but not all of the following:

- Salary
- Start-up funds
- Computer and software

- Teaching load
- Teaching release
- Guaranteed junior sabbatical
- Research funding
- Conference travel
- Summer salary
- Delayed start
- Early start/pre-contract advance
- Maternity leave
- Paid visit to look at houses
- Moving expenses
- Partner position
- Family/housing benefits
- Grant support
- Equipment
- Lab space and supplies
- Office furniture (if specialty)
- Library acquisitions
- Subscriptions to journals and memberships
- Tenure expectations (if coming in with tenure credit)
- Extension of decision timeline

What you ask for will depend on your circumstances and your goals. A single person with no children might decide to prioritize research support—for example, additional leave time and a larger research budget to pay for overseas research. A person supporting a family might forgo additional research funding to prioritize a higher salary. A person seeking a position for their partner might forgo both research support and a higher salary in order to prioritize a partner appointment. The point is, in all cases, this is the one and only time in your early years in the department that you can attempt to turn circumstances in your favor, so be clear on your goals and pursue them.

Negotiations should be approached holistically. In other words, if your offer encompasses ten of the above elements, you should not expect to seek drastic increases in all ten. You will, with the help of your mentor, decide on your bottom-line elements, and those that can be compromised on. As you decide on your approach to the negotiation, consider four things: the status and rank of the institution and department, what other recent hires have gotten (as far as you can determine this), how badly they seem to want you, whether you sense or know that there is a viable backup candidate, and any red flags you may have picked up in the course of your interactions with the department.

The most important rule of negotiating: Match your negotiation to the type and rank of the institution. Do not attempt an R1 negotiation at a small, resource-poor teaching college. That is the scenario in which most rescinded offers occur. Likewise, don't undersell yourself with a few paltry requests appropriate for a teaching college when you're dealing with an R1 or Ivy League. In chapter 11 I explained the types and ranks of institutions. As I suggested there, R1s, Ivy Leagues, and elite SLACs will have the deepest pockets and the greatest scope for negotiation; middle-tier institutions will have some, but far less. When it comes to regional teaching colleges or community colleges, there may be none at all.

One perennial question is whether to conduct negotiations by email or phone. Many senior faculty insist that phone is de rigueur, but I disagree. In my opinion, inexperienced junior hires are in no position to effectively comprehend and evaluate the many elements of an offer in a phone call, and spontaneously improvise successful responses. I believe that inexperienced negotiators need the pacing of email to study the offer, discuss it with trusted advisors, and carefully construct their replies.

Of course tone is always tricky in email, and misunderstandings are possible. Nevertheless, I continue to advocate for email, particularly for women candidates who struggle to express their wants and needs. Savvy department heads know that junior women candidates can often be pressured to accept less. It is not that the department head is out to cheat you; any good department head will simply prioritize saving money wherever she can. Therefore as a general rule I believe it is wise to resist pressure to proceed by phone if you can. However, if the department is insistent, and there is no graceful way to refuse, or conversely if you feel strongly that you are a person who does best in the personal interaction of the phone, then by all means take that route. Just be sure you prepare your requests ahead of time, and have them written out in front of you, with explanations, to refer to if you find yourself panicked or tongue-tied.

Always proceed courteously and professionally. Respond quickly to emails and calls, and never leave them hanging, even if just to say, "I received your latest email; thank you. I will study it and respond by tomorrow." Don't apologize, make excuses, offer elaborate justifications for your requests, or instantly back down. Although they might grumble a bit as the negotiations carry on for a week or so, they will respect your process and will not hold it against you. Just remember that this process establishes the tenor of your relationships with future colleagues, so remain courteous and professional in all things.

Regarding salary, be aware that many public institutions suffer from salary compression. That means that associate and full professors' salaries have not kept pace with the national market, and consequently new assistant professors are offered salaries as high as or higher than those of the tenured faculty who have been on campus for years, even decades. Salary compression creates terrible feelings of resentment and low morale. The department head will be well aware of these feelings. When the department head tells you, "We cannot go higher than $70,000 for your starting salary due to pay scale issues in the department," you can probably take that as a hard no, because it most likely reflects associate level salary compression. This doesn't mean no additional money is possible, however. Rather, you must now seek short-term or "nonrecurring" obligations instead of a recurring annual salary commitment. Nonrecurring commitments include start-up funding, summer salary, teaching release, research funding, conference and travel funding, and so forth. When salary negotiations have been exhausted, turn your efforts to shorter-term forms of compensation that don't put pressure on an already overburdened salary structure.

Never, ever dictate to a department what you believe to be a salary or research support "norm" for your field. As in, "I should be given a salary of $80,000 because I know that is what other assistant professors at peer institutions in the field have been offered." Nothing, and I mean nothing, will offend and alienate a department more thoroughly than being lectured to by a clueless yet arrogant new Ph.D. The fact is, you have no idea what the conditions are prevailing in that department or in any department. You don't know the current and future budgetary context, the state of salary compression, the presence or absence of endowments, questions of morale, and a host of other issues. Take your cue from the initial offer, and negotiate within a reasonable percentage of that. A reasonable percentage at the assistant professor level is generally in the neighborhood of 5 to 15 percent. The lower end is appropriate for small teaching colleges; the upper end is appropriate for science and professional school offers. For the vast majority of humanities and social science offers at most institutions, 10 percent is an appropriate increase to request. I'm not saying you will get it, but it is a substantial and meaningful ask that at the same time is not likely to offend or alienate your prospective department.

Get everything you negotiate in writing. Email typically constitutes "in writing." Keep in mind that not all elements of the offer will necessarily show up in the formal signed contract, which at some institutions is quite minimal and covers only the salary and teaching load. In those cases, the other negotiated items will be present in an email exchange that you print out and file. Any understandings that are not in writing will have no standing in the future, when the department head or dean with whom you negotiated has been replaced.

Now, one aspect to consider is if you have another competing offer or possible offer. If you do, first off, lucky you—this is the best position to negotiate from. Although note that the new offer, to be usable in the negotiation, must be equal or better in all respects of rank and status. You cannot use a visiting or temporary job as leverage for a tenure track offer, no matter how high ranking that other institution is, nor will a low-ranking tenure track offer serve as leverage vis-à-vis an elite offer. If you are waiting on an offer from a second school, you may contact that second school and inform them of the offer you received from school A. You will write something to this effect:

DEAR STEVE,

Thank you again for having me out to visit your department at X U. I enjoyed the visit immensely. I am writing to let you know that I have received an offer from another institution. My timeline for accepting this offer is approximately one week. I wonder if I could receive a response regarding your search within that time frame. I want to reiterate my interest in your position. I hope to hear from you soon.

SINCERELY,

NAME

You can be assured that this email will send a jolt of terror through the spine of Steve, if you are his department's first choice. The greatest fear of departments once a hiring decision has been made is that the candidate will be unavailable. The department may have a solid alternate candidate available, but often they do not. Departments often end up voting all but the top candidate as "unacceptable," so failure to get the top candidate means a failed search, and the risk of losing authorization to hire that year. So all their eggs may be in one basket, and that basket is you.

If you are their top candidate, and they just haven't told you yet because they haven't had a chance to complete their voting and offer process (offers may need time to be vetted by the dean, for example), this small email will send the department into a panic. And a panicked department is what you want. Because a panicked department, sensing that they might lose you to institution A, will be more likely to agree to your negotiating requests, although, as always, within institutional limits.

All departments have financial and logistical limitations. You cannot negotiate above those. If you try, you will quickly alienate your future colleagues. They may resent you, and those feelings of resentment are dangerous for a soon-to-be junior colleague. The key to negotiating is to always maintain good faith and honesty, and always have a highly delicate sense for when you are hitting a true wall of "we can't do that." Because when you hit that, that's when you stop.

In the event you are negotiating two offers, once you make your decision, call or email both departments immediately, courteously express your gratitude for their offers, and accept one with warmth and enthusiasm, and turn down the other with (nonapologetic) respect. Remember that the colleagues in the rejected department will continue to play a role in your professional life for many years to come. You will see them at conferences, they might be external reviewers for your journal article or book manuscript, and, who knows, one of them might end up one of your tenure writers one day. So preserve your good relations with these people. They will not be angry that you rejected their offer. They will just be disappointed. Be very friendly when you next run into them at a conference.

FORTY-NINE
....

The Rare and Elusive Partner Hire

The dreaded partner issue: This is the hardest negotiation of all.
Many R1 and elite campuses have explicit partner hiring policies as a recruitment method; ideally this will provide a tenure
track line for the partner, but the policy may instead provide only
teaching opportunities, an affiliation, office space, and other limited resources. Don't immediately accept the first accommodations
suggested if they fall short of the tenure track hire you seek. Fight
for the partner hire, and remember that in importance it dwarfs
all other negotiation points. Think about it—with a partner hire
you get twice the collective income, research funding, retirement,
and benefits. So if you come into a negotiation seeking a tenure
track partner position, know that this is the big-ticket item and you
should plan to adjust other requests accordingly.

By the way, same-sex and domestic partners will be recognized
for the purposes of partner hiring at most major institutions, unless there is a religious affiliation that objects to them.

It is my position that you should wait until you have a firm offer before you bring up the partner. Any mention earlier than that could
well work against you in the minds of the faculty, consciously or unconsciously. Understand, however, that this advice is contested. A
number of experienced commenters to my blog believe that partner hires should be raised immediately, at the point of invitation to
the campus visit or even earlier. I have seen clients succeed with this

approach, and I see the rationale for this advice. A department may be able to do more for your partner with substantial lead time than it can if the partner is suddenly sprung on them at the last minute.

Nevertheless, my experience on actual searches suggests to me that search committees may have a conscious or unconscious bias against the candidate who is known to be dragging along a partner. Partner hires are a hassle and an expense. If the department is confronted with two equivalent candidates, one of whom has a partner and one of whom doesn't . . . to whom will the offer go? I never saw a candidate openly rejected on the basis of a potential partner issue, but I certainly witnessed telling silences and vague circumlocutions. In all things, of course, you are the best judge of the institutional context and your own comfort with ambiguity.

Whenever you mention your partner, be aware that this is the only chance you will have to negotiate for a partner hire, so do not waste it. Don't be immediately put off with the range of one-year, two-year, three-year, instructor, adjunct, and visiting positions that they will try to pawn off on you. They may say something like "Oh, we can revisit your husband's tenure case later, when this contract is up," but don't believe it. The partner's position is never revisited after you lose the leverage of your initial negotiation. That is, until you gain the leverage of an external offer, and that's likely several years of tense domestic relations down the line. Push as firmly as you can for the actual tenure track offer, until you feel certain that it is simply not possible. Understand that outside of the most elite institutions, and even at them, it is often (usually?) impossible.

It is especially important in the case of partner negotiations that you accept absolutely nothing that is not in writing. Again, any "informal" agreements or understandings that you may have with the current department head or dean will be void when the head or dean moves on.

Make sure that your partner is debut ready. His or her record should be unassailable, the CV should be flawless, the dissertation finished, and a polished research and teaching statement prepared. Do your own research about which departments the partner would be eligible for an appointment in, and the full range of positions for which he or she is qualified. Be proactive; do not passively write that you "hope some accommodation can be made for my wife." Be specific. "My wife has a Ph.D. in X and has taught courses in X, Y, and Z. She would be an excellent fit for your departments of A and B, and could also teach in programs such as C and D. We are seeking a tenure track hire."

Be flexible about any offered position that is tenure track. Many difficult negotiations have to take place among administrators to line up a partner hire, and some department heads will be better at this than others. To some extent you are at the administrators' mercy. It is common for the cost of a partner hire to be paid for from three sources. The original department will pay one-third of the partner hire's salary, the dean's office will pay one-third, and then the receiving department will pay one-third. This deal may appeal to the receiving department, as they are getting a new line for one-third cost. On the other hand, the receiving department may instead balk at this new line imposed from outside, and may fear that the partner hire will derail the other hiring goals they have in place. This is a valid fear—the dean may well deny their hiring requests the following year by pointing to the "new line" they got with the spousal hire. Because of this fear, administrators may have to knock on several doors to find a department willing to take the "gift," and they may well find it impossible, in the end, to accomplish.

The important thing, once again, is to hold firm and politely repeat, "My biggest priority is a tenure track position for my partner," without any escalation or emotionalism or drama, day after day, to person after person, until you either get the partner offer, or get a flat-out no that you read as unmistakable. As long as they are still talking to you about it, don't waver. When it is clear that it isn't going to happen, let it go without recriminations, and move on with a request for the best possible non-tenure-track option available. Make sure that you prioritize ongoing positions with security and research support, so that your partner can remain productive and competitive for future hire opportunities. And keep your eyes open for external offers that provide the leverage to raise the issue again a few years down the line.

FIFTY

The Rescinded Offer—
Who Is In the Wrong?

The rescinded offer has grown more common in recent years, but it is still quite rare. Out of about one hundred negotiating assistance clients with whom I worked over a two-year period, three had offers rescinded. In all cases that I know of, at the junior level, the institution abruptly canceled the offer when the client sought to negotiate it.[1]

Many readers have written panicked messages asking if negotiating is now out of the question for successful tenure track job seekers. It is not. You should still expect to negotiate your tenure track job offer in nearly all cases. Just be aware that you must match your approach to the type and rank of institution. And be cautious with small colleges (especially those with current or former religious affiliations), which seem to be the most likely to rescind.

The rescinded offer rose to national consciousness in 2013, with the case of "W," who blogged about an offer in philosophy she received from Nazareth College that was rescinded when she sent an email launching into negotiations. This incident prompted an outpouring of anguished and outraged commentary. What exactly happened? W attempted an R1 negotiation at a small teaching college. That is a dangerous move indeed.

Here is the email that W wrote to the department:

As you know, I am very enthusiastic about the possibility of coming to Nazareth. Granting some of the following provisions would make my decision easier.

An increase of my starting salary to $65,000, which is more in line with what assistant professors in philosophy have been getting in the last few years.

An official semester of maternity leave.

A pre-tenure sabbatical at some point during the bottom half of my tenure clock.

No more than three new class preps per year for the first three years.

A start date of academic year 2015 so I can complete my postdoc.

I know that some of these might be easier to grant than others. Let me know what you think.

I will break down the errors of approach based on institutional type.

Salary: She asked for a significant increase in salary (in her later follow-up comment she says it was an increase of less than 20 percent, which I am going to take to mean somewhere between 15 and 20 percent). That is unreasonably high for any new assistant professor position in the humanities, even at an R1 or elite SLAC. At a small, resource-poor teaching college it is entirely out of the question. Junior candidate raise requests should fall in the 5 to 15 percent range, and at tiny teaching colleges, the low end of that range.

She also informs the department that this salary request "is more in line with what assistant professors in philosophy have been getting in the last few years." This is presumptuous and inaccurate. An assistant professor candidate is not privy to national salary standards across departments at every rank of school. Reliance on published average salary tables from the *Chronicle of Higher Education* and the like is an ill-conceived move in this context as these don't reliably reflect any given institution's circumstances. Salaries for new assistant professors in the same discipline routinely vary by some

$30,000 across ranks of schools. For example, one humanities client I worked with on negotiating, in 2013, was offered $75,000 at an R1, while another client in the identical field was offered $45,000 at a small teaching college. You do not get to dictate to the institution what their salary "norm" is or should be. That is determined entirely at the institutional level.

Maternity Leave: W writes in a follow-up that the department had informally agreed to maternity leave. However, preemptively listing maternity leave in a contract before the new hire is even pregnant is not standard university practice. It's not that departments won't grant maternity leave. It's that they rarely guarantee it ahead of time.

Pre-tenure Sabbatical: While this is the norm at R1s and elite SLACs, it is categorically not done at small teaching colleges. Its presence on this list of requests displays a serious misunderstanding of the nature of the institution and its position. This may well have been the decisive factor in the collapse of negotiations.

Three Years of Reduced New Class Preps: It is standard for a new hire to ask for some teaching or new prep release for the first year. Asking for this much, in this way, is not only arrogant, it is also entirely inappropriate for an institution like Nazareth College, where the job is, quite simply, a teaching job.

A Delayed Start Date: While a delayed start date can be accommodated at R1s and elite SLACs, it is almost impossible to manage for other institutions. The school has to staff its classes; if you don't show up, they have to scramble to find someone else. Large elite schools will have a pool of potential adjuncts to choose from, but a school like Nazareth will not. They need a warm body to stand in front of those classes, and that warm body is you. You need to show up.

If W had worked with me on negotiating, I would have told her to remove or rephrase many of the elements on her list of requests, because they were inappropriate to such a small, teaching-oriented, resource-poor, service-heavy kind of institution. W certainly made some grievous errors of both substance and tone in her approach to the negotiations.

However, let me make myself perfectly clear: W's errors do not justify the rescinding of her offer. Nazareth could have responded, "We can do X, but not Y or Z. With regard to Q, we already have policy in place to provide it when it becomes necessary. At our institution the expectations for teaching are X. We do not commonly support X and Y. We can explain further in a phone call if you'd like."

Rescinding an offer for errors of tone is unethical. New hires are typically fresh, wet behind the ears Ph.D.'s who have experience only at the R1s where they were trained. Departments should give new hires the chance to hear and understand the conditions that prevail at their rank and type of institution, and should respond with information so that the candidate can make an educated decision about fit. Many, many former elite Ph.D.'s have found meaningful careers at teaching colleges. Sometimes it just takes a little time for them to grasp the context.

If you are the recipient of an offer, be alert to the rank and type of institution, and move particularly cautiously if you are dealing with a small teaching college, especially one with a current or former religious affiliation. Institutions like this have low salaries and high teaching expectations, and may have little to offer by way of perks. They may have an insular and secretive culture and dictatorial administrative tendencies (this characterization comes from clients at such institutions and has been borne out by my own observations when assisting with negotiations for them). Approach your negotiations cautiously, and demonstrate a willingness to work within the circumstances that prevail on the campus.

When you do negotiate any position, do not succumb to a culture of fear. While W made an error of arrogance, far more new hires fall into the error of excessive diffidence. Do not think that timorousness will stop an offer from being rescinded; nor will it make you more "liked" by a department. And it certainly won't aid in your negotiations.

The following is an example of an excessively diffident attempt at negotiation by a client. I have emphasized all the language by which the client diminishes, juvenilizes, sabotages, or makes excuses for herself.

DEAR DEPARTMENT HEAD,

I *just* wanted to get back to you and discuss *a little more* about the offer.

I *would again like to let you know* that X is my priority but I also have an offer from Y which is offering me $Z. *I understand that you may have some constraints* but *would you consider* increasing the starting salary *to some extent?* Also, *I was wondering if* you could *add* a start-up research fund. *I understand that* conference travels are generally covered, but *I would like to make sure* that I get covered for two conferences each year *in order to stay productive.* In terms of teaching load, *would it be possible to* have an X course load during the second year? In addition, *I will really appreciate if I could* get covered for the house-hunting trip for my husband and myself. *It is going to be a long move from Y*, so *we would like to* visit and *make sure that we find a nice place for our family.*

Also, *I would really appreciate if* you *could consider* extending the deadline *just a few more days.* Again, my priority is X but *I just want to* make sure that I know all the options before I make my decision, and I am expecting to hear from a few schools within the next week.

I worked with this client to transform her timorous and evasive language into confident and clear requests.

DEAR DEPARTMENT HEAD,

Thank you again for the generous offer. X U is my top choice and I'm excited about joining the faculty there. However, I have a few issues related to the offer that need to be resolved before I can give a final commitment. I want you to know that I have another offer in hand as well as several possible offers that I am to hear about shortly.

My current offer brings a salary of $Y. I would like to request that X U match that.

I would also like a start-up research fund of $Z, to fund things like travel for research and a research assistant.

In terms of teaching load, I'd like to request a course release for the second year as well.

I would like to make a trip to Q with my partner to look at houses, and I'd like to know if the department can cover some or all of that expense.

And, finally, I want to ask for a further extension of the deadline by one week. I am very grateful for your flexibility on the deadline so far. But because several offers seem to be pending, I wish to know all of my options before I make a final decision.

I want to reiterate my seriousness about the X U position, and hope that we can reach an agreement quickly.

SINCERELY,

NAME

The client got everything she asked for.

The question of what one is entitled to ask for is always fraught for inexperienced candidates. I once worked with a negotiating assistance client from the humanities who insisted, over and over, that he should be entitled to tens of thousands of dollars of start-up funding, a significant raise to support his struggling family, and a host of other perks far beyond the scope of the small rural college from which he had finally scored an offer, after years of searching. "You can't really ask for *all* of that!" I said to him each time. "You'll have to pick and choose." Finally, the client cried out (over email), "But why? Why have I no power?"

At first I laughed—I thought it was hyperbole for comic effect. But then I realized he was serious. Then I got annoyed—well, of course you have no power, I thought. Why would you think you had power? But then, as days went by, I found myself reflecting on this cri de coeur. Why does he have no power? Does he actually have *no* power? What is power, for a successful job candidate negotiating his first job? Answering this query accurately requires a rather careful parsing of the successful candidate's real position vis-à-vis the hiring body. So before leaving this chapter, let's delve into that question.

First of all, remember Marx: You are the labor, not the owner of the means of production. Ipso facto, you really have almost no power. This is fact. Add to this that your labor market is vastly, obscenely oversaturated. There are hundreds if not thousands of you who would leap at the job. Thus, at the entry level position in the academy, you have almost no power, which in this case might be better called leverage. As I explain above, if you are the happy recipient of more than one equivalent offer (and they must be equivalent in type and status), then you have more leverage.

Once the department has chosen you as their top candidate, they've invested thousands of dollars in the search already, and may well have voted all other candidates unacceptable. Therefore, although there are, in theory, hundreds or thousands of you to take the slot, in fact, there may be few immediately available other than you. A little leverage appears on the horizon! However, because well-known cases of rescinded offers have gained much exposure recently, the generalized atmosphere of fear mitigates against leverage for you.

So . . . do you have any power? Well, it's my opinion that yes, you do. Even without a second offer, you have a little. The department has invested an enormous amount of money and time into finding you, and you can use their desire not to have the search fail to your advantage. You have a little bit of leverage, and it is in that "little" that the work of negotiating happens. You can ask for X but not Y, Z but not Q. You can ask for A, B, and C, but not A through H, inclusive. And so on.

Traumatized survivors of the market tend to be so desperate and craven and codependent and eager to please that, left to their own devices, they barely utter a squeak in negotiations. That is a mistake. Job offers should be appropriately negotiated. At the same time, occasionally an offeree suffers from delusions of grandeur and believes that tens or hundreds of thousands of dollars should be provided as tribute to his or her greatness, as was the case with the client above who inspired these musings. Most often, offerees simply have no conception of how budgets associated with a line are actually funded—that is, what pots of money are available, where they reside, to whom they may be given, and what strings are attached to them that tie the negotiating department head's hands.

Unless you have it on good authority that the institution you are dealing with is a known rescinder, all job offers should be negotiated. Negotiations can cover salary, moving expenses, teaching release, a guaranteed junior sabbatical, research funds, start-up funds, conference funds, and so on, but how many of these things you can ask for, and how much of an increase, will hinge on the status of the institution, and your field. Hard science and life science offers are quite breathtaking from a humanities point of view. When I help clients from science fields negotiate, I routinely stand by flabbergasted at what they get. Many science discipline hires will easily get ten to one hundred times (in dollar value) what a humanities hire can expect at the same institution (for example, $10,000 in start-up funding for the assistant professor in English versus $1 million for the assistant professor in astronomy).

Negotiating is really an art. I have clients give me a rundown not just of their initial offer but of how warm or cold the department felt, how eagerly they feel they're being recruited, their sense of what recent hires have been given, the overall financial outlook of the institution, and a range of other factors. Then we carefully construct the negotiating request playbook over an extended series of email exchanges. These things take careful thought and consideration.

It may be a hard lesson that at the end of all those years toiling away in the Ph.D. program and on the job market, and perhaps as an itinerant adjunct, when you finally grab the gold ring of the tenure track position, you still have little power indeed. But that is the case. However, never confuse little power with no power. You have some, and a successful negotiation will extract every last little bit of benefit from it.

PART VIII

······················

GRANTS AND POSTDOCS

FIFTY-ONE

The Foolproof Grant Template

G rants are essential to a competitive record. First, because they are evidence of peer review that demonstrates the intellectual viability of your project. A major grant shows you to be, in a sense, "pre-vetted" by a set of scholars in your field. And second, because you need the money to finish the work without adding to your debt.

Grant writing is the most formulaic of all genres of academic writing. I learned this as a new assistant professor through the good graces of a senior colleague, a full professor who had recently moved to West Coast U from an Ivy League institution. He kindly took me under his wing, and one of the things that he told me in my first year was to apply for major national fellowships, and not stop until I got a year of research leave to write my book. He had received the National Endowment for the Humanities Fellowship a few years earlier, and he urged me to apply.

I demurred—how could I compete for a major fellowship that even senior scholars struggled to win? Nevertheless, he encouraged me, and passed on to me his own successful proposal to use as a model. He explained that this proposal drew from another proposal written by one of his former senior colleagues at his previous institution. I was at least the third generation to draw from the model. The projects of the three proposals were not remotely similar in terms of topic or geographical area; rather, it was only the proposal structure that he was telling me to study. The first iteration, and then my colleague's, and then my own, all followed a consistent organization. And, lo and behold, it worked for me for the NEH competition, just as it had worked for them.

I immediately saw the utility of the proposal structure, and used it again and again. Once I mastered it, I won virtually every grant and fellowship for which I applied. When I had graduate students of my own, I passed my NEH application on to them, calling it my "grant template." All of my students used it to organize their grant and fellowship applications and they, too, won almost every major fellowship for which they applied.

I freely shared my proposal with any grad student who asked during my years of teaching. Eventually I left my academic career and came back to West Coast U, where I briefly worked as an advisor in the McNair Scholars Program, a program providing graduate school preparation and application support for first-generation and underrepresented advanced undergraduate students, very green in the ways of the academic world. These students were all working on applications for much-needed fellowships, and I knew that the template would help them, but I saw that they were too inexperienced to be able to decipher the organization themselves. So I took the next step, and I broke it down for them.

I reduced my old NEH proposal into its elemental building blocks, and provided a basic explanation for its parts. I saw that the formula is, at root, a Hero Narrative, and that it establishes the three goals of legitimacy, urgency, and viability.

The first step is to identify the general topic of wide interest that your specific project relates to. This will be a topic that anyone in your field would agree is significant. If your work concerns urgent topics such as immigration, sustainable energy, curing cancer, new social technologies, environmental degradation, global climate change, and so forth, this is easy. But even if you work in an obscure area of study, you must begin at the widest possible level of interest. Until you can identify a broadly interesting theme, you will never be completely successful in applying for grants. Your application must excite readers, and the readers are likely from a range of different disciplinary locations. They will not be compelled by intellectual minutiae and the angels on the heads of the pins of your

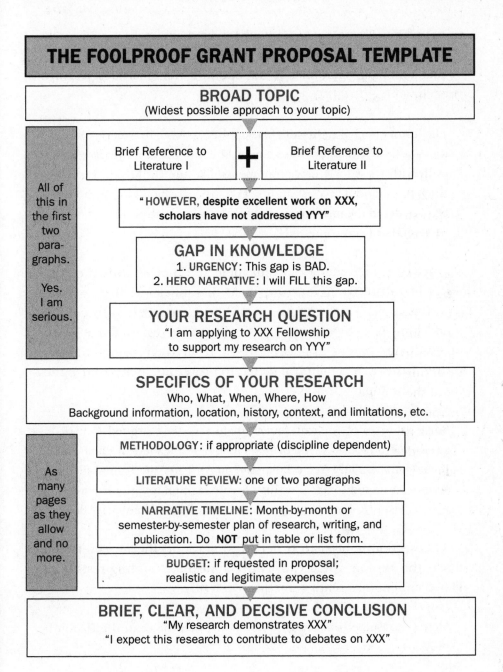

micro-niche. They want to know that your work and your scholarly vision are broad and encompassing.

The following example of an opening demonstrates the approach.[1]

> The history of civil rights and black power activism in American history and public memory has come to the fore in recent years, especially with the rise of new monuments, like the Dr. Martin Luther King Jr. Memorial in Washington, D.C. The question of who should be considered the most important black leaders in these movements, however, has been contested.

Once you have established your topic, you then identify two bodies of literature from your own field or subfields that have dealt with this topic. This brief survey will be no more than three sentences long. It is not a comprehensive literature review, the bugbear of graduate student applicants fresh from their comprehensive exams. Instead, it is merely a sketch to prove the intellectual legitimacy of the topic.

> Some scholars of African American history have argued that research should focus on the primary ideological leaders of the movement (Jeffries 2002). Yet, scholarship on African American women's history has noted that leadership narratives often marginalize women's activism (Robinett 2000, Gore, Woodard, and Theoharis 2009).

This section is brief in order to foreground the However Sentence, the axis on which your entire appeal for funding rests. The However Sentence reads something like this:

> However, none of these works have addressed the central question of X.

X in this case is what your research has revealed to be essential to an accurate understanding of the big topic identified in the first one or two sentences.

In our case:

To date, however, little work has thoroughly examined African American women's central role as intellectual and ideological leaders in the black power movement.

Notice that the However Sentence operates without any passive aggressive or judgmental rhetoric about other scholars' failings ("the stunning failure of the field to account for X"). A neutral observation of a gap in the literature suffices.

This brings us to urgency. What are the stakes of not knowing this thing?

As a result, scholarship endorses a narrative that characterizes African American women primarily as activists, making their intellectual role marginal or nonexistent in one of the largest social movements in American history. Without an adequate analysis of African American women as activists and intellectuals, we undervalue their impact in the civil rights and black power movements, ultimately leading to a one-sided conceptualization of the movements' importance and legacy.

Enter the Hero. As the Hero, you are the one who shall save us from ourselves, and our devastating ignorance about the true significance of X.

My project, *Title*, remedies this gap by analyzing the intellectual production of black women radicals during the black power movement.

This is immediately followed by a concrete statement of the proposed work. This is one of the most often forgotten elements.

I am applying to the X University Postdoctoral Fellowship in order to transform my dissertation into a monograph, *Title*, a study of the impact of African American women on the ideological and organizational direction of the black power movement.

This can be followed by a brief preliminary elaboration of the methods and the argument of the research.

Through close examinations of the political speeches, pamphlets, and drawings of women in black power organizations, I argue that African American women developed gender-specific political identity models that connected their gendered interests to black power ideology. I contend that the political models that African American women developed caused black power organizations, and the movement at large, to be more inclusive in their ideological and political priorities. Ultimately, my research shows that the models created through African American women's intellectual production caused the movement to be as radical in its critique of patriarchy as it was in its critique of racism.

The most important single rule of the Foolproof Grant Template is controlling the length of this opening. All of the above must be accomplished in two paragraphs, and no more. The tendency of far too many grant writers is to front-load obscure arguments and complaints, and to bury their topics in a sea of literature review and citation, leading to an organization in which the point of the grant is not arrived at until five or more pages into the proposal (or never!).

This is an error, because it doesn't take into account the state of mind of the reviewer. The reviewer is skimming what could well be hundreds of these proposals. The reviewer is exhausted and distracted. If the legitimacy and urgency of the project are not established immediately on the first pages, the proposal will be passed over.

The rest of the proposal provides substantiating evidence that the project is a feasible one, according to reasonable and well-thought-out disciplinary methods and timeline. That is, it establishes viability—that the project can and will be finished during the term of, and using the resources of, the grant or fellowship.

Specifics and Background: One or two paragraphs of specific information about the background, context, history, and scope of the research. This section often answers basic questions such as when, where, who, what, and how.

Literature Review: A brief sketch of the major literature related to the topic, no more than one or two paragraphs in length. This is not your comprehensive exams. All sources may be listed in an attached bibliography, which will likely not count against length or word count.

Methodology: If appropriate to your field, include the methods that you will use to conduct the research. These differ by discipline, and are not always required.

Timeline: A narrative, semester-by-semester, or month-by-month, plan of research. What will you do when? Be specific and give dates. Here is an example:

> The X Postdoctoral Fellowship will allow me to revise this project for publication as a scholarly monograph. During the first semester of the fellowship, I will continue conducting interviews with women like Q, who organized women's meetings and speeches at major political events. I will also finalize chapter 4, using this new material. During the Spring semester, I will finalize chapter 5, revise the conclusion, and submit the manuscript to scholarly presses such as University of X Press and University of Y Press. During the second year of the award, I will begin researching my next scholarly project, *"Title."* This project will examine A and B [about two sentences]. My preliminary research shows that . . . [about 1 sentence]. Resources for this project are located in the S Center for Research on Black Culture, etc.

Budget: This is not required in all proposal narratives. If it is, include both anticipated costs and any already committed funding sources. Break down your legitimate research expenses, including lab supplies, field supplies, travel both large and small, books and materials, Internet or computer access fees, and so forth.

Conclusion: Finish with a clear conclusion. Even one sentence suffices, but do not neglect to include it. It may read like this: "I expect this research to contribute to debates on X and play an important role in shaping research on X and Y in the coming years."

> My scholarship reveals black women's previously hidden intellectual production, making their theoretical contributions more accessible. In the process, it reveals black women activists as key figures in the development and direction of black power activism, ultimately contributing to debates about the public memory of African American liberation movements.

This conclusion pulls together the disparate elements of the application and returns the reader to the urgency of the subject.

Do all of this, my friend, and you will walk away with abundant funding for every project. You will have the leisure to do the best work, and the best work will, in turn, legitimize you for the next major grant for which you apply. You will be on the grant gravy train, and that is the key to the most successful academic careers. As you gain these successes, be sure to pass on your own grant proposals as models to those coming after you. Stay alert to this kind of capital when it crosses your path, and always be ready to pass it on. It's good karma.

FIFTY-TWO

Proving Your Project Is Worthy

While the Foolproof Grant Template is highly formulaic, that doesn't mean it is easy to apply in practice. There are two places where grant writers working with the template routinely fall down: The first is in the first "large topic" sentence. And the second is in the articulation of the "gap" that occurs in the However Sentence.

In the Foolproof Grant Template, I ask for an opening sentence or two that quickly engages the reader in the topic of the research. This is more difficult than it seems. Young academics have been so disciplined to think in terms of analysis and citation that they cannot easily step back to remember that there is a phenomenon that precedes scholarly argumentation about the phenomenon. This phenomenon exists or existed in the world at large—the world in which people live, as opposed to the world that is inside your or your advisor's mind.

You will note that the Foolproof Grant Template does not open with the tedious line, "My/this research/dissertation is about . . ." That is because this is one of the most self-absorbed openings possible, and it displays indifference to the wants and needs of readers.

Consider these four opening sentences:

"My dissertation is about declining polar bear populations."

"I am applying to the X Fellowship to support my dissertation, which is on declining polar bear populations."

"Many scientists in the field of environmental studies have been debating the causes of polar bear population decline."

"Polar bear populations are plummeting due to recent changes in the climate."

Only the last actually rises up to articulate the phenomenon that precedes any studies, arguments, or analyses, and inspires the reader to take notice.

It is true that to continue in this vein would be to move into a kind of journalistic sensationalism, but as you are a scholar, that is easily avoided. In sentence 2 and 3 of the template, you situate the phenomenon within a scholarly dialogue, and then demonstrate the existence of a scholarly gap. Grant writing is, let it not be forgotten, PR. You are selling a project, and the reader needs to buy it.

You do that by remembering that we live in a world of big issues. This is true even when your work is on a relatively obscure topic—for example, fourteenth-century Japanese Buddhist iconography, or, say, compositional structure in early modern opera—as long as it is one meaningful in your particular field. "Big" is a relative term, and while the truly big issues of our times—immigration, global climate change, and the like—garner the largest grants, any academic subject can be shown to speak to important disciplinary questions.

Once you have established your topic and the bodies of literature that relate to it, the next problem arises at the point where you identify a gap, in order to legitimize your specific research topic. The difficulty here is that just because something has never been studied before does not in and of itself mean that it should be. And just because you chose to spend a decade of your life on a subject does not in and of itself mean that we, as readers, find the subject worthy of interest or financial support.

Many new grant writers are confused on these two points, and fondly and naïvely believe that because they found a gap, and because they spent a decade trying to fill that gap, the importance of the gap will be immediately compelling to funders. It is not.

In short, too many grant writers imagine that the gap is the exact micro-topic of their dissertation.

I once had a colleague who used to mock the annoying academics who bring every discussion back to their own interests. "Why did that job talk [on, for example, postwar American ethnic literature] not discuss elephants?" she'd slyly ask. In other words, why aren't you discussing the thing *I'm* interested in?

This is the problem of the Foolproof Grant Template gap, except that here it is the grant writer who has taken on the role of the self-absorbed academic: "Why has the field failed to address elephants, i.e., my particularly scholarly preoccupations? Outrageous, I say!"

This is the reason that so many grant applications devolve into sour complaints about those "other" scholars who have "badly neglected" or "incomprehensibly overlooked" or "shockingly failed to address" this microscopically small topic. Remember: Just because people have not yet discussed topic X does not in and of itself persuade us, the readers, that topic X is worthy of being discussed.

Readers are under no obligation to consider your micro-topic of any inherent interest or urgency, until you actually use your words to demonstrate that it is. That does not mean adding five new sentences to construct a fatiguingly wordy rationale. It means using one sentence effectively to shake the reader into awareness that the literature, while excellent, has overlooked a point that upon further reflection is of great significance.

Let's take a dissertation on emergent racial minority activism in Japan. Here is a self-absorbed gap sentence:

> Stunningly, scholars to date have failed completely to adequately address the imagery of historical and geographical identity used in websites created by groups such as the Buraku Liberation League.

Here is an effective gap sentence:

> Scholars to date have not attended to the increasing mobilization of social media and Internet technology in minority activism in Japan; these new technologies, however, have transformed activism by providing new anonymous sites for members to safely debate racial identity and plan real-world mobilizations.

The first example reads like a passive-aggressive indictment of other scholars for their failure to study *your* project. The second example educates the reader in an emergent phenomenon, and catalyzes curiosity about what the phenomenon really means. That curiosity is what keeps committees reading, and grant money flowing.

It is a perennial danger for dissertation writers to be obsessed by their narrow dissertation topics. To write an effective grant application, however, you need to step back, and be able to tell a wider story of why your topic is necessary and timely for an understanding of your subject writ large.

FIFTY-THREE

The Postdoc Application:
How It's Different and Why

Postdoctoral fellowships in the humanities and social sciences have emerged in the past twenty years or so as a kind of stopgap alternative to elusive first tenure track jobs. Sponsored by universities or foundations, they support research and writing work for scholars within a few years of their Ph.D.'s. Prominent examples include the Princeton Society of Fellows, the Harvard Society of Fellows, the Michigan Society of Fellows, and the Andrew W. Mellon Fellowship of Scholars, which places scholars at R1 institutions and elite liberal arts colleges around the country.

These postdocs are usually between one and three years in length, and they're typically organized around a theme that changes with each annual round of review. To take one example, the Princeton Society of Fellows science competition for 2015–18 will award four fellowships. Two of these are open to any area of the humanities or social sciences, one is focused on the study of "race and/or ethnicity," and one is reserved for what they are calling "humanistic studies."

These postdoctoral fellowships are distinct from science postdocs, which are arranged individually, last for an indefinite number of years, and constitute a required phase of training for the academic science career. The humanities and social science postdoc is an optional step, although an increasingly desirable one. It is worth noting that there is an emerging genre of teaching postdoc that is not an elite research-oriented post such as I have described so far, but instead an adjunct position in sheep's clothing. Study all postdoc advertisements carefully to ensure that you apply only for those that provide acceptable conditions related to your goals.[1]

Many junior people do not have a clear picture of the requirements of a postdoc application. Some treat the postdoc application too much like a job application, and some treat it too differently. The fact is, it falls somewhere in the middle. The principle that animates the postdoc application is this: You are there to serve the postdoc; the postdoc is not there to serve you. It is a misunderstanding of this basic principle that causes most errors of the postdoc application.

For the purposes of this chapter, I'm going to assume that the postdoc application requires a cover letter, a four-page research proposal, a description of a proposed course, and a brief statement of participation in the scholarly community. While these are not universally required, they will illuminate the general expectations and potential pitfalls of the typical postdoc application.

Cover Letter

The postdoc application cover letter is similar to the tenure track job cover letter. The letter will be no more than two pages long, and will include the same initial paragraphs devoted to introduction, dissertation, dissertation import, and publications. In all of this, the content must be oriented to the stated mission of the postdoc. If your research topic is Brazilian female immigrant workers to Japan, then for a gender postdoc, you will emphasize the ways this population exemplifies changing gender relations in Brazil and/or Japan; for a globalization postdoc, you will emphasize changing labor mobility globally; for an Asian Studies postdoc, you will emphasize economic, social, or political transformations specific to Japan. This tailoring requires an original recasting or reframing of your work to meet the mission of the postdoc; failure to do this means failure to get the postdoc.

The postdoc letter departs from the tenure track job cover letter after the descriptions of research and publishing; at this point, it must turn to a quick sketch of the plan of work for the fellowship year or years. It will articulate, month by month, or semester by semester, the timeline for research and writing and submission for publication.

If the postdoctoral fellowship includes a teaching component, the letter will then turn to teaching. It will articulate general teaching competencies and skills, but it will focus primarily on any proposed class required by the postdoc, and how the proposed class will also advance the mission of the postdoc.

This connection to the mission cannot be simply left implicit. If the postdoc is on food studies, it is not enough to simply propose a course on food. Rather, the connection must be made explicit:

> I propose to teach a course titled Food and Danger. By focusing on contemporary discourses of food purity and food threat, this course examines contemporary anxieties about food safety, obesity, and nutrition in the United States and beyond. Bridging scientific and media texts, and capitalizing on the dynamic Internet world of food blogs, this course will advance the mission of the X postdoc by inquiring into the ways that science and popular culture collide in contemporary understandings of food as threat.

Lastly, in place of the typical tailoring paragraph, the letter will conclude with a brief paragraph explaining how the candidate will participate in the scholarly community on campus, and use the resources provided by the campus. The campus is funding this expensive postdoc not so some random academic can come and sit in an office and write for a year, but rather, to "buy" the energy, contributions, and participation of an additional world-class scholar to their campus community for the period of that year. Everybody knows that you are frantic to get your writing done and desperate to find a location to do it. Who isn't? This does not distinguish you. What they care about is that you serve the postdoc by participating in campus/departmental scholarly life. You do this, however, as in all professional documents, without flattering, pandering, or begging.

Do not waste their time by telling them they are illustrious, brilliant, dynamic, or vibrant. Rather, identify specific faculty on campus with whom you would collaborate, and initiatives and programs on campus that are likely to house interdisciplinary conversations and debates to which your project relates. Articulate, without any desperate, emotional rhetoric, how you will participate in them.

Four-Page Research Proposal

This research proposal looks very much like a grant application, and the Foolproof Grant Template will serve you well here, at least for the opening paragraphs. As in all research proposals you will want to open by proving the importance and urgency of your topic. You will construct the proposal as Hero Narrative, and follow the Foolproof Grant Template all the way through to the point where it breaks off into things like budget and methodology. In place of those sections, you will focus entirely on timeline. The point of a postdoc research proposal is to, first, articulate an important and significant project, and second, demonstrate that the project can be completed during the period of the postdoctoral fellowship. For U.S. postdocs, the expected project for at least the first year or two is transforming your dissertation into publications or a book.

The postdoc committee wants to see that the applicant is going to efficiently use the time on campus to complete specific research tasks, and a clear set of publications. Postdoc committees like publications. They like to be mentioned in the acknowledgments of books: "This research was completed while I was in residence at . . ." To repeat, they are not inviting someone and paying them good money to come and pretend they are still in graduate school. They are inviting you to produce. They will appreciate a month-by-month timeline/plan of work that shows explicitly what new archival research you will conduct, and when; what journal articles you will finish and submit, and when; and, if you are in a book field, what book chapters you will complete, and when the book manuscript will be sent to publishers.

After the timeline of work, you'll end with a strong conclusion that shows how the postdoc year will play into your larger career trajectory as a scholar.

Prestigious postdocs are in the business of supporting the next generation of leaders in the scholarly world. To the extent that you represent yourself as a leader, you will do well. To the extent that you harp on and on about how much you need the postdoc to get out of an oppressive teaching load, you will do poorly. Be aware that the vast majority of postdoc applications do the latter.

Proposed Course Description

Many applicants do not clearly grasp the difference between the postdoc and an adjunct, and they propose courses that are generic and basic. This is a mistake. Postdocs are expensive. If a campus wanted a generic and basic course, it would hire a cheap adjunct. There are many available. Instead, they are advertising for a postdoc. That means they want a highly specialized course that reflects the postdoctoral scholar's distinctive scholarly program.

The class can't be absurdly specialized, of course. If the applicant's dissertation topic is the emerging gay male community in Jakarta, the course cannot be Emerging Gay Male Communities in Jakarta. Too narrow. Neither should it be Introduction to Indonesia or Gender and Sexuality. Too broad. Rather, it should be pitched somewhere around Global Sexualities, or Gender and Sexuality in Southeast Asia, or Queer Globalizations. The final choice for how to pitch the course will hinge on the climate of the department and the campus, and the postdoc mission itself—if it's an Asian studies postdoc, then you would prioritize Gender and Sexuality in Southeast Asia; if it's a gender postdoc, then you would prioritize Global Sexualities; if it's a transnational studies postdoc, then you would prioritize Queer Globalizations. Tailoring to the mission of the postdoc happens here, too. The specific elements of the course description can follow the template I introduce in chapter 31.

Statement of Participation in Campus Community

Not all postdocs require this separate statement, and even if they do, you should still sketch this information in your cover letter. It is important enough to bear repetition. The postdoc committee does not want someone who arrives, walks into their allotted office, and is never seen again for the rest of the year. What they want is someone who arrives and dives into the scholarly community of the department and the campus. A postdoctoral scholar is typically exempted from all service work on campus, which leaves time for the scholar to make herself visible as an involved departmental member. She should show up for brown bags and talks, symposia and conferences, and coffee and lunch with colleagues.

It is in this statement of participation that you articulate your orientation in that direction. Identify programs and initiatives in the department and on campus, by name, and discuss how you anticipate participating. Mention two or three faculty members by name, and how you look forward to engaging with them.

Do not default to graduate student behavior. In the humanities and social sciences, the postdoc is not meant to be a continuation of your graduate training, in which you "study under" the important and illustrious faculty at the institution. You are not awarded a prestigious postdoc to be a student. They have plenty of students, and do not need any more. You are awarded a prestigious postdoc to be an important, albeit temporary, member of the scholarly community. This is a major point of difference with science postdocs, where the postdoc *is* conceived as a continuation of training, and the postdoc advisor often plays a role somewhat analogous to the dissertation advisor.

Thus, in humanities and social science postdoc applications, do not write that you wish to go to campus to "learn from" or "study with" the "esteemed" and "illustrious" scholars there. Rather, you *are* one of the scholars there. They may well learn from you. The proper stance here is that of a colleague who brings her own dynamic field of expertise to the campus, and who looks forward to energetic interactions with colleagues.

FIFTY-FOUR

The Good and the Bad of Postdocs

Before leaving the subject of postdocs, we must pause to consider their larger value to the academic career for scholars in the humanities and social sciences. For those in the sciences, postdocs have long been an expected part of early career training, and their value is relatively clear. But for humanists and social scientists, how should they be weighed?

With depressing regularity, I hear about advisors who tell their advisees that they are "not ready" for the tenure track job market and should thus limit their job search to only postdocs. Or, conversely, that they have told their advisees that postdocs are "pointless" and should be ignored in the search for tenure track jobs. Both pieces of advice are preposterous.

Anyone who can apply for a postdoc can apply for a tenure track job. And anyone seeking a tenure track job would do well to score a prestigious postdoc. The prestigious research postdoc is not only a major line on the CV, but also provides the money, time, and resources to generate the publishing record necessary to get a tenure track job. Aside from what is usually a nonexistent or minimal teaching requirement (except in the case of the "teaching postdoc"), the recipient is free to write in ways that are unavailable to anyone else, whether grad student, adjunct, or tenure line faculty. The postdoctoral scholar gets many of the advantages of a tenure line professor in terms of access to library resources and funding for conference and research travel without any onerous service or administrative duties. Thus, these postdocs are a marvelous opportunity for new Ph.D.'s to devote one or more years to revising their dissertation into a book or other publications.

So what is the best way to use the one to three years at a humanities or social science postdoc? Task number one is get your writing done. You should expect to finish your book manuscript by the end of year one or, if you have a multiyear postdoc, by the middle of year two at the latest. If you have a two- or three-year postdoc, expect to devote the latter part to a major second monograph or research project.

Go into the postdoc with a writing plan, and stick to it. Don't dawdle! Once you get into a tenure line job or fall into a cycle of adjuncting, you'll never have this kind of time again.

Because postdocs are temporary, you must calculate the timing of your writing and submissions for publication carefully with an eye to the job market, and be fiercely conscious of unexpectedly looming fall job application deadlines for your next position to follow.

Imagine that you have a two-year postdoc. While you ostensibly have two years of open and unfettered writing time, for the purposes of the job search, you have only one year, because only the publications you completed and references you cultivated during the first year will be available by, say, October 15 of the second year, which is the deadline for many applications. Countless postdoctoral scholars have been caught unaware by this matter of timing, and fail to front-load lines on the CV for applications they must send out immediately for their *next* position a year hence.

With a one-year postdoc, it is even harder. You have to submit applications for next year's positions before you've barely even arrived to take up residence at the postdoc! Plan ahead to have one or more manuscripts in submission over the summer, or at latest by early fall of the postdoc year. As one reader wrote in a guest post for my blog, "I did not calculate that the glorious three-year postdoc in fact translated to two years before I'd be on the job market. . . . It also goes without saying that I had no idea how journal submissions or timelines functioned. Little did I know that for fast-track journals, if all goes well, the time from submission to acceptance could be the same length of time to create a human being."

Besides publishing, the second major task for the postdoc is networking. There you are, on the Harvard/Princeton/Michigan/etc. campus. Don't waste it. You'll already be in a cohort sharing nearby office space. You'll see those colleagues every day, and they are likely working—if the postdoc competition is based on a theme—on topics close to your own. In addition, some of the leading scholars in your field are either there, or visiting there. Meet them and get to know them. Create a scholarly community among the faculty on campus in all relevant departments, and the scholars who pass through giving talks.

I am often asked whether it's better to take a tenure track job at a low-ranked, teaching-heavy institution, or an elite and luxurious, but temporary, postdoc. I can't answer this question. The decision hinges entirely on your personal circumstances. The unbroken writing time and networking possible at an elite institution are invaluable for anyone's career. But what is the cost? If you are exhausted from spending years moving from one temporary position to another, need job security because of family or other obligations, or wish to avoid the publish-or-perish elite career track, then the tenure line job at a lesser institution is the right choice. Much depends on your stomach for risk. And then, the risk itself is always in flux and unpredictable. How bad is the market in your field now, and how much worse is it likely to get in the future? Nearly all fields and subfields are declining in terms of tenure track hires, but not all are declining at the same pace. If yours is one that is still hiring, then the risk of waiting an additional year on the hope of a second offer later is not as dire as it is in fields that are nearing extinction. In the end, nobody knows your circumstances but you.

PART IX

. . . .

SOME ADVICE ABOUT ADVISORS

FIFTY-FIVE

······················

Best Advisors, Worst Advisors

I had a rocky road into graduate school. I had won the prestigious, and completely portable, National Science Foundation Graduate Research Fellowship, and had been recruited with a generous package of supplemental funding by an Ivy League university. I was on the path to finish graduate school with a nest egg.

Then I traveled to a major national conference to have a personal meeting with my soon-to-be Ivy anthropology advisor . . . and he behaved like a toad. He was rude. He was dismissive. He sighed at my proposed topic, the one that had won the six years of full funding—an innovative (for the late '80s) study of the impact of Japanese corporate culture on Southeast Asian workers in Japanese factories opening in countries such as Thailand and Malaysia. He kept looking over my shoulder to find other, more important people to talk to.

At the end of our brief talk in the conference hallway, I was stunned, heartbroken, and mostly confused. I cried, slunk back to my hotel room, and raged to friends. A week or so later, recovering some of my equilibrium, and never one to suffer in silence, I called up the department to complain. I learned that the graduate college at the university had happily recruited me (and my NSF award) without first gaining the buy-in of the one faculty member—the lone Japan anthropologist—who would have to be my primary advisor. If I had entered that program, I would have entered a world of hurt.

Outraged and disgusted, I made a quick decision, withdrew from the program, and turned to another program that had also offered me generous funding to work with a well-known Japan anthropologist there. I was happy and well funded at that institution, and things worked out OK with my advisor for quite a while ... and then they didn't. Suffice to say, for most of the years I worked with her, she was good enough.

But over the years I learned a lot about what makes advisors good, bad, excellent, and terrible. Not just from my advisor, but from watching my friends in the program and their struggles with their advisors, and then coming to advise students myself, and observing the advising practices of my colleagues.

What should you expect from an advisor?

A good advisor will likely be very busy and require some careful scheduling to meet. However, once tracked down, he should do the following: Read and comment on your work in a timely fashion, pass you through the stages of your program in an ethical and transparent fashion, write letters of recommendation and submit them by the deadline, educate himself about the contemporary job market and tell you bluntly what you're doing wrong in your job search, read your CV and cover letter and provide intensive edits, inform you of the necessity of publishing and instruct you on how to do it, encourage you to apply for national and international grants, remind you of submission deadlines for your national conference and teach you how to apply, and, while at the conference, make time to introduce you to his colleagues from other campuses, especially the well-known and influential ones.

A good advisor is rare indeed. With apologies to Proverbs 31 and King James, the following shows you what to expect:

Who can find a virtuous advisor? For his price is far above rubies.

The heart of his advisee doth safely trust in him, so that she shall have no need of panic.

He will do her good and not evil all the days of his life.

*He seeketh publishing opportunities for her, and worketh willingly to
promote her.*

He is like the merchants' ships; he bringeth her funding from afar.

*He riseth also while it is yet night, and giveth feedback to his students
and a portion to his female students.*

*He considereth an application and readeth it; with the fruit of his
hands he provides extensive comments.*

*He girdeth his loins with timely career advice, and strengtheneth his
understanding of the current job market, and not the one from the 1970s.*

*He perceiveth that his advisee is highly qualified; his candle goeth not out
by night when writing recommendation letters for every job and postdoc.*

*He stretcheth out his hand to the adjunct; yea, he reacheth forth his hands
to the underemployed.*

*He provideth advice on appropriate clothing; his grooming is a model
to his male students.*

He openeth his mouth with wisdom, and on his tongue is the law of kindness.

*His advisees arise up and call him blessed; his department head also,
and she praiseth him:*

Many faculty have done virtuously, but thou excellest them all."

Here are the five top traits of the worst advisors. If you are still
considering graduate school, test for these before you commit
yourself to an advisor or a program. If you are already in graduate
school, and you recognize your advisor in this list, see if you can
switch out. If not, work to protect yourself. And if you are in graduate school and your advisor has none of these traits, you've won the
advisor lottery, appreciate your good fortune (and good judgment),
and prepare to pay it forward with your own students later.

5. Steals Your Work

This doesn't happen too often. But when it does, it means you have
the very worst advisor. This is a toxic advisor, and you need to get
out immediately. Talk to your department head, and the graduate
dean.

4. Is Maddeningly Inconsistent

This advisor insists on one path of action one week, and the next week, insists on its perfect opposite. One meeting they tear apart your dissertation chapter with "Too much poststructuralist feminist theory! It's completely unnecessary to your argument!" You make the revisions, send in the new version, and the next meeting, she responds with "Where's your poststructuralist feminist theory? How can you possibly write this chapter without it?"

Don't give up in despair. Just follow up every meeting with a clear, short email that summarizes what was said. Then include that email when you submit the next set of revisions, and be ready to whip it out if you find the advisor contradicting it some time later.

3. Is Abusive, Negative, and Undermining

This is sadly common. This is the advisor that can't manage a positive comment. Avoid these advisors if you can, but it's possible you can't. If you're already committed to one, surround yourself with other, positive, mentors. Remember that with all negative, undermining people, they are actually talking to and about themselves, and not anyone else.

Ironically, the best path with an advisor like this is to stand up for yourself. Bow and scrape and apologize and trust me, the abuse will intensify. Set firm boundaries and stand up for your ideas . . . and chances are, she'll back off.

2. Is Never Around

The more famous your advisor is, the more likely he is always jetting off to Amsterdam, South Africa, or Singapore for some high-powered conference or symposium or keynote address. This is also a risk if you have an assistant professor advisor in about his fourth or fifth year in the department: always away giving the next big talk.

Get self-sufficient fast, find mentors on campus who are more available, and schedule meetings with your advisor well in advance.

This one, you can work around. With email, Google Docs, Face-Time, and Skype . . . nobody really needs to be anywhere these days.

1. Is Nice, Friendly, and Available

Wait, what?

Yes: is nice, friendly, and available . . . and never gives you the fierce criticism and the tough pushback that force you to confront your weaknesses, take risks, stop whining, cut the excuses, get over your fears, and make hard decisions about reputation, money, and jobs.

This advisor has been the downfall of countless graduate students. Too wussy to go after the big guns, these students circle around the nice associate professor ladies (and the occasional man) in the department, the ones who remember their birthdays and sometimes bring in homemade bread.

Example conversation with a nice advisor:

You: I'm getting ready to submit a proposal for a poster at the MLA!

Nice advisor: Awesome! You'll be great!

Example conversation with an effective advisor:

You: I'm getting ready to submit a proposal for a poster at the MLA!

Effective advisor: Really? Didn't you submit a poster last year? Now that you've advanced to candidacy you need to stop that; it's time you were presenting papers. Papers are lines that count on your CV, and they give you the experience that you need of speaking in front of an audience or handling the Q and A. You still have time before the deadline, so write a paper proposal and give it to me for a check before you submit it.

Do not attach yourself to someone nice. Attach yourself to someone intense. They might not be warm and fuzzy, but they'll have you prepared to succeed. If you've never cried before, during, or after a meeting with your advisor, something is amiss. This does not mean ongoing abuse, of course, or sabotage or undermining. It means that your self-satisfied assumptions have been shaken, your too-low bar of achievement abruptly raised. Do athletes make the Olympics working with nice trainers who tell them everything they do is great? In the academy as it's currently constituted, you need to surround yourself with those who, from a place of care, push you far outside your own complacent comfort zone.

If you are early in your grad school career and already know your advisor's a dud, change advisors. If you are late in your grad school career and only just realized your advisor's a dud, you can still protect yourself by getting help from other sources.

Bonus Worst Advisor: The Emeritus

Do not have an emeritus as your advisor. Emeriti are old. They made their reputation in decades past. They may have been highly successful and powerful. But that was in the past. Now, their work is old, their peers are old, their connections are old, their publications are old, and their theoretical foundations are old.

I can hear some of you indignantly defending the preciousness of your emeritus advisor and his still-vibrant contributions to the field. Maybe you have a good one, maybe not. I've never personally seen a case where it worked out. I have seen far too many examples of graduate students' lives and careers destroyed by emeritus advisors who were too out of touch to be able to help their students cope with the brutality of the current job market. You, my reader, are about the future. The emeritus is about the past. Do not be seduced by their corduroy patches, their leisurely gait, their home-brewed beer, and the endless, endless hours they have to spare for you. Stay clear; keep a wide berth.

Don't ever forget this rule: If your advisor seems to have infinite amounts of time to talk to you . . . be skeptical.

FIFTY-SIX

A Good Advisor Is Not Nice

I received an email once from someone who signed herself "Nice Lady Advisor":

> I wish you would write a post on the "nice advisor" problem, addressed to us nice advisors. I aspire to your level of effective bluntness, but I often find myself choking up and couching my criticisms in such "constructive" terms that my advisees can miss the underlying hard truths. Many times I long to say, "This writing sample is boring and shallow, and nobody is going to give you a job/fellowship based on it." But I don't want to be toxic or undermining, so instead I say, "Use active verbs to make your writing more vivid! Make sure each paragraph has a topic sentence and evidence to support a claim! Frame your argument and claims as a response to arguments and claims in the current literature—refer to scholars X and Y!" And my advisees think their work is basically okay, when it's not.

All advisors, but particularly nice advisors, beware the impulse to water down your critique. The truth, if it is really the truth, and not some expression of your own private twisted agenda, is never toxic or undermining. It is empowering.

I say it again: The Truth Is Empowering.

The harm of the nice advisor lies in letting students believe there is no problem, that everything is fine. So the students cruise on, turning in chapters and defending their dissertation and sending out applications . . . until one day, they realize, at the hands of the unyielding job market: Everything is not fine. They are not brilliant. They should have been worried.

The last thing a student needs is a nice advisor, if by nice you are saying, or implying through your silences, "You have nothing to worry about." That is not adequate advising. That's abnegating responsibility. You empower your students when you tell them the truth. Even when the truth is hard and disappointing.

Nice advisors are the most insidious because their damage is hidden from view. At least with an abusive advisor the advisee knows there's a problem. Against a nice advisor, she is defenseless.

A client once told me about an interview she missed by mistake: "I had an interview scheduled with a great college in my town about a year ago, but when I drove out on the freeway to get there, I got mixed up and turned the wrong way. I couldn't get turned around in time to make the interview. By the time I got there, I was a half hour late, and I'd missed the interview."

She wrote to ask me if I felt she still had a chance at the department, which was advertising again. I felt myself start to say, "Oh, I'm sure you still have a chance." But then I stopped. Did I believe that? No, I did not. Truthfully, I thought she blew it. So was I helping her by saying otherwise? No, I was not. Had she come to me to make her feel good about herself? No, she had not. She came to me to hear the truth. So, I paused a moment and said instead, "Yeah, I think you blew it. I don't think a search committee will be likely to give you consideration when you flaked on an interview with them a year before."

And I realized again that, in Ph.D. advising, nice is wrong.

Of course, the advisor can't just criticize ("This writing sample is boring and shallow"). The advisor must *critique and teach*: "This writing sample is boring and shallow because it repeats an empty assertion multiple times without developing it with additional evidence and argumentation. To make it work for you you'll need to revise it to move crisply through an organization that lays out a question, then describes bodies of scholarship on the question, then advances an argument, then proves the argument with evidence, and then offers a conclusion. I can help you sketch the outline for that in the next five minutes. Then go away and do it, and send me back the revision."

This is advising. This is the job. This is what advisees should expect, and what advisors should provide.

If you're an advisor and do this, yes, your advisees may cry. They may resent you. No, they may not do what you say. It may not be comfortable. It may involve strife. But that is your job, as an advisor. To show them what they're doing poorly and teach them how to do it better.

If you want to go home and be nice to your cat or your kids or your friends, that's fine. But don't be nice to your advisees.

FIFTY-SEVEN

Ph.D. Debt and Ethical Advising

Graduate students: attend closely to the degree of transparency you find in your graduate department and advisor around the escalating scandal of Ph.D. debt. Ph.D. students in all fields, especially the humanities, routinely bear five- and six-figure debt, sometimes reaching over $200,000. As the *Wall Street Journal* pointed out in 2014, the debt of those with advanced degrees jumped an inflation-adjusted 43 percent between 2004 and 2012. In 2012 the median loan debt for this group reached $57,600. One in five graduate students now carry debt over $100,000, and the same figures show that one in ten graduate student borrowers owe more than $153,000.[1] The *WSJ* went on: "The increases were sharper for those pursuing advanced degrees in the social sciences and humanities, versus professional degrees such as M.B.A.s or medical degrees that tend to yield greater long-term returns."[2] Meaning that the graduate students with the fastest-increasing debt are those in the fields least likely to yield jobs and/or salaries sufficient to even contemplate full repayment.

Graduate students encounter this level of debt even when they are "fully funded" by their programs. Why? Because graduate stipends in the humanities and social sciences have stagnated during the past decades, and are rarely adequate to cover the actual costs of living in the regions in which most graduate programs are located.

(The same is sometimes true in the sciences and sometimes not; it hinges on the field and the institution.)

The recruitment of new Ph.D. students into humanities and social science degree programs that routinely offer inadequate "full" funding packages is the academic equivalent of subprime lending—the predatory lending practices that target vulnerable and unqualified borrowers. The inevitable foreclosures on these borrowers' properties, while catastrophic to the borrowers, only increase the banks' profits. In academia, the university is the bank, and the faculty are the bankers. Faculty are incentivized to increase graduate student enrollment, and suffer no personal consequences from graduate students' ruinous circumstances post-graduation. The university benefits from—indeed depends upon—graduate student labor in teaching and research, and transfers the costs of maintaining that labor force back on the laborers themselves, in the form of personal debt.[3] The Work of the Mind mythology enables (and simultaneously mystifies) a large-scale transfer of assets from the young and vulnerable to professor and administrator salaries through cheap grad student/Ph.D. labor, and also to bank profits through indebtedness.

Some might argue that the highly educated applicants to graduate programs are far from a vulnerable population. I disagree. Graduate school applicants are typically young, and like most young people they lack training in financial literacy. Indeed, this particular population is one that is wont to pride itself on its esoteric, otherworldly orientation and lack of financial self-interest; it considers those qualities a virtue and often a form of sophisticated cultural critique. And these applicants have been systematically misled by the blandishments of their undergraduate professors who flatter their intelligence, and market a vision of the academic life that includes only its allures (intellectual community, scholarly training, independence, and the company of like-minded souls) while hiding its costs (insufficient stipends, a collapsing job market, lost wages, staggering opportunity costs, and crushing debt).

Faculty do not inquire too deeply into how their graduate students are making ends meet on the stipends they offer. The average humanities stipend is around $15,000 a year, or $1,250 a month. It is not a stretch to imagine a modest budget (rent: $500, gas: $100, food: $300, utilities: $200, books and research: $200, misc.: $200 = $1,500) that immediately exceeds this. Include the university fees that are typically not covered by waivers (up to $1,000 a year), and professionalization activities required to search for a tenure track job, such as attending conferences, which will cost about $1,000 per conference, and the stipend falls far short. Now add dependents, or any kind of medical issue. Without help from family or spouse, the only option to stay afloat in the program is a loan. A modest loan of $10,000 a year seems not too extravagant, but multiply it by 7 or 10 years in a program, add interest, which for graduate students accrues while they are still enrolled . . . and voilà, the student bears a debt burden of $125,000. Add to this the typical debt from an undergraduate degree, and the Ph.D. now owes $150,000 to $175,000 for the privilege of a graduate degree that brings limited likelihood of employment.

Offer letters make no mention of this truth, and prospective graduate students lack the financial literacy to understand its implications for their future. Once a student is accepted into the program and under way, sunk costs accrue, and quitting looks like "failure." Conversely, finishing is defined as "success," even when finishing requires the borrowing of hundreds of thousands of dollars, with virtually no chance for an income sufficient to pay it off.

When I was a faculty member sitting on our admissions committee, proudly and grandiosely handing out our offers of "full-ride" fellowships to "deserving" incoming students, I often secretly wondered how any student could possibly live on the stipend we were offering. I never spoke this concern aloud, and neither did any of my colleagues. Now, of course, it's obvious. They can't. Certainly not if they live in a city, or have a child, or get sick, or lack a family subsidy.

Do I think humanities and social science Ph.D.'s with six-figure debt have made the most responsible of all possible life choices? No, I do not. I believe the level of denial about the repercussions of this debt is a direct reflection of the larger denial of economic reality that permeates all aspects of the Ph.D. enterprise. But I also understand the cultlike nature of the academy that prevents people from being able to imagine quitting, and that makes this debt appear logical and good, as if it's in the service of some higher calling.

In 2013, I created an open-source spreadsheet called the Ph.D. Debt Survey to gather some numbers and stories around the subject of Ph.D. debt.[4] It quickly went viral and garnered more than two thousand anonymous entries in the space of a week. It makes no claims to be a scientific survey.[5] I share the summaries of a few of its entries here (emphases my own). I urge graduate students to study these stories carefully, and direct other graduate students, as well as undergraduates considering grad school, to read them.

Case 1: Rhetoric and Composition, 2014 Ph.D.
Total Debt: $140,000

This current job-seeker took out loans to supplement her Ph.D. stipend in the $10,000 to $15,000 range. She was told that student debt is "good debt." She took out the loans based on the expectation she would earn around $40k/year upon graduation. Instead, she found no employment for months, despite looking broadly across the fields of teaching, technical writing, communications, and events. She wrote, "I have supplemented my income with freelance work and adjuncting each summer, which delayed my dissertation; am on fellowship this year to finish on time but am ineligible for loans and *am maxing out credit cards while on the job market, paying for campus visits and anxiously awaiting reimbursement.*"

Case 2: Psychology, 2009 Ph.D.
Total Debt: $275,000

This single mother went back to school in her 30s to complete a BA, MA, and then Ph.D. Preschool tuition costs were higher than those for her master's program, and she could only cover total expenses with loans. Separated from her husband by the time she began her Ph.D., and with a five-year-old at home, she struggled to cover the costs of full-day kindergarten, a home, car, tuition, books, etc., and took out additional loans to manage it. She is presently employed in a nonacademic position at a university and pays a little each month toward the debt. She writes, "I am now too scared to apply for a home loan because I'm sure I'll be turned down, since I make in the $50s and have this massive student loan debt. It is overwhelming and I wake often thinking about the fact that my fourteen-year-old will soon go to college, and I have my own enormous debt. I work in a job where I will hopefully get it wiped away after ten years, but I fear that won't happen by then. *It's a HORRIBLE feeling to owe this much. I wish I had never gone back to school.*"

Case 3: Anthropology, 2013 Ph.D.
Total Debt: $0

This securely employed person had undergraduate and master's programs paid for by family, and five years funding for her Ph.D. She wrote, *"It was only possible to not take loans because of family support."*

Case 4: Art History, 2007 Ph.D.
Total Debt: $0 (formerly $50,000)

This securely employed person took out loans to be able to live in an expensive area and "not to have to eat popcorn or ramen for dinner all the time" while in a grad program that paid only $11,500 in annual stipend. He was able to pay off debt and make a down payment on a house only due to a $100,000 inheritance his wife received after the death of her father. Prior to that they were paying more on debt service than on their mortgage. "Although I am employed and out of debt, I understand the severity of the debt question. My current university, a low-ranked, regional public institution, pays 25 percent less than our peers and has done so for a long time. We don't get raises. And this is an expensive town to live in. I don't see how other people who have debt manage it. *I could only pay off the debt due to a family inheritance.*"

Case 5: Anthropology, 2006 Ph.D.
Total Debt: $75,000 (formerly $90,000)

This tenured associate professor took out loans for undergraduate and graduate studies, to supplement fellowship and dissertation grants. She wrote, "I just keep chipping away at it. Month by month. *I am hopeful to one day experience loan forgiveness.*"

Case 6: Visual Art/Art History, 2011 Ph.D.
Total Debt: $57,000

This Ph.D. on the tenure track job market took out loans in graduate school to cover the costs of a life-threatening cancer diagnosis. With treatments, surgeries, radiation, and chemotherapy, he had to stop working for several years. Student loans helped cover the cost of living and paid for cancer treatments, many of which were not covered fully by limited student health insurance. Student debt seemed safer than accumulating more credit card debt. He worked multiple jobs and freelanced on weekends, paying back minimal amounts through the income-based repayment plan option. He has suffered some recent relapses in health, and wrote, "I can't even see past the next year let alone the next ten years of my life because my debt hampers my decision-making so much. *I doubt I will ever own a home, let alone retire. I hope that I can eventually get to a place where my debt doesn't make me feel suicidal every day.*"

Case 7: Archaeology, 2010 Ph.D.
Total Debt: $67,000

This person, who works at Starbucks while living with family, had a TA-ship funding package that covered only the eight-month academic year for eight years. The teaching assistant salary was not sufficient to allow savings for the four summer months. Funding ran out in the final semester, which had to be paid for out of pocket in order to defend. She needs to earn at least $45,000 per year in order to make the minimum payment on her student loans. She spent two years in non-tenure-track work, moving three times in twenty-four months. She was eventually unable to find another adjunct teaching contract and could no longer afford the intrastate moving expenses of going from one temporary postdoc/teaching job to another. She wrote, "I decided to 'leave' academia when I passed up the last relevant job posting because it was for a non-tenure-track, temporary teaching job at UCLA for which the salary was $25,000 *before* taxes, and required a move of 3,000 miles across the continent with no moving expenses reimbursement. *I wouldn't have been able to afford to take the job, even if I had been offered it.*"

Case 8: History, 2013 Ph.D.
Total Debt: $100,000

This securely employed person has loans from both undergraduate and graduate programs. His "full funding" package in graduate school paid $17,500 per year for five years, which barely covered rent and living expenses in the urban location. After that funded stage, while writing the dissertation, he taught, but for only $15,000 to $20,000 per year. The final year required additional loans to cover travel to three professional conferences. He has no repayment plan currently. He wrote, *"This debt is my deepest secret."*

What does the Ph.D. Debt Survey show us?

It shows us that without monetary support from either parents, grandparents, some other relative, or a working spouse, someone doing a Ph.D. in the humanities or social sciences will probably be unable to finish his or her program without five- or six-figure debt. It shows us that in the humanities and social sciences, "full funding" is a myth. As one anthropologist who owes $176,000 wrote, "I was 'fully funded' but that full funding barely covered travel expenses and rent on an inexpensive local apartment." Another anthropologist who owes almost $300,000 explained that when it was time to apply to graduate schools at the peak of the recession, programs had just cut their funding packages by 50 percent. In addition, because graduate student loans are unsubsidized, the interest rate is crushing. That entrant went on, "The 8.5+ percent of the Grad PLUS rape, I mean rate, is criminal. It has done much to inflate my debt amount."

It shows us that in the sciences, debt is far more rare. Few participants in the survey from the sciences had significant debt to begin with; those who did described quick repayment during well-compensated postdoctoral positions. As one wrote, "As soon as I graduate I can continue to live like a poor graduate student, but the increase in salary to the postdoc level should allow me to pay off all of my student loans within five years and then be able to finally live like an adult." One chemistry Ph.D. with $100,000 in debt expects to repay it by finding an "industry job." One psychology Ph.D. is having half of his debt paid off by the National Institutes of Health Loan Repayment Program. In order to qualify for the program, she had to choose a lab science (rather than teaching) based career track. "To increase my chances of obtaining the LRP, I based my job decisions and research topics on what the NIH valued. It kept me as a postdoc and a research assistant professor in a school of medicine versus the tenure track route . . . but just knowing my debt is likely resolved is the biggest weight off my shoulders."

By contrast, the majority of humanists and social scientists state that they are on a ten-year, twenty-year, or thirty-year federal repayment plan, vaguely hope for loan forgiveness, or have no plan (one wrote in the "Plans for Repayment" box: "HAHAHAHAHA-HAHAHA"). Even successful repayment puts a strain on all, delaying or hampering a range of life decisions. One environmental planning Ph.D. explained that she, at age thirty-eight, gave up her home, moved away from her partner for a postdoc position, and moved back in with her elderly father to save on rent. She wrote, "I put more than half my postdoc salary towards debt and paid it off in fourteen months. However, my adult life, relationship, and self-confidence have taken a significant hit from the sacrifice, and I fear we may not be able to afford to start a family while I am still young enough to have children."

Graduate school debt is where the tawdry financial reality behind the Work of the Mind mythology demands its due. Intellectual dreams have a price tag, and that price can wreck lives. One film

studies ABD called it a "deal with the devil." She wrote, "I could either believe in my abilities and passions and take the loans, or know
that my point of view would be excluded from knowledge production because of the lack of real economic support for accessible
higher education in the U.S."

The problem of course is that the choice to "believe in one's
abilities and passions," as this ABD asserts, is to lay a veneer of
self-empowerment over what is fundamentally exploitation. Many
intelligent people who can easily apply their critical faculties outward, to a critique of systemic exploitation in society, fail to correctly
identify the ways that graduate school has become a mechanism to
co-opt their own scarce resources, funneling them toward institutional and corporate gain, with "encouraging" undergraduate and
graduate faculty advisors as the enablers. As William Pannapacker
wrote in his *Chronicle of Higher Education* column "Graduate School
in the Humanities: Just Don't Go," "It's hard to tell young people
that universities recognize that their idealism and energy—and
lack of information—are an exploitable resource."[6]

Why is it so hard to see the operations and repercussions of this
systemic debt clearly? The cases provide insights.

- They are told that education debt is good debt.
- They believe, at the time, that the Work of the Mind is
  "priceless."
- They don't understand the long-term consequences of loans.
- They don't grasp the severity of the collapse in tenure track
  hiring.
- They experience unexpected health crises not covered by
  low-quality graduate student insurance.
- They struggle to accurately weigh sunk costs versus
  opportunity costs.
- They are debilitated by secrecy and shame.

Secrecy and shame create a vicious circle of debt, in which the loans
themselves become the reason for not quitting. One reader explained:
"I have some grad school debt, and to be honest with you, I do feel a

strange sort of shame about it. I was 'funded,' after all. I think I stayed in my program longer than I should have because I started taking out loans. How could I justify the loans if I didn't finish?"

The Ph.D. Debt Survey is evidence for Pannapacker's argument that at this time only a certain kind of student can pursue an advanced degree in the humanities without incurring serious financial risk. He writes,

> As things stand, I can only identify a few circumstances under which one might reasonably consider going to graduate school in the humanities:
>
> • You are independently wealthy, and you have no need to earn a living for yourself or provide for anyone else.
> • You come from that small class of well-connected people in academe who will be able to find a place for you somewhere.
> • You can rely on a partner to provide all of the income and benefits needed by your household.
> • You are earning a credential for a position that you already hold—such as a high-school teacher—and your employer is paying for it.
>
> Those are the only people who can safely undertake doctoral education in the humanities. Everyone else who does so is taking an enormous personal risk, the full consequences of which they cannot assess because they do not understand how the academic-labor system works and will not listen to people who try to tell them.[7]

This passage infuriated readers who wrote (and continue to write) enraged comments to the effect that the academy "should" accommodate anyone regardless of class or financial status. Indeed the academy should. But the academy does not. Pannapacker is not prescribing anyone's behavior; he is describing a financial reality.

Too many advisors turn a blind eye to the inherent conflict of interest in their position recruiting new graduate students (or encouraging talented undergraduates) to graduate programs within the predatory graduate labor/debt scheme on which universities depend (and from which tenured faculty benefit).

Indeed, many advisors actively insist that they should be allowed to continue to grow their graduate programs without qualms. In 2013 I attended a panel at the Modern Language Association conference called "Who Benefits? Competing Agendas and Ethics in Graduate Reform." The point of the panel was to acknowledge the lack of jobs for Ph.D.'s in English and promote reforms of graduate training in that field. Yet almost every panelist refuted calls to cut Ph.D. recruitment. One presenter even recommended expanding it. When an audience member spoke up on the urgency of reducing graduate admissions, the panel chair responded, "Absolutely not. Any move that we would make to cut our graduate programs would be professional suicide for us."

At which point I raised my hand and asked, "Who is this 'us'?"

Let's examine his statement: Any move that *we* would make to cut *our* graduate programs would be professional suicide for *us*.

Professional suicide is what graduate students are already committing on a daily basis as they confront the reality of a Ph.D. that cannot be turned into meaningful work, and the looming default on what are often hundreds of thousands of dollars in loans.

Professional suicide is what adjuncts are committing each year that they spill out their time, energy, and spirit in an endless, pointless, and ultimately fruitless quest for job security.

Professional suicide is what Ph.D.'s contemplate when they have to painfully and laboriously attempt to reinvent themselves for a nonacademic position, for which the Ph.D. is appallingly expensive, slow, and imprecise training, when they are already often in their midforties or beyond.

Professional suicide is what Ph.D.'s face when they discover ten or more years of their peak earning years (when they should have been paying into Social Security) have been lost in the black hole of a graduate program that yields nothing but devastating opportunity costs.

This panel set out to ask "who benefits" from graduate training. It could not have answered the question more clearly. The tenured benefit. They are the "us" that cannot contemplate or countenance a change in their privileged position.

Do not wait for your advisor and department to tell you the truth about their complicity in a predatory structure that exploits graduate students. Understand for yourself that they are entirely complicit. Faculty are absorbed by the ego gratification of producing replicas of themselves, and are explicitly and implicitly incentivized to keep the recruitment flow open and the TA courses staffed, regardless of the impact on you. To protect your well-being and financial future, beware the debt that is now a requisite element of graduate school training in many fields, and refuse to participate in any graduate school scheme that imposes it.

PART X

·············

LEAVING THE CULT

FIFTY-EIGHT

It's OK to Quit

It is OK to quit. It is OK to decide to move on and do something else. What started out as an inspired quest for new knowledge and social impact can devolve into endless days in an airless room, broke, in debt, staring at a computer, exploited by departments, dismissed by professors, ignored by colleagues, disrespected by students.

It is OK to decide that's not what you want. There is life outside of academia. But academia is a kind of cult, and deviation from the normative values of the group is not permitted or accepted within its walls.

If you decide to leave, make no mistake: You will be judged harshly by others and, yes, you will lose some of your academic friends, who can't tolerate the threat you represent to their most cherished values. When I began the earliest stirrings of my post-academic transition by making handmade jewelry from Japanese paper and selling it at my little card table in the parking lot of the Saturday farmers market in my Midwestern college town, I learned this, to my chagrin. A few tenured colleagues and friends, there to shop for the week's organic greens, would stop by to say hello. But far, far more would catch a glimpse of me, and stop in their tracks some distance away, faces registering first shock, then consternation, then horror: "She's a, a, a . . . *crafter?*" Then they would sidle by, eyes carefully averted. The pattern was painful, to say the least, although with time I came to appreciate it as a kind of test of character, or at least of their level of indoctrination into the cult.

More important, to the extent you've been properly socialized into the cult during graduate school, you will judge yourself. Making the decision to leave involves confronting that judgment, working through it, and coming out the other side. It is long and hard and involves profound shame. Heck, for a long time I was embarrassed for *myself*, at that card table in the parking lot.

If you're an adjunct you may well be caught in a delusional belief system that on the one hand you will get one of the tenure track jobs to which you apply (some possibility), and on the other hand that your excellent teaching, selfless service, and continued loyalty to the institution at which you adjunct will be rewarded with permanent employment at that institution (virtually zero possibility). You pour your heart into adjunct teaching because this teaching is your only concrete connection to the academic career. You also pour your heart into adjunct teaching because you do, in fact, love to teach and believe in its redemptive power. Nathaniel C. Oliver described this belief system in his post, "To Adjunct or Not to Adjunct: How Long Must We Suffer the Slings and Arrows?"

> In past years, I would not have hesitated to take on as many classes as my school would offer, believing that my efforts would be recognized and that, in due course, I would be given a full-time position. In four years of teaching, I had never expressed a preference in my choice of courses, assuming that my willingness to teach any subject, any time, any where would demonstrate my indispensability to the school. I did my utmost to show that I was both a hard worker and a team player who was devoted to the goals of my institution, my colleagues, and most importantly, my students.[1]

But universities cold-bloodedly exploit this passion and desperation, knowing that adjuncts will keep showing up to teach, and teach well, no matter how little they are paid. You teach more and harder in a desperate effort to impress the (indifferent) institution, make ends meet, and prop up your belief that you and your work matter. But at what cost to physical and mental health?

"I can't stand the thought of half-assing things," one adjunct told me. "Every cell cries out against it. I feel disloyal if I shirk on my teaching to focus on looking for a job."

When teaching well as an adjunct becomes an end in itself, and becomes the goal to which all else is sacrificed, including the adjunct's economic self-protection and psychological self-care, then something is terribly wrong. That's where the adjunct becomes a willing participant in the mechanisms of his own exploitation. That is Stockholm syndrome.

Higher education critic Josh Boldt has called adjuncting an addiction. Borrowing from Alcoholics Anonymous, he asked adjuncts to "admit that we are powerless over [teaching]—that our lives have become unmanageable." He asked adjuncts to recognize that they are in an "abusive relationship," and that living as a full-time adjunct "is a lot like living as a drug-addled tweaker."

He went on:

As long as we refuse to admit we have a problem, we'll never be able to change anything. Too many of us continue to sacrifice over and over again for this addiction. And why? For the students? They wouldn't know the difference. For the institution? God, I hope not, because they obviously are not sacrificing for us. For ourselves? That doesn't even make sense. For the craft? A romantic ideal, but the only craft you can eat begins with a K.

The fact of the matter is tens of thousands of us fall on our swords every year. Just like any good addict, we are expert manipulators— except we are the victims of our own justifications.

[Each class we get] only gets us back to normal. We'll never get ahead, never have enough. The system is designed that way.[2]

Never forget that the institution will dispose of you when you are no longer of use to it. Whether some of the faculty at your adjunct institution are nice people is immaterial. As Oliver explained: "Yes, my students may have liked me; yes, staff members may have liked me; yes, even other faculty members, including the chairs of the departments for which I taught, may have liked me. Unfortunately, none of those groups had much, if any, impact on hiring me for anything other than what I was already doing: teaching a full course load while being paid less than anyone else at the school."

Do not waste your time raging about how they should "appreciate" all you do for them and their students. They have no economic incentive to do so.

Adjuncts cannot necessarily just walk away from the exploitation of the system at large, when adjuncting may be the best immediate option to turn the Ph.D. into income while seeking permanent work, and create a record that will help in that search. But don't cathect onto or identify with the adjunct labor that is being extracted. Because that is to identify with—to form an identity around—the exploitation itself.

Adjunct exploitation will stop only when Ph.D.'s stop sacrificing themselves up to exploitative conditions. Oliver explained: "As long as I work as an adjunct, I am complicit not only in my own abuse, but in the abuse of education itself, which I will never cease believing in as an ideal, even if its reality is all too often marred by the demands of a corporatist, bottom-line mentality."

Yes, the students are underserved by the corporatized university as it is currently constituted. Yes, it is heartbreaking to watch the steady capitulation of an institution we all love to values we abhor. Yes, the students deserve better. However, saving the students is not your job; indeed, if you are an adjunct you cannot save them from the depredations of the university-cum-business dedicated to cost cutting and the abandonment of the educational mission. Your job must be to take care of yourself, protect your time and mental health, do your best to get the tenure track job you want, and, when you've tried as long as you're willing, reorient yourself for nonacademic work.

Unionization is one critical alternative in this process. Find out about union efforts at your institution and get involved. Unions are virtually the only thing that has ever effectively intervened in adjunct exploitation at a collective level. However, joining unionization efforts, as I pointed out in the beginning of the book, means dropping the self-defeating delusion that academic work is somehow separate from labor. And it requires rejecting the shame that is imposed by the elitist agents of academic "meritocracy," who insist that adjuncts are failures who deserve their fate. As Sarah Kendzior wrote in an Al Jazeera column, "Academia's Indentured Servants," "We have a pervasive self-degradation among low-earning academics—a sweeping sense of shame that strikes adjunct workers before adjunct workers can strike."[3]

In the end, you may decide to stay, or you may decide to leave. The goal is to act with purpose. As Josh Boldt wrote, "Some might interpret [my] message as . . . telling you to quit. I'm not. I'm telling you to step back from your situation and think clearly about it. Defamiliarize. Decide if you are spending your time, intelligence, and money in the best way."

So, continue on in your search if it is what you truly want, and blessings upon your head. Quit if it is what you truly want, and blessings upon your head. Either way, proceed armed not with self-delusion and blind hope, but with knowledge and a plan.

FIFTY-NINE

· · · · · · · · · · · · · · · · ·

Let Yourself Dream

Moving from the academic to the nonacademic, post-academic, or alt-academic job market requires a revolution in your thinking about yourself and your abilities. The single biggest transformation is moving from a focus on singular identity to a focus on disparate skills. Think about it—until now, you've been able to describe yourself in nouns: an "anthropologist," a "political scientist," a "theorist," a "specialist" in X, or Y, or Z. But outside the academy, nobody is looking for those categories of nouns, which only make sense within the university system. How many employers post job ads seeking a specialist in Renaissance Italian literature? Outside the academy, employers are looking for skills.

The task confronting you is to disaggregate your skills from your identity. This requires moving from the singular to the plural, and from the linear track model (from graduate school to tenure track job) to the flexible opportunity model (imagining and trying out a host of new options).

The Professor Is In opened a post-academic advising wing in fall 2014, which links post-academic job seekers to one of a team of experts: people with Ph.D.'s who have successfully navigated the shift to nonacademic work and who generously share their knowledge of these conventions with clients and me both.[1] One of these post-academic experts, Karen Cardozo, wrote a guest post on the blog called "Beyond Tenurecentrism," that articulates the revolution in thinking required to make this transition:

> [The post-academic] mindset requires assiduous participation in a head game that is antithetical to the disciplinary thinking or single-minded focus that is the hallmark of most doctoral programs. Instead, think of your life as a Windows operating system. The ONLY program that was automatically installed when you matriculated into your graduate program was Preparing for Your Academic Career (and as the Professor has amply argued, that is a shoddy program with a lot of bugs and very few updates).
>
> You will need to download and open other applications, such as Keeping Your Options Open, Acquiring Additional Experiences and Skills, and Building a Broader Network (both within and beyond the academy).[2]

Academics tend to assume they have no skills for the nonacademic job market, but that's entirely untrue. All you lack is experience in framing your skills as such. For example, as a cultural anthropologist of Japan, I might not recognize the multitude of skills I mastered in the course of creating that identity, but if I take a moment to disaggregate them from the unitary identity of anthropologist, I discover I can quickly create this list: writing, public speaking, ethnographic research, textual research, interviewing, administering surveys and questionnaires, data entry, data analysis, fluency in Japanese, Japanese cultural expertise, publishing, editing, reasoning . . . to name just a few.

Because academics operate in such an insular world of similarly trained people, most of these skills are simply taken for granted. Of course I can edit, I might think, or, of course I can speak Japanese! What Japan anthropologist can't? But if my frame is no longer "Japan anthropologist," but expanded to encompass the larger world, Japanese fluency is indeed a rare skill, and one sorely needed by many in business and other fields.

The first task for anyone considering a leap into the nonacademic job market is to identify those skills and past experiences that are hidden, assumed, or taken for granted within your previous scholarly identity, and recognize each one as the achievement that it is.

A good prompt for this work is to construct three categories of skills and experiences that are distinct to you. Call these your *Skills* Differentiator, *Knowledge* Differentiator, and *Achievements* Differentiator. Under "Skills," you can include proficiency in qualitative data analysis, statistics, public speaking, and so on. Under "Knowledge," you can include your areas of expertise—disciplinary, geographical, methodological. And under "Achievements" you can include specific accomplishments: managed a lab, wrote a book, organized a conference, ran a program.[3] Brainstorm freely, and don't be shy. You don't need to show this list to anyone but yourself. As you give yourself permission to acknowledge everything you are capable of doing, you'll see that anyone with a Ph.D. commands a substantial list of skills indeed. (See chapter 60 for a list of more than one hundred skills that translate out of the academic career.)

As you contemplate your skills and experiences, don't limit yourself to those you gained in the Ph.D. process alone. You may well carry forward a range of skills from other phases in your life, other jobs, and outside interests. Do not discount these. Remember that to make the post-academic leap you must wrench yourself out of old patterns of "tenurecentric" judgment that perceive only a narrow list of academic achievements as valuable. It may take you time to even register that you possess these other skills, they've been so soundly dismissed in the academic realm.

In my own case, as I became more and more alienated from my academic career, I found solace in art and jewelry making, drawing from the Japanese paper crafting I'd mastered as a hobby over the course of my twenty-some years of involvement with Japan. As I mentioned above, I started a small business to sell that art and jewelry at local markets in my Midwestern college town, and found that not only did I do reasonably well in sales, but also that the artistic process soothed and healed my damaged psyche. I also found unexpected pleasure in the wholly unfamiliar challenges of running a business—interacting with customers, setting prices, and promoting my work. I found myself inspired and satisfied in ways I hadn't felt in years. That little business was the precursor to The

Professor Is In, and taught me the skills I continue to use every day in this much larger enterprise.

In other words, my current business exists because I took a tiny first step to mobilize a "silly" nonacademic skill (origami) to heal myself, and make a change: a skill that, truth be told, I'd always considered a bit of an embarrassment, and hidden from my colleagues. Did I know that my origami hobby would eventually lead to the launch of a successful consulting business? Absolutely not. I only knew that each new task felt right, and inspiring. I mobilized the skills I had, and the new skills I eagerly gained (managing PayPal, building a website) while I constantly queried myself: What do I want? Am I happy? Is this satisfying? Am I making what I consider to be enough money? Am I offering something of value to the world?

Because the post-ac transition is also about motivation. That is, you must query not just what you can do, but also, what you want to do. And that can be hard to discern, when you've just spent a decade (maybe longer) focused entirely on one academic goal. In my own case, I spent about a year, when I wasn't managing my small jewelry business, curled in a fetal position on the sofa, unable to discern a larger purpose to my life outside the academy. Who was I, if not a professor? What could I be? What could I do? And how could I make enough money to support my family? The jewelry business was great, but it did not bring in enough. I had to find something else.

I fretted and I fretted. I complained endlessly to my partner, Kellee. I cried. I cursed. I chewed my nails. I lost sleep. I lay on the sofa some more. I asked over and over, What can I do?

Finally, one day, Kellee—bored with this nondialogue that never seemed to progress—turned to me in exasperation and said, "Karen. Listen to me. Here is what you have to do. As long as I've known you, you've been motivated by one thing. That thing is rage. You are motivated by rage. So, you need to figure out what you're angry about. Because whatever that is, whatever you're angry about, that's what you need to focus on. That will be your thing."

I stopped short. Right there in the kitchen, I stared at her. I could not deny it. She was right. Rage was my motivator. It always had been. (Whether that's a good thing or not is the subject of another book.) In any case, she was right.

What was I angry about? Turns out, that was not difficult to discern. I took a breath.

"What am I angry about?" I practically shouted. "What am I ANGRY ABOUT? I'll tell you what I'm angry about! You KNOW what I'm angry about! [She did.] I'm angry about all those f-ing professors sitting in their f-ing offices earning good f-ing salaries while the entire academy is going to shit, and their grad students are milling around like a bunch of lost sheep without a f-ing clue, and the professors don't lift a f-ing finger to help them or even tell them the f-ing truth that they are not going to get a f-ing tenure track job, but that they are CERTAINLY not going to get a job unless they stop ACTING like f-ing grad students and start getting a grip and publishing and FACING REALITY, but their advisors do nothing and NOBODY IS TELLING THE GODDAMNED TRUTH." I paused for breath. "THAT is what I'm angry about."

And at that moment, The Professor Is In was born.

(I'll also take this opportunity to say that this is why my partner, Kellee, is an amazing career and life coach.[4] She somehow always knows the right question to ask.)

I had my calling. All I needed to do then was figure out how to turn that fury into something constructive. Eventually, after more brainstorming with the ever-insightful Kellee, the path became clear: a blog, and professional advising/editing services for academics. Then I had to build a website. I already knew how to do that, in a rudimentary fashion, from my jewelry business, so over one weekend I did it. I spent a few more weeks hammering out the website message explaining what I was trying to do, and why I was doing it, and the services, and rates. And then I started writing: post after post after post, on all the fundamentals that I wanted Ph.D. job seekers and graduate students to know about the job market and the academic career.

I didn't realize it at the time, but my project was an anthropological one. Anthropologists' stock in trade is to take taken-for-granted, implicit knowledge and defamiliarize it, and then analyze it for the ways it expresses unspoken norms of power, privilege, and hierarchy. I didn't think of my task as anthropology; I just knew it made sense to study the graduate training apparatus as a system that reproduced status hierarchy, especially at its points of transition from grad student to job seeker and from job seeker to new hire. As a former insider, I knew exactly how we tenured faculty on search committees (during my years at the university) judged and evaluated job applications; how we deconstructed interviews; how we fought out ranked short-lists; how (as a department head) I managed new hires through the offer and negotiation process. And, I knew with perfect certainty that none of this knowledge was ever shared, in any methodical, transparent way, with the graduate students we advised. Why? Many reasons. But more important: Not sharing it was wrong. It needed to change. I could change it. My business was born.

I did not know then whether The Professor Is In would be successful. I just knew I had to do it. It has been successful, and that's very gratifying. But even if it had not been, it would have been valuable. It would have opened new doors, and revealed new avenues to pursue. It would have played a role in my post-academic transition, just like the jewelry business did.

From this story, I want you to take the message: Look at what moves you. And build a life around that. What moves you doesn't have to be rage—you may be emotionally healthier than me (I hope you are)! But whatever it is, it emerges only when you dig down beneath the shame, the narrow judgments of value, and the debilitating sense of failure and loss, and begin to see the skills you have gained and the contributions you are poised to make. Not everything we throw at the wall sticks in the post-academic realm. But everything is meaningful.

SIXTY

100+ Skills That Translate
Outside the Academy

One of the most popular post-academic webinars we offer at The Professor Is In is the one created and led by Margy Horton called "Targeting Your Skills for Your Postacademic Career." Margy is an academic writing coach, consultant, and editor. She has a Ph.D. in English, and is the founder and principal of ScholarShape, a business dedicated to helping academics achieve their writing goals.[1]

Her webinar is successful because it so perfectly balances the vision work of reimagining your post-academic identity with the practical information you need to compose your new résumé and cover letter. One of the most valuable parts of the webinar is her list of skills that Ph.D.'s may not realize they have. She calls it "100+ Skills That Translate Outside the Academy."[2]

As you peruse job advertisements, you'll begin to see many keywords crop up—words such as "analysis," "assessment," "modeling," "data collection," "leadership," "fund-raising," and "training." These terms may seem like a foreign language to you at first, but a quick glance at the list that follows reveals that you will be able to lay claim to them as part of your scope of expertise.

One of the most harmful habits of mind for Ph.D.'s who seek to move out of the academy is our collective overinvestment in impossibly high standards of expertise. Out in the nonacademic world, you don't have to be the leading authority on X. It is enough that you have a skill and know how to talk about it and use it. Read this list, and claim your rightful skills. And know that these can be part of the foundation of your next career.

Research and coursework

1. Quickly reading and processing large amounts of complex material, often while writing summary notes
2. Framing: Breaking down information, sequencing it, and creating an organizational framework for it
3. Concentration: Intense, sustained focus on a particular task or subject
4. Fairness: Looking at an issue from multiple perspectives
5. Synthesizing: Finding connections among disparate ideas or viewpoints; determining how the viewpoints are similar and/or different
6. Weighing: Assessing evidence for its soundness and its relevance to a particular argument
7. Modeling: Developing and testing various solutions to a problem to find the best solution, that is, through experimentation
8. Problem recognition: Identifying and defining problems
9. Problem analysis: Determining potential causes of a problem
10. Data assessment: Developing effective methods for sorting data and determining which data are good and usable
11. Navigating ethical considerations, as in securing institutional review board approval
12. Pressuring or cajoling busy superiors to read your work and give feedback
13. International and multicultural awareness
14. Public speaking: Both as a specialist to an audience of specialists, and as a specialist to a general, multidisciplinary audience of educated listeners
15. Information gathering: Locating and navigating databases, archives, or other appropriate sources of information
16. Qualitative data collection (interviews, surveys, questionnaires, case studies, ethnographies)

17. Quantitative data collection (observation, measurement, use of proxies)
18. Qualitative data analysis (coding and identifying themes)
19. Quantitative data analysis (statistics and so forth)
20. Data commentary: Selecting which findings to highlight and describing them in a coherent, concise way that tells a story
21. Induction: Generalizing a theory from specific cases
22. Deduction: Interpreting a specific case in light of a theory or multiple theories
23. Comparing multiple theories and assessing their respective robustness
24. Developing a cohesive project: One in which the various components are aligned, including the problem to be solved, the statement of the project's purpose, and the methods for solving the problem.
25. Developing an independent claim that is worth arguing, that is, neither self-evidently true nor indefensible
26. Writing quickly and concisely
27. Managing multiple deadlines and meeting them
28. Editing others' written work
29. Revision of one's own writing: The task that, according to rhetoric scholar George Gopen, is one of the greatest intellectual challenges there is
30. Critiquing peers' work, as in a writing group or workshop
31. Critiquing experts' work, as in book reviews or literature reviews
32. Storytelling: Creating a meaningful narrative by artfully selecting and arranging facts
33. Assessing which "experts" are really experts and which journals are really respected/respectable.
34. Comfortably disagreeing with experts and defending yourself from their attacks on your work
35. Genre awareness: Ability to distinguish the nuances of micro-genres, some of them artificial (such as variations among journals, course assignments, different committee members' ideas of good academic writing)

36. Market positioning: Distinguishing your voice, identity, research, and/or findings from everyone else's
37. Rational debate, in writing or in person
38. Defining: Developing definitions of complex, abstract terms
39. Causal analysis: Understanding complex causal relationships
40. Curiosity: Compulsion to learn and ability to learn quickly
41. Domain expertise: Knowledge that in some way, however tangential, can be used to illuminate big-picture, real-life problems
42. Ability to format Microsoft Word documents (it can be lucrative to do this for others)
43. Thought leadership: Looking the opposite direction from everyone around you to see what no one else has noticed
44. Facilitating communication among multiple stakeholders (for example, committee members)
45. Ability to get to the heart of the matter (for example, boiling your dissertation down into a brief thesis or pitch to publishers)
46. Graphic design: making tables, figures, and other graphics to illustrate your research
47. Fund-raising: Raising funds through grant writing, fellowships, or other means
48. Proposal writing: "Selling" a project that doesn't exist yet
49. Writing standard academic English (formal, grammatically correct, evidence-based prose)
50. Writing with purpose, focus, and style

Teaching

51. Motivating groups and individuals to complete projects
52. Facilitating group discussions
53. Running purposeful, efficient meetings
54. Preparing people for future learning by teaching foundational concepts and skills
55. Public speaking as an expert who translates specialized knowledge to a general audience

56. Course design, curriculum design
57. Content development: Gathering and organizing facts into information on a given subject
58. Identifying training objectives
59. Giving critical feedback: Evaluating and critiquing the work of subordinates
60. Classifying and ranking various feedback items (distinguishing when to emphasize content issues versus formal characteristics)
61. "Reading" an audience to determine their knowledge and interest level in the subject you're discussing
62. Coaching, tutoring, and mentoring subordinates (for example, in office hours)
63. Peer mentoring (such as helping fellow teachers)
64. Intuiting when a subordinate is cheating and using good judgment to decide on the most appropriate action
65. Constructing an argument to defend a specific action you have taken (such as your grading decisions)
66. Managing mini-deadlines on the route to a major deadline
67. Finding and nurturing others' strengths
68. Articulating overall goals for other people and creating a realistic schedule of mini-goals to structure the people's pursuit of the goal
69. Program assessment (such as reviewing curricula, learning objectives, and assignments, and the alignment of these elements)
70. Assessing others' writing quickly and thoroughly
71. Weighing positive and negative feedback on your performance (such as from students, peer mentors, and supervisors) and making adjustments as necessary
72. Balancing competing demands from a direct supervisor, subordinates, and the institution

Service

73. Navigating a bureaucracy (which forms need to be signed by whom, and sent where, and by what date)

74. Managing a team
75. Getting your voice heard in a meeting
76. Identifying problems in a community
77. Locating and funneling institutional resources to solve problems
78. Motivating peers
79. Enlisting superiors to get your task done (such as getting a dean on board with your initiative)
80. Delegating tasks: Assigning a task to the most suitable team member
81. Collaborating with a team to produce something tangible ("deliverables")
82. "Hiring" or recruiting people for your committees

Intangibles, extracurricular activities, and miscellaneous
83. Finding the humor in dire situations
84. Making intelligent-sounding comments when you have no idea what anyone is talking about (the fine art of BS)
85. Blogging: writing for a general audience about complicated subjects
86. Using social media effectively
87. Growing a network
88. Adapting quickly to changing constituents' needs; remaining flexible
89. Working under pressure
90. Working without supervision
91. Ability to invent or improve a get-to-know-you activity
92. Learning unwritten mores; cultural awareness
93. Foreign languages: Reading, speaking, translating
94. Using software
95. Ability to strategize
96. Applying concepts to multiple scenarios
97. Ability to switch rapidly among different tasks
98. Preternatural understanding of "ordinary" things that are related to your domain knowledge or discipline
99. Discussing current events intelligently

100. Agitating for change; community organization
101. Stretching a shoestring budget
102. Efficiently learning about new, major trends
103. "Future foresight" (see Daniel Burrus's book *Flash Foresight: How to See the Invisible and Do the Impossible*)
104. Structured problem solving
105. Schmoozing, entertaining a crowd
106. Engaging in, understanding, and talking about politics
107. Organizing a workspace for maximum efficiency
108. Tolerating risk and uncertainty
109. Finding the bright side; optimism
110. Willingness to go against the grain
111. Appreciating the absurd and wondrous

SIXTY-ONE

·················

Collecting Information

Reinvention does not happen in a vacuum. You cannot expect to know what you might want to do, or what skills you have or need to do it, without experimentation and study. It's an open-ended process with multiple parts, and in this it is entirely different from the regimented, linear, and predictable academic job market.

Once you have a handle on your skills, begin to brainstorm different kinds of work that might utilize them—whether in a non-profit, a museum, a corporation, your own small business, K–12 teaching, or something else. You can find examples of what's possible by reading widely in the now abundant Internet resources on post-academic careers. A few good places to start include:

- The Versatile Ph.D. (http://versatilephd.com/)
- From Ph.D. to Life (http://fromphdtolife.com/)
- The Leaving Academe forum of the *Chronicle of Higher Education* (http://chronicle.com/forums/)
- The Adjunct Project (http://adjunct.chronicle.com/)
- How to Leave Academia (http://howtoleaveacademia.com/)
- Jobs on Toast (http://jobsontoast.com/)
- Life After the Ph.D. (http://lifeafterthephd.com/)

Don't rush this work. You need time to think, reflect, imagine, talk, dream. This is a difficult transition, and it won't happen overnight. As Karen Cardozo writes in her post "Freeing the Academic Elephant": "In a tenurecentric universe, Alt/Post-Ac discourse inevitably comes across as elegiac—a consolation prize for the lost academic career. But what makes you so sure that an academic career was the right choice for you in the first place? . . . Instead of viewing your Alt/Post-Ac situation as imposed upon you by external factors out of your control, carve out some time and space to heed whatever vocational desires are bubbling up from within—possibly long-buried ones rendered inert by your time in the academic trenches."[1]

As you meditate on the new vocational desires that might bubble up, there are steps you can take to gain both knowledge and inspiration:

1. Nurture Relationships with Mentors in Your Field.

Relationships are never more important than in the transition out of the academy. You will feel isolated, depressed, judged, and rejected. You will also be confused and bewildered, and perhaps frightened out of your mind. You need a team of allies to support you, boost your flagging spirits, and provide examples of what's possible. The community of recovering academics is large, proud, passionate, and, above all—generous. They are always willing to help someone new save themselves.

Don't be shy. Reach out. Don't expect every connection you pursue to "stick"; it doesn't have to. This is not an advisor-advisee relationship that has to shape you for years to come. Sometimes all you need is a referral, a link, an email address, or just an idea to feed your vision.

2. Find Internships or Volunteer Opportunities.

Sometimes you have to work for free to get experience in a new field of work. Is this a sustainable post-academic path? No. The increasing reliance on unpaid internships is a problematic element of the new low-wage economy. But for you, in the thick of a radical reinvention—you may need to volunteer your time while you gain hands-on experience that you can put on your résumé.

3. Conduct Informational Interviews.

In an informational interview you seek out an established person in an industry or field in which you may be interested in working, and schedule thirty minutes or so to ask questions about the industry or field. These are not interviews for specific positions, and should not be used to try to sell yourself for a job. Rather, use the time to ask questions about the types of work available, trends in the field, and what employers are looking for. But make no mistake—your interviewee is drawing impressions of you as well. If you make a good impression, he or she may well remember you for the next opening, or pass your name along to someone else.

4. Set Aside Time for Additional Training.

It took you ten or so years to become a Ph.D., and you won't become a post-academic overnight. You may need additional training. I don't mean more graduate schooling, although in a few select cases you may need some formal schooling, to get a teaching certificate or the like. More often, this just means filling some gaps. You can sign up at your local chamber of commerce for mentorship on starting a small business; you can take a class on building and managing a website; you can polish up a rusty language skill; you can take a university class in statistical analysis. Remember that the perfect is the enemy of the good. You don't have to become an unassailable expert in the new skill as you once felt you must in your dissertation topic. You just have to be good enough at it to offer your services.

5. Contemplate the Problems You Can Help Solve.

What problems do people have that you're situated to assist with? They may be big problems—managing trade with China. Or they may be small problems—finding the right necklace for a gift. All problems need solutions, and providing solutions is the foundation of paying work. What can you do that solves a problem that people have? Locate that, and you have your direction. And, of course, you may have several. I, for example, can help people in their quest to find interesting Japanese-themed handmade jewelry. And it turns out I can also help people in their quest to find tenure track jobs. I have found both of these missions profoundly satisfying.

6. Network Like Mad.

You have no idea where your next job ultimately awaits. In contrast to the academy, where open positions are finite, public, and cyclical, in the nonacademic world, positions pop up unpredictably, and are rarely advertised. In that context, networking does not mean trying to ingratiate yourself with influential leaders. Rather it means knowing a lot of people, and making sure those people know you, know that you're available, and know the kind of things you have to offer. Networking in the post-ac world is not hierarchical and linear; rather, it's holistic and spherical. Your neighbor, the guy who teaches your statistics class, the mother of the kid your daughter babysits, the woman you always see at the gym, the retired businessman at your synagogue: All of these are people who need to know who you are and what you're trying to do. It goes without saying that you'll also mobilize the resources of the Internet with your LinkedIn profile, your Facebook page, your profile on appropriate networking sites, and your website.

Whether in person or online, in the post-academic transition, relationships matter, and you need them now more than ever as you launch into this new and unknown territory. Networking is not about manipulating people to get what you want, but knowing people to learn what they need. It's not a highly regarded academic skill, but out in the rest of the world, you neglect it at your peril.

SIXTY-TWO

·················

Applying While Ph.D.

The post-academic community is filled with experts on job applications for nonacademic jobs. The cover letter, résumé, and interview in these contexts all have conventions that differ substantially from those in the academy that I have described in this book. In this chapter, I will sketch a few points related to the résumé and the cover letter, and then discuss possible challenges that people with Ph.D.'s might confront in their encounters with nonacademic employers. The fact is, academics don't have the best reputations for adaptability and accessibility. A little care in your applications can go a long way in laying possible employer concerns to rest.

A business résumé is a marketing document introducing your skills to a potential employer. It should identify employer and position needs, describe how your background makes you suited to fulfill these needs, and do so in a way that is reader friendly.[1] The length should be job appropriate, and two pages is the norm.

While the "Objective" section has gone out of style, a focal line is still valuable. For example:

Committed to improving company profits by contributing bilingual skills and knowledge of civil-law countries to legal department of a firm doing business in Latin America.

Under "Employment," list your job titles on the left, and dates of that employment on the right, in reverse chronological order. Each job title should be followed by three to five bullet points of responsibilities for entry-level positions or five to ten responsibilities for managerial positions.

Remember that on a résumé, education typically goes at the end.

The résumé, unlike the CV, should be fluid and dynamic. You should modify it for each specific job listing. The skills you highlight and the order of their appearance should change to fit the job description. Résumés not written for a specific position should highlight the skills that are expected in that type of position.

Whenever applying for nonacademic jobs, remember that employers now use digital tracking systems to sort applications, and these systems depend on keywords. The savvy job-seeker understands how to find and mobilize these keywords. You can usually draw these from the ad itself, as well as from a survey of company or institutional websites in the field. One tactic is to use Wordle .net to generate a word cloud from the ad, and deploy the keywords in both the résumé and letter. You can easily find examples of keywords by Googling "common keywords for jobs." Some frequently seen keywords for K–12 teaching positions, for example, include: "credentials," "education," "teaching experience," "subject areas," "curriculum development or design," "student teaching," "teaching mentorships," "key accomplishments," "in-service training," "English as a second language (ESL)," "classroom management," "teaching and learning," "curriculum planning," "peer mentoring," "lead teacher," "teacher-parent relations," "special needs students," "gifted/talented students," "testing," "technology integration."[2]

As you highlight your experiences and skills, remember that these do not have to map perfectly onto job titles. Separate your skills and achievements from the formal positions you held. Always use action words and be specific.

A good example: "Was responsible for filing documents"

A better example: "Filed and maintained confidential student records"

Describe specific accomplishments whenever possible.

A good example: "Raised funds for annual service project"
A better example: "Raised $11,050 for the annual Kids Read benefit, a 15 percent increase from the previous year."

When constructing your cover letter, remember that these are typically about one page in length. You can use a four-paragraph structure. Always employ proper business letter formatting, with the date and address of the recipient at the top left. After your salutation, in the first paragraph, introduce who you are, the position for which you are applying, and, if appropriate, where you learned of the position. Follow with no more than two body paragraphs in which you make a connection between yourself and this particular job/company, highlight the parts of your résumé that speak directly to the job listing, and briefly explain anything that might be considered strange or a weakness in your résumé. As you brainstorm the content of these two paragraphs, consider the connection between yourself and this particular company:

- Why are you interested in this company? Have you worked, interned, or had interactions with this company in the past?
- What is interesting to you about this particular job?
- What is distinctive about you that this employer might find valuable?

If you, as a former academic, constitute an unusual applicant for the position, address that directly. If you appear to be changing careers, explain why and what you are hoping to find in this next career. If you appear overqualified for the position, explain why you are still interested in it. Explain any gaps in your résumé, but without defensiveness, emotionalism, bewildering quantities of text, or academic jargon such as "subjectivity," "positionality," and the like.

Conclude crisply, by inviting further communication. End with a complimentary close and your contact information.

As you construct your cover letter for nonacademic jobs, don't assume that your Ph.D. automatically renders you "overqualified." Indeed, many employers may have conscious or unconscious biases against people with Ph.D.'s, which you should indirectly address in your materials. Margaret Gover, director of Graduate Student Professional Development at the University of California–Riverside, has assisted numerous Ph.D.'s in their post-academic employment search. She recommends that you foreground four areas:

1. Adaptability and Perseverance

Employers may worry that Ph.D.'s are only interested in arcane scholarly pursuits. They need to know that you can adapt to different situations and accomplish challenging tasks.

How Do You Show It? Show how you overcame challenges and troubleshot technical problems. Demonstrate problem-solving: how you evaluated and/or assessed the effectiveness of one approach and determined a new course of action.

2. Ability to Work with Others

Employers may worry that Ph.D.'s are misanthropes who work in isolation. They need to know that you will be generally well liked by the other employees, that you will be able to work in a collaborative environment, and that you will be able to work with customers.

How Do You Show It? Highlight collaborative projects and research. Talk about times that you used conflict resolution skills. Show yourself to be an empathetic person who can see problems from many points of view.

3. Communication Skills

Employers may worry that Ph.D.'s use jargon and obscure vocabulary that others can't easily understand. They want people who can communicate effectively both orally and in writing.

How Do You Show It? Make sure that your résumé and cover letter are well written, without jargon or difficult language. Demonstrate times when you have communicated the mission of an organization/employer to the larger community. Talk about the variety of people you have worked with for different purposes.

4. Knowledge of the Job

Employers may worry that Ph.D.'s understand only the university environment. They need to know that you can do the job and that you can grow in that position.

How Do You Show It? Show that you have had positions in the past where you had to plan, organize, or execute complex tasks that relate to the advertised position. Show problems you solved or data you analyzed in ways that translate pragmatically. Show that you made the effort to understand the job, and relate your skills to it.

In all of these steps remember that your biggest enemy may be yourself. Your sense of failure in one realm (academia) may imperil your ability to imagine success in any others. The most important work you must do is turn your powerful mind to a critical analysis of the cultlike judgments of the academy. Identify the judgment and shame that continues to hold you back, and, piece by piece, bit by bit, let it go.

SIXTY-THREE

Breaking Free:
The Path of the Entrepreneur

When you're considering your next steps, please don't stop at the notion of finding a "job" or "position" that has been defined and advertised by others. Consider creating your own. That is the path of the entrepreneur, and it is a vital one. Unfortunately, it is also a path little recognized by people in the humanities and social sciences. Scientists have many models of scholars who have transformed their patented ideas into successful businesses, and indeed the intensive grant-based model of science funding promotes a high degree of entrepreneurialism. But humanists and social scientists tend to be so tied to institutional dependency that it's hard for them (us) to see the possibility of breaking free.

It took me many years to make the transition myself. Even after leaving my tenured position to return to the Northwest, and running a small but successful jewelry business, I still remained wedded to the idea that for "real" work, I needed to find a "job" at some kind of institution. To that end, I found a position working half-time at West Coast U's McNair Scholars Program, a federally funded program that trains first-generation and underrepresented undergraduates to apply to and succeed in graduate school. It was a terrific program that I believed in fiercely; however, it paid somewhere in the vicinity of nothing. Nationally, the program was reeling from federal budget cuts. Our much-needed services were suffering continual cutbacks.

It was while I was working at McNair that I opened The Professor Is In. Indeed, it was the advising I provided for those McNair undergraduates that crystallized my idea for the company. The new business did well, and the more it grew, the more torn I felt between the time I wanted to devote to it and the time I owed to my university advising job.

But I couldn't contemplate leaving the university position. After all, it was a university. It represented security, safety, and legitimacy. As my eighty-five-year-old mother said, "You can't possibly give up a university position to put all your eggs in the basket of a new business, Karen! It's too risky!"

But in the weeks and months that followed, I watched the financial footing of my federal program crumble and The Professor Is In grow. And one day I realized the risk did not lie in leaving. It lay in staying. The risk was in being too frightened to let go of my institutional location, identity, and (minuscule) paycheck, to launch out entirely on my own.

I was reminded of the movie *World War Z,* a postapocalyptic zombie film that I had just seen with my then-twelve-year-old son. In the movie there is one nice family that is too afraid to leave their apartment as the zombies overtake the city. They were sure that staying put was the safer path. But as you may imagine, staying put got them eaten. They clung to the familiar, even as the familiar crumbled around them. In the zombie landscape of higher education, clinging to the dream of an institutional position, when institutions are crumbling (and inhabited increasingly by walking dead administrators), is a profoundly unsafe choice.

For those tenure line faculty and mid-program graduate students who are in secure, continuing positions, the university is like a giant teat from which all good things flow. From it you gain your legitimacy, standing, funding, resources, library card, and salary. And it is the cornerstone of your identity and worth. Faculty and graduate students sit with hands outstretched, waiting for the institutional parent to squirt out the "support" to which they feel so aggrievedly entitled.

It is this stance of dependency, and the profound fear of risk it inculcates, that holds Ph.D.'s back from imagining the full range of possible alternative careers. When my academic clients first tentatively begin to imagine alternatives, they nearly always start by looking for a replacement teat—another institutional motherlode of jobs, salary, benefits, and security. While those jobs do still exist, they're scarce and getting scarcer. "Good" jobs—with a living wage and benefits—are in decline in all sectors of the economy.

I urge you to consider releasing yourself from institutional dependency. Kerry Ann Rockquemore, founder and president of the National Center for Faculty Development and Diversity, has identified five differences between the academic and entrepreneurial mind-set:

1. Academics move slow; entrepreneurs move fast.
2. Academics study problems; entrepreneurs solve problems.
3. Academics function in constraint; entrepreneurs create possibility.
4. Academics focus on patterns; entrepreneurs focus on exceptions.
5. Academics loathe promotion; entrepreneurs live to sell.[1]

Study these five points and inquire of yourself: How does my thinking remain slow, problem focused, pattern seeking, promotion phobic, and limited by a sense of institutional constraint? If you released your mind to embrace speed, problem-solving, exceptions to rules, selling your skills, and possibilities not authorized within an academic value system—what will you find? You will find something, I promise you. Here are three steps to get you started.

1. Examine Your State of Dependency on Institutional Validation. Ask yourself what ways you depend on the institution for money, resources, and identity. Then ask yourself what role that dependency might be playing in your thinking. Be alert to the ways you attach an image of "failure" to the loss of institutional validation. I'm not telling you to throw this dependency off in a grand gesture. I'm just asking you to examine it and call it what it is. Academics are conformists. Aca-

demics are "company men" with the false self-image of radical indi-
vidualists. Just naming a thing weakens its hold on you. Ask yourself:
If I were to imagine myself as my own "institution," how would that
feel? Sit with that.

2. Ask Yourself: What Skills Do I Have That Have Value to Others? As I explained in chapter 59, my first business involved making tiny origami cranes, frogs, and flowers into jewelry. That was a skill that had
value to others. People liked the jewelry, and I created a tiny business selling it. It never made much money, but it taught me to build
a website, run a blog, handle PayPal, and a host of other small business skills. In another case, a former student—a primatologist—was
always good at statistics. Her graduate school friends and colleagues
continually asked for her help in their statistical analyses. Eventually the demand grew to the point she started charging money. Suddenly, she's running a business. Ask yourself what you can do that
could help someone else solve a problem.

3. Try. Don't be intimidated by the word "entrepreneur." You don't
necessarily need an office or a fancy website or logo, or capital or in-
vestors. I started with a server fee and a box of manila folders. And it
turns out I didn't even need the manila folders. Be open to the pleasure of earning money by concrete services you provide. Academic
work is so abstract. The work and the paycheck seem far apart, separated by a wide campus and a labyrinth of offices. But when you
offer a service, get an inquiry, quote a rate, have it accepted, do the
work, and get paid, it is gratifying on a whole different level. I used
to love the little money box full of dollar bills I came home with
from my jewelry booth at the Saturday market. It was just pennies
compared to my university salary, but it meant so much more, because it came from something I believed had value.

Entrepreneurs start from the premise that it might be possible to
generate their own institutional location and income. The dependency that Ph.D.'s have on external validation and institutional location squelches the risk taking that is increasingly required in the
new post-institutional economy. This is profoundly frightening for

academics raised up in the conformist environment of the academy, where intellectual "risks" always must be validated by others, and always are taken on somebody else's dime.

However, it is not impossible. I can't tell you what your options will be, but I can tell you that you almost certainly have some. The trick is to identify them, and then to have the independence to validate them yourself. They aren't valuable because some department or committee or university said they are. They are valuable because you know their value. As you conceive of your alternative career path, be willing to embrace the possibility that you can be the source of your own funding, legitimacy, and identity. If you're in a precarious relationship to the academy, you've got zombies on your tail. You are not safe. You do not have security. Staying is the risk. Don't hunker down on your campus while the zombies scale the walls.

CONCLUSION

....

Declaring Independence

As I write this, I've been post-academic for almost four years. Four years since I left my tenured position to move back to the Pacific Northwest town where I had once been a tenured professor, with no job and no idea what I'd do next.

It took three years before I finally started to walk freely about town, knowing that I might run into my former faculty colleagues. Before that I mostly skulked and hid, hoping to avoid them.

When I began to spend time with them, many of these former colleagues remarked at how much happier I seemed. One said to my partner, "It's been fun getting to know Karen this time. I never talked to her when she was here before. Back then she always seemed so angry."

I was indeed angry back then. Because back then, I was living entirely according to the principle of external validation. I was in thrall to the academic cult, which dictates that you have value only if others in authority have validated your work. Your comprehensive exams, your dissertation, your articles, your grant proposals, your book, your job search, your tenure case: All succeed or fail based on the judgment and approval of people above you. The properly socialized academic makes that validation the core of her identity.

No wonder the young of the profession are so servile.

Dependency on external validation is the enemy of contentment and joy. My process of becoming post-academic has been 100 percent a process of finding my own inner source of validation. My work is valuable because I say it is. This was a brutally hard stance to achieve. A piece of advice by Cheryl Strayed, in a collection of her *Dear Sugar* advice columns, helped to crystallize it for me. Strayed was responding to a young woman, a frustrated writer, who wrote in asking for help overcoming her depression, her defeatism, her inability to get words on paper. The young woman wasn't an academic, but her anguish is familiar: "I want to jump out the window for what I've boiled down to is one reason: I can't write a book. But it's not that I want to die so much as have an entirely different life. I start to think that I should choose another profession—as Lorrie Moore suggests, 'movie star/astronaut, a movie star/missionary, a movie star/kindergarten teacher.' I want to throw off everything I've accumulated and begin as someone new, someone better."[1]

Strayed tells her many things, many wise and wonderful things, in a long and deep response. She focuses on the young would-be writer's lament that "I write like a girl. I write about my lady life experiences, and that usually comes out as unfiltered emotion, unrequited love, and eventual discussion of my vagina as metaphor."

Strayed responds: "Nobody is going to give you permission to write about your vagina, hon. Nobody is going to give you a thing. You have to give it yourself. You have to tell us what you have to say."

Strayed ends her advice: "So write. . . . Not like a girl. Not like a boy. Write like a motherfucker."

Write like a motherfucker. Or, in other words, declare independence from external validation. Don't wait for approval, whether it's for your writing, your teaching, your research, or even your identity as an academic or as a post-academic who has moved on.

Yes, it's true, if you stay in the academy all those reviews and evaluations must be endured to get the dissertation passed, get the grant, get the job. That's for your work, and it's unavoidable. This whole book is dedicated, after all, to helping you understand exactly how those evaluations work and in what corners validation lies.

But for your life, in academia or out, remember that your self and your voice and your truth come not from the approval of others, but from within. Don't confuse external validation of your work with validation of your worth. Especially if you're an adjunct. As Ms. Mentor concluded a 2014 column in the *Chronicle of Higher Education*, "If you're an adjunct, and there doesn't seem to be any change on the horizon in your field, be ruthless in appraising your possibilities. Do not listen to Them. Listen to your own inner voice."[2]

A reader once wrote to describe her journey after finishing an Ivy League humanities Ph.D. She spoke about the typical birth metaphors of the dissertation—the gestation process of an idea, dissertation as baby. But, "I truly felt as though I had given birth to a stillborn," she wrote. "I knew that I would never turn the dissertation into a book because I knew that I had no interest in an academic career, no desire to go on the job market, no interest in moving to a remote location, kissing more professor ass, continuing my serf-like status, and so on."

She went through a long, dark phase of confusion, feeling like a "failure and a loser." How could she not? The Work of the Mind mythology dictates that the only outcome deserving of validation is reproduction of more Work of the Mind. But my reader, and many others like her, discovered the opposite: Accepting rigid judgments of academic success and failure makes for chronic anxiety and depression, and prevents those in the academy from realizing the full scope of their own potential.

Eventually this reader turned to my blog, but not to learn to package herself for an academic career. Rather, she read for information on "how to deprogram myself and recover my own sense of value as a person and professional." In the end, she succeeded in her efforts to deprogram herself. Once she left behind her shame at "failing" in her academic career, she found clarity about her goals. She soon applied for, and got, a full-time position teaching outside the academy, at a school she loves.

Stay in academia if you want. Or leave it. Search for the tenure track job, by all means, if that's your life's goal. I wish you the very best of luck in that quest. Leave the academy, by all means, if it is destroying your finances and your spirit. I send you all my support. The academic career can be good. The academic career can be bad. Whatever path you choose, know that it is your own. Say no to the less-than status, the linking of your identity to others' judgment, the servile dependence on others' approval. Advisors, professors, employers, peers—they will make their judgments. But only you can say what counts as your success.

ACKNOWLEDGMENTS

I want to thank every job candidate who ever submitted an application, or suffered through an interview, for a job at one of my former departments. You all taught me something.

I want to thank my clients at The Professor Is In, who constantly challenge me to find new ways to explain how the academy works (or doesn't) and whose stories never fail to move, enrage, and inspire me.

I want to thank the readers of The Professor Is In blog, who don't accept anything at face value, but who always keep the mood there on the blog positive, constructive, and mutually supportive. That's a rarity on the Internet, and I am grateful.

I want to thank my former Ph.D. students. I'm not going to name you, but you know who you are. You taught me to be a better mentor. I only wish I'd known then what I know now.

Now for some people I can name. I want to thank William Pannapacker, Sarah Kendzior, and Rebecca Schuman for exposing the "big lies" of the academy and poking at its self-serving pretentions. And for provoking me to think ever more deeply about the nature of academic labor. Roger Whitson, Jesse Stommel, and Adeline Koh all contributed inimitable insights into the changing landscape of the humanities, and the enduring mystery of the MLA.

I appreciate Carole McGranahan for being a sounding board. And Susan Schultz—former professor and longtime friend—for fighting the good fight against the corruption of corporatized universities and the administrators who serve them.

During my own graduate studies, Rob Wilson and Geoffrey White were examples of humane and generous mentoring. You showed me what's possible.

It's a pleasure to thank my awesome agent, Alia Habib, who "got" the project instantly, shepherded it along patiently, and helped this former professor figure out how to write and sell a trade book. And my editor at Random House, Nathan Roberson, who likewise needed no persuading that this was a book worth writing and helped me hone its message.

Maggie Gover, Karen Cardozo, Jessica Langer, Maggie Horton, Stephanie Day, Allessandria Pollizzi, Sarita Jackson, Jason Tebbe, and Joe Fruscione have been endlessly, endlessly generous with post-academic ideas, blog posts, and hands-on help both for me and for the clients who so need them.

I want to give Joe Fruscione and David Luebke a special shout-out for all they've taught me about faculty unions. Thank you for all your work on that critical front; I hope in a small way this book will support those efforts.

Petra Shenk, Nica Davidov, Verena Hutter, Maggie Levantoskaya, and Kristy Lewis: I could not have written this book without you, as you are well aware.

Thank you to Jodi Schneider for help with research, Bradley Baker for help with numbers, and Rebecca Schuman for help with conference cost-cutting ideas.

Thank you to T. J. Tallie for some 11th-hour insights into the job-search escapades of a queer person of color.

Former colleagues (and dear friends!) from the University of Oregon—Julee Raiskin, Lizzie Reis, Maram Epstein, David Luebke, Matt Dennis, Eileen Otis, Diane Baxter, Shaul Cohen, Carol Silverman, Geraldine Moreno-Black, David Wacks—thank you for keeping me informed about the lives of humanists at a public university that, like most, prefers football to the humanities.

Former colleagues (and dear friends!) from the University of Illinois at Urbana Champaign—Kirstin Wilcox, Stephanie Foote—you inspire me, provoke me, inform me, and argue with me. And, let me be the first to put in print: your Facebook updates are the finest writing on the current state of the academy available today.

My gratitude goes to Gail Unruh, director of the University of Oregon McNair Scholars Program, who first helped me realize what I could offer on the subject of professionalization. The program he built, and the services he provides to undergraduates, gave me a model to emulate as I conceived of my own fledgling business.

Thank you, Lizzie, Stephanie, and Verena, for your valuable comments on the whole manuscript.

Here in Eugene, LeAnn McArthur and Lillian Almeida have shared the insights of their respective professional worlds, and far more important, their steady friendship and support. And my Zumba gals—Cynthia Valentine Healey, Shelley Galvin, Leah Ann Dunbar, Rena Dunbar, Lisa Milton—you keep me surrounded with love and dance. Judy Goldstein and Nina Korican—you kept food and movies coming.

David Burdelski, dearest old friend: you believed in The Professor Is In before it even existed. You gave it legs. Thank you.

Adam Goodheart, newly discovered First Cousin Once Removed: thank you for being family and for sharing your wide knowledge of the world of books, agents, and writing.

I wrote part of this book in my sister's hospital room, where she was recovering from a catastrophic car accident. Thank you, Janine, for recovering. And for always supporting your sister's odd path. Thank you to my mother, Kathleen Kelsky, for constantly checking in on "how the book is going." Thank you to my in-laws, Lynda and Ron Weinhold, for your unfailing encouragement.

Finally, Kellee Weinhold: you've been there from the start, for this tumultuous, wonderful ride. You made this whole enterprise possible. And you've brought your fierce advice and compassionate encouragement to The Professor Is In—and its clients—in countless ways, large and small. Words cannot express my love and thanks. And Miyako and Seiji, my darling teenagers: Thank you for keeping me honest. Whether it's how many hours I'm really spending on the computer, or what exactly I'm telling "Mom's struggling Ph.D.s," you always insist that it be the truth.

NOTES

ONE: THE END OF AN ERA

1. Much of the following discussion is based on Michael Mitchell, Vincent Palacios, and Michael Leachman, "States Are Still Funding Higher Education Below Pre-Recession Levels," Center on Budget Policy and Priorities, March 1, 2014, http://www.cbpp.org/cms/?fa=view&id=4135.

2. Douglas Belkin and Scott Thurm, "Deans List: Hiring Spree Fattens College Bureaucracy—And Tuition," *Wall Street Journal*, December 28, 2012, http://online.wsj.com/news/articles/SB10001424127887323316804578161490716042814.

3. Institute for College Access and Success, "Student Debt and the Class of 2012," http://www.projectonstudentdebt.org/.

4. Steven Odland, "College Costs Out of Control," *Forbes*, March 24, 2012, http://www.forbes.com/sites/steveodland/2012/03/24/college-costs-are-soaring.

5. Belkin and Thurm, "Deans List."

6. Phil Oliff, Vincent Palacios, Ingrid Johnson, and Michael Leachman, "Recent Deep State Higher Education Cuts May Harm Students and the Economy for Years to Come," Center on Budget Policy and Priorities, March 19, 2013, http://www.cbpp.org/cms/?fa=view&id=3927.

7. Adrianna Kezar, Daniel Maxey, and Judith Eaton, "An Examination of the Changing Faculty: Ensuring Institutional Quality and Achieving Desired Student Learning Outcomes," p. 4. Council for Higher Education Accreditation Occasional Paper, January 2014. Institute for Research and Study of Accreditation and Quality Assurance. http://www.chea.org/pdf/Examination_Changing_Faculty_2013.pdf. This publication, based on the ongoing research and advocacy of the Delphi project, is the most thorough and comprehensive overview available of the forty-year adjunctification trend in university staffing.

8. Reprinted with permission from "Here's the News: The Annual Report on the Economic Status of the Profession, 2012–13" (Academe, March–April 2013) by the American Association of University Professors Figure 1,

http://www.aaup.org/report/heres-news-annual-report-economic-status
-profession-2012–13.

9. American Association of University Professors, "Losing Focus: The Annual Report on the Economic Status of the Profession, 2013–14," Table 4, http:// www.aaup.org/reports-publications/2013–14salarysurvey.

10. Ibid.

11. Coleman McCarthy, "Adjunct Professors Fight for Crumbs on Campus," *Washington Post,* August 22, 2014, http://www.washingtonpost.com/opinions/ adjunct-professors-fight-for-crumbs-on-campus/2014/08/22/ca92eb38–28b1 –11e4–8593-da634b334390_story.html.

12. Charlotte Allen, "The Highly Educated, Badly Paid, Often Abused Adjunct Professors," *Los Angeles Times,* December 22, 2013, http://www.latimes .com/opinion/op-ed/la-oe-allen-adjunct-professors-20131222-story.html.

13. Allie Bidwell, "How Much Loan Debt Is from Graduate Students? More Than You Think," *U.S. News and World Report,* March 25, 2014, http://www .usnews.com/news/articles/2014/03/25/how-much-outstanding-loan-debt-is -from-grad-students-more-than-you-think.

14. Steve Street, Maria Maisto, Esther Merves, and Gary Rhoades, "Who Is Professor 'Staff' and How Can This Person Teach So Many Classes?" Center for the Future of Higher Education, August 2012. See also "Research," Adjunct action.org, http://adjunctaction.org/facts-figures.

15. Alice Umber [pseud.], "I Used to Be a Good Teacher," August 20, 2014, *Chronicle Vitae,* https://chroniclevitae.com/news/668-i-used-to-be-a-good -teacher?cid=oh&utm_source=oh&utm_medium=en#sthash.4GFlbjOL.dpuf.

16. Adam Davidson, "Why Are Harvard Graduates in the Mailroom?" *New York Times Magazine,* February 22, 2012, http://www.nytimes.com/2012/02/26 /magazine/why-are-harvard-graduates-in-the-mailroom.html?_r=0; Eric Garland, "Sarah Kendzior Exposes the Ponzi Scheme That Is Academic Jobs," August 12, 2012, http://www.ericgarland.co/2012/08/24/sarah-kendzior -exposes-the-ponzi-scheme-of-academic-jobs; Atlas Odinshoot, "The Odds Are Never in Your Favor," *Chronicle of Higher Education,* January 20, 2014, http:// chronicle.com/article/The-Odds-Are-Never-in-Your/144079; Alexandre Alfonso, "How Academia Resembles a Drug Gang," November 21, 2013, http:// alexandrealfonso.wordpress.com/2013/11/21/how-academia-resembles-a -drug-gang.

17. See the New Faculty Majority, www.newfacultymajority.info. See also the Coalition of Contingent Academic Labor, http://cocalinternational.org/index .html.

18. Vimal Patel, "Graduate Students Seek to Build on Momentum for Unions," *Chronicle of Higher Education,* May 12, 2014, http://chronicle.com/ article/Graduate-Students-Seek-to/146487/?cid=wb&utm_source=wb&utm _medium=en.

19. Rick Perlstein, "Professors to Grad Students: Focus on Studies,

Not Wages," *The Nation,* December 4, 2014, http://www.thenation.com/blog/177472/professors-grad-students-focus-studies-not-wages#.

20. Tamar Lewin, "More College Adjuncts See Strength in Union Numbers," *New York Times,* December 3, 2013, http://www.nytimes.com/2013/12/04/us/more-college-adjuncts-see-strength-in-union-numbers.html?page wanted=all&r=o.

21. Thomas Benton [William Pannapacker], "Graduate School in the Humanities: Just Don't Go," *Chronicle of Higher Education,* January 30, 2009, http://chronicle.com/article/Graduate-School-in-the/44846.

22. Robert Oprisko, "Just Visiting: How to Give an Internal Candidate the Bad News," *Chronicle Vitae,* January 30, 2014, https://chroniclevitae.com/news/305-just-visiting-how-to-give-an-internal-candidate-the-bad-news.

23. Rebecca Schuman, "True Academia Story of 'Thesis Hatement,' vol. 1: Rock Bottom," pankisseskafka.com, March 30, 2014, http://pankisseskafka.com/2014/03/30/true-academia-story-of-thesis-hatementvol-1-rock-bottom/.

TWO: BREAKING OUT OF THE IVORY TOWER

1. Karen Kelsky, "Death of a Soul (On Campus)," July 18, 2011, http://techin translation.com/guest-post-death-of-a-soul-on-campus.

2. Thomas Benton [William Pannapacker], "The Big Lie About the Life of the Mind," February 8, 2010, http://chronicle.com/article/The-Big-Lie-About-the-Life-of/63937.

3. David Perry, "Faculty Refuse to See Themselves as Workers. Why?" May 22, 2014, https://chroniclevitae.com/news/509-faculty-refuse-to-see-themselves-as-workers-why?cid=vem#sthash.rjoVWSvG.dpuf.

4. Ian Bogost, "Academic Paydom: Tactical Solutions from the Steven Salaita Situation," Bogost.com, August 9, 2014, http://bogost.com/writing/blog/academic-paydom.

5. Marc Bousquet, *How the University Works: Higher Education and the Low-Wage Nation* (New York: New York University Press, 2008).

6. Ann Larson, "Rhetoric and Composition: Academic Capitalism and Cheap Teachers," AnnLarson.org, March 3, 2012, http://annlarson.org/2012/03/03/rhetoric-and-composition-academic-capitalism-and-cheap-teachers.

THREE: THE MYTHS GRAD STUDENTS BELIEVE

1. Torrey Trust, "The Professor Is In: At UCSB," UCSB GradPost, October 21, 2013, http://gradpost.ucsb.edu/career/2013/10/21/the-professor-is-in-at-ucsb.html.

2. Nathaniel C. Oliver. "To Adjunct or Not to Adjunct—How Long Must We Suffer the Slings and Arrows?" Nathanielcoliver.com, July 31, 2014, http://

nathanielcoliver.com/2014/07/31/to-adjunct-or-not-to-adjunct-how-long-must
-we-suffer-the-slings-and-arrows.

3. Pannapacker (Benton), "Graduate School in the Humanities: Just Don't Go."

FIVE: STOP ACTING LIKE A GRAD STUDENT!

1. Amy Cuddy, "Your Body Language Shapes Who You Are," TED.com, http://www.ted.com/talks/amy_cuddy_your_body_language_shapes_who _you_are.

SIX: THE ATTRIBUTES OF A COMPETITIVE TENURE TRACK CANDIDATE

1. Thank you to Verena Hutter for creating this five-year plan.

SEVEN: BUILDING A COMPETITIVE RECORD

1. Karen Kelsky, Ph.D. Debt Survey, http://theprofessorisin.com/ph-d-debt -survey.

ELEVEN: WHERE ARE THE JOBS? INSTITUTION TYPES AND RANKS

1. This long-standing classification and ranking system has been taken over by the Indiana University Center for Postsecondary Research, but retains the Carnegie name, http://classifications.carnegiefoundation.org/.

2. Sydni Dunn, "Public, Private Pay Gap Widens," April 8, 2013, http:// chronicle.com/article/As-Public-Private-Pay-Gap/138359/.

3. John H. Ball, Ph.D., "Teaching at a Community College: Some Personal Observations," American Historical Association, April 2010, http://www .historians.org/publications-and-directories/perspectives-on-history /april-2010/teaching-at-a-community-college-some-personal-observations.

NINETEEN: APPLYING TO CONFERENCES

1. Thanks to Carole McGranahan for these insights.

TWENTY: HOW TO WORK THE CONFERENCE

1. Claire Potter, "It's Safe to Go Back to the National Meetings: A Radical Guide to Days 1 and 2 of the 2011 AHA," January 5, 2011, http://chronicle .com/blognetwork/tenuredradical/2011/01/its-safe-to-go-back-to-annual -meeting/.

TWENTY-EIGHT: **WHAT IS A DIVERSITY STATEMENT, ANYWAY?**

1. This diversity statement example is shared with permission of its author, Mara A. Evans, Ph.D. Dr. Evans is currently a postdoctoral research associate in the Department of Biochemistry and Molecular Biology at the University of Georgia.

2. Keisha Ray. " 'How Are You Diverse?' How the Academic Job Market Aggravated My Racial Insecurities." Bioethics.net. January 5, 2015. http://www.bioethics.net/2015/01/how-are-you-diverse-how-the-academic-job-market-aggravated-my-racial-insecurities/.

THIRTY-EIGHT: **WAITING, WONDERING, WIKI**

1. Rebecca Schuman, "Market Crash Course: Wallowing in a Wiki Wonderland," December 17, 2013, https://chroniclevitae.com/news/227-market-crash-course-wallowing-in-a-wiki-wonderland?cid=at&utm_source=at&utm_medium=en.

2. Ibid.

THIRTY-NINE: **GOOD JOB CANDIDATES GONE BAD**

1. Terry McGlynn, "Getting the Emphasis Right," *Inside Higher Ed,* January 24, 2014, https://www.insidehighered.com/advice/2014/01/24/essay-writing-cover-letter-academic-job-teaching-institution.

FORTY-TWO: **MANAGING YOUR ONLINE PRESENCE**

1. Kelli Marshall, "How to Curate Your Digital Identity as an Academic," January 5, 2015. http://chronicle.com/article/How-to-Curate-Your-Digital/151001/?cid=at&utm_source=at&utm_medium=en.

FORTY-FOUR: **WHEN YOU FEEL LIKE YOU DON'T BELONG**

1. Victor Ray, "Reflections on Nominal Diversity in Academia," Conditionally Accepted. April 1, 2014. http://conditionallyaccepted.com/2014/04/01/nominal-diversity/.

2. Keisha Ray, " 'How Are You Diverse?' How the Academic Job Market Aggravated My Racial Insecurities." Bioethics.net. January 5, 2015. http://www.bioethics.net/2015/01/how-are-you-diverse-how-the-academic-job-market-aggravated-my-racial-insecurities/.

3. Kate Weisshaar, quoted in "Productivity or Sexism?" August 18, 2014, https://www.insidehighered.com/news/2014/08/18/study-raises-questions-about-why-women-are-less-likely-men-earn-tenure-research.

FORTY-SEVEN: **COVERING THE COSTS**

1. Sarah Kendzior, "The Closing of American Academia," Al Jazeera, August 20, 2012. http://www.aljazeera.com/indepth/opinion/2012/08/2012820102749246453.html.

FORTY-EIGHT: **DON'T BE AFRAID TO NEGOTIATE**

1. Thanks to Bradley Baker for these calculations.

2. Michelle Marks and Crystal Harold, "Who Asks and Who Receives in Salary Negotiation," 32, no. 3 (2009): 371–94.

3. Sara Laschever, quoted in Audrey Williams June, "Negotiating Tactics for Women, November 27, 2011, http://chronicle.com/blogs/onhiring/negotiating-tactics-for-women/29883.

FIFTY: **THE RESCINDED OFFER—WHO IS IN THE WRONG?**

1. This differs from the case of Steven Salaita in summer 2014, who saw his tenured offer rescinded as a result of inflammatory anti-Israel tweets. Rescindment of new assistant professor offers are generally not, at time of this writing, associated with the hires' political stances.

FIFTY-ONE: **THE FOOLPROOF GRANT TEMPLATE**

1. This proposal is shared with permission of its author, a former client.

FIFTY-THREE: **THE POSTDOC APPLICATION: HOW IT'S DIFFERENT AND WHY**

1. Sydni Dunn, "A Brief History of the Humanities Postdoc," July 7, 2014, https://chroniclevitae.com/news/593-a-brief-history-of-the-humanities-postdoc.

FIFTY-SEVEN: **PH.D. DEBT AND ETHICAL ADVISING**

1. Jason Delisle, Owen Phillips, and Ross Van Der Linde, "The Graduate Student Debt Review: The State of Graduate Student Borrowing," March 2014, www.newamerica.org/.

2. Josh Mitchell, "Grad Students Driving the Growing Debt Burden," March 25, 2014, http://online.wsj.com/news/articles/SB10001424052702303949704579459803223202602?mod=WSJ_WSJ_US_News_5&mg=reno64-wsj.

3. Marc Bousquet argued this point as early as 2008 in his book *How the University Works: Higher Education and the Low-Wage Nation* (New York: New York University Press, 2008).

4. Kelsky, Ph.D. Debt Survey.

5. For those who like official sorts of figures, the NSF gathers data on graduate school debt. Find it here: http://www.nsf.gov/statistics/sed/2013/data/tab38.pdf. To me, as an anthropologist, it is, of course, the stories that tell the real story.

6. Pannapacker (Benton), "Graduate School in the Humanities: Just Don't Go."

7. Ibid.

FIFTY-EIGHT: IT'S OK TO QUIT

1. Oliver, "To Adjunct or Not to Adjunct: How Long Must We Suffer the Slings and Arrows?"

2. Josh Boldt, "Off Track: Adjuncts Are Addicts," October 29, 2013, https://chroniclevitae.com/news/91-off-track-adjuncts-are-addicts. To address this addiction, Boldt created the Adjunct Project, an online repository of data about adjunct exploitation, as well as information and support: http://adjunct.chronicle.com/.

3. Sarah Kendzior, "Academia's Indentured Servants," April 11, 2013, http://www.aljazeera.com/indepth/opinion/2013/04/20134119156459616.html.

FIFTY-NINE: LET YOURSELF DREAM

1. In fall 2014 this team included Karen Cardozo, Stephanie Day, Joe Fruscione, Maggie Gover, Margy Horton, Jessica Langer, Allessandria Polizzi, and Jason Tebbe.

2. Karen Cardozo, "Beyond Tenurecentrism," February 12, 2014, http://theprofessorisin.com/2014/02/12/beyond-tenurecentrism-cardozo-1/.

3. I thank corporate ethnographer Stephanie Day for the Differentiator rubric.

4. Find her at http://www.kelleeweinhold.com.

SIXTY: 100+ SKILLS THAT TRANSLATE OUTSIDE THE ACADEMY

1. www.scholarshape.com.

2. Shared here with permission from Margy Horton, Ph.D.

SIXTY-ONE: COLLECTING INFORMATION

1. Karen Cardozo, "Freeing the Academic Elephant." February 18, 2014, http://theprofessorisin.com/2014/02/18/freeing-the-academic-elephant-cardozo-2/.

SIXTY-TWO: **APPLYING WHILE PH.D.**

1. The discussion on this page draws from the work of Margaret Gover, Director of Graduate Student Professional Development at UC-Riverside.

2. This list is drawn from Candace Davies, "How to Use Teaching Keywords to Your Advantage," Monster.com, http://teaching.monster.com/careers/articles/6788-how-to-use-teaching-keywords-to-your-advantage.

SIXTY-THREE: **BREAKING FREE: THE PATH OF THE ENTREPRENEUR**

1. Kerry Ann Rockquemore, "Shifting Your Mindset," July 14, 2014, http://www.insidehighered.207elmp01.blackmesh.com/advice/2014/07/14/essay-difference-between-academic-and-entrepreneurial-mindset.

CONCLUSION: **DECLARING INDEPENDENCE**

1. Cheryl Strayed, *Tiny Beautiful Things: Advice on Love and Life from Dear Sugar* (New York: Vintage Press, 2012), 53, 59.

2. Ms. Mentor, "Who Are You Trying to Impress? Don't Let 'Them' Make You Feel Like a Failure," October 27, 2014, http://www.chroniclecareers.com/article/Who-Are-You-Trying-to-Impress-/149659/.

INDEX